Seoul
서울

Martin Robinson

LONELY PLANET PUBLICATIONS
Melbourne • Oakland • London • Paris

Seoul
4th edition – July 2003
First published – May 1993

Published by
Lonely Planet Publications Pty Ltd ABN 36 005 607 983
90 Maribyrnong St, Footscray, Victoria 3011, Australia

Lonely Planet offices
Australia Locked Bag 1, Footscray, Victoria 3011
USA 150 Linden St, Oakland, CA 94607
UK 72-82 Rosebery Ave, London, EC1R 4RW
France 1 rue du Dahomey, 75011 Paris

Photographs
Many of the images in this guide are available for licensing from Lonely Planet Images.
w www.lonelyplanetimages.com

Front cover photograph
Jongno 2-ga after dark (Jeff Yates)

ISBN 1 74059 218 2

Printed through Colorcraft Ltd, Hong Kong
Printed in China

Contents – Text

Contents – Maps

The Author

Martin Robinson

Martin lived in South Korea for two years teaching English, working in the local provincial governor's office and writing a comprehensive hiking guide to Jeollabuk-do. Before that he was employed by the British Council in Tokyo for three years but took time off to explore Asia and contribute regular travel articles to newspapers and magazines. He has been a UN volunteer in South Africa and once spent a year on the islands of Samoa where he worked as a freelance journalist and photographer and wrote a book on traditional Polynesian culture.

Born in London and educated at Oxford University, he now lives in New Zealand. He is married but still attached to the nomadic life of a global information gatherer.

FROM THE AUTHOR

Thanks to Mrs Dho, David Mason, Hank Kim, Jang Young-bok, Ok Ja-shin, Joe from Incheon, Park Gi-hwan and Han He-jean. Special thanks to Evelyn Cheah and my wife.

This Book

From the Publisher

Martin Robinson thoroughly revised and updated this 4th edition of *Seoul*. His work built on the efforts of Robert Storey who authored the 3rd and 2nd editions, and Chris Taylor who wrote the 1st edition.

This edition of *Seoul* was superbly coordinated in Lonely Planet's Melbourne office by our dear departing Rebecca Lalor (editing) – good luck in Taiwan Bec. Melanie Dankel and Simone Egger assisted with editing; Kristin Odijk proofread the book. Hunor Csutoros coordinated the mapping, and Nicholas Stebbing was in charge of colour and design. Michael Day commissioned the book, Chris Love kept it in check, Leonie Mugavin cast an eye over travel information, Quentin Frayne organised the language chapter with help from Emma Koch, Daniel New and Gerilyn Attebery designed the cover, and LPI provided the photographs.

Jane Thompson provided editorial supervision, and Corinne Waddell supervised cartography. Kate McDonald and Adriana Mammarella were responsible for layout checks.

Thanks to Mr Bang Sun-gyu, Cultural Attaché, Consulate General of the Republic of Korea, Sydney; and the Seoul Metropolitan Subway Corp for allowing us to use their map.

Thanks

Many thanks to the travellers who used the last edition and wrote to us with helpful hints, useful advice and interesting anecdotes. Your names follow:

Dennis Arthur, Jesse Baehm, David Benner, Grace Blake, Paul Boucher, Michael Brantley, Geoff Brooks, Lyndal & Murray Brown, Aafke & Dennis Bruin, Irene Calder, Peter Caruana, Michael Copenhafer, Francesco Diodato, Hugues Donato, Macdara Ferris, Joseph Fette, Tony Fitzcarl, Robin Fletcher, Del Ford, Mike Fowler, Nelson Fung, Donald Gillies, Leigh Hardy, Andy Hatfield, Gilles Hurtebize, Lee Jeong Im, Sheldon Johnston, Ben Jordan, Philip Jurecky, Daichi Kawashima, David Kendall, Bartosz Kozik, Eric Leeou, Volker Lehmann, Tim Lehnert, Claire Lessard, Claudia Li, Joann Lichtenberger, Jonathan Lim, Kathrin Linderer, Jennifer Martin, Mike Martin, Peter Martyn, Mark McKibbin, Stan Meihaus, Gary Mink, Hong Minsuk, Tony Osborne, JF Paitel, Ryan Parker, Shaun Petty, Laura Pohl, Abel Polese, Renata Ramos, Michael Richter, Jennifer Roberts, Hector Rodriguez, Ma Rosario Lapus, Alejandro Salvatierra, Marilyn Schick, Brandon Si, Chua Siaw Hui, Mr Sigeki, Reda Sijiny, Aileen Simarro, Leif Soderlund, Nicolas Sotnikoff, Mathieu Stewart, Joshua Taaffe, Mathilde Teuben, Aairam Thomas, Dan Thompson, Steven P Tseng, Nick van der Leek, Eric van Dort, Vicky Vitallo, Harry Weide, Andy Westall, Joerg Winkelmann, Derek Yokota, Se-Joon You, Ruth Zanker, David Zuman

Foreword

ABOUT LONELY PLANET GUIDEBOOKS

The story begins with a classic travel adventure: Tony and Maureen Wheeler's 1972 journey across Europe and Asia to Australia. There was no useful information about the overland trail then, so Tony and Maureen published the first Lonely Planet guidebook to meet a growing need.

From a kitchen table, Lonely Planet has grown to become the largest independent travel publisher in the world, with offices in Melbourne (Australia), Oakland (USA), London (UK) and Paris (France).

Today Lonely Planet guidebooks cover the globe. There is an ever-growing list of books and information in a variety of media. Some things haven't changed. The main aim is still to make it possible for adventurous travellers to get out there – to explore and better understand the world.

At Lonely Planet we believe travellers can make a positive contribution to the countries they visit – if they respect their host communities and spend their money wisely. Since 1986 a percentage of the income from each book has been donated to aid projects and human rights campaigns, and, more recently, to wildlife conservation.

Although inclusion in a guidebook usually implies a recommendation we cannot list every good place. Exclusion does not necessarily imply criticism. In fact there are a number of reasons why we might exclude a place – sometimes it is simply inappropriate to encourage an influx of travellers.

UPDATES & READER FEEDBACK

Things change – prices go up, schedules change, good places go bad and bad places go bankrupt. Nothing stays the same. So, if you find things better or worse, recently opened or long-since closed, please tell us and help make the next edition even more accurate and useful.

Lonely Planet thoroughly updates each guidebook as often as possible – usually every two years, although for some destinations the gap can be longer. Between editions, up-to-date information is available in our free, monthly email bulletin *Comet* (w www.lonelyplanet.com/newsletters). You can also check out the *Thorn Tree* bulletin board and *Postcards* section of our website which carry unverified, but fascinating, reports from travellers.

Tell us about it! We genuinely value your feedback. A well-travelled team at Lonely Planet reads and acknowledges every email and letter we receive and ensures that every morsel of information finds its way to the relevant authors, editors and cartographers.

Everyone who writes to us will find their name listed in the next edition of the appropriate guidebook. The very best contributions will be rewarded with a free guidebook.

We may edit, reproduce and incorporate your comments in Lonely Planet products such as guidebooks, websites and digital products, so let us know if you don't want your comments reproduced or your name acknowledged.

How to contact Lonely Planet:
Online: e talk2us@lonelyplanet.com.au, w www.lonelyplanet.com
Australia: Locked Bag 1, Footscray, Victoria 3011
UK: 72-82 Rosebery Ave, London EC1R 4RW
USA: 150 Linden St, Oakland, CA 94607

Introduction

No other Korean city approaches the size and importance of Seoul. It is the political, financial, educational and cultural hub of the country, with nearly all roads, bus routes, railway lines and flight paths in the country leading to it.

It is also a buzzing and modern Asian city with a high standard of living. Seoul's busy streets are lined with smart shops, dazzling high-rise shopping malls bulging with the latest in clothing and accessories, unusual cafés, reasonably priced restaurants, lively bars and luxury cinemas. Entertainment districts are packed with billiard halls, bowling alleys, live-jazz clubs, raging nightclubs and private rooms where you can sing and dance to karaoke.

Yet reminders of Seoul's traditional aristocratic society remain – five ancient palaces where re-enactments of court ceremonies are held, fortress walls and gates, royal shrines and tombs, and one-storey wooden houses with tiled roofs that were built by the *yangban* (aristocrats).

Traditional cultural performances, annual festivals, folk villages and folk museums give visitors the opportunity to experience the rural lifestyle that existed on the peninsula for centuries. You can stay in a guesthouse or hotel and sleep on a padded quilt on an *ondol*-heated floor, or sit on floor cushions in a traditional restaurant, eating a Korean banquet and drinking local liquors.

Buddhist monks still live, work and meditate in monasteries and temples whose origins go back many centuries, and travellers can share their life for a day or two on temple-stay programmes. Offerings to the spirits are still made at shamanist shrines in the nearby mountains, but Seoul is also one of the most Christian cities in Asia, with Protestant and Catholic churches in every neighbourhood.

Korean cuisine is another of the city's attractions. Restaurants in every price range offer the chance to sample a wide variety of meals, snacks and drinks unique to Korea, while Japanese, Chinese and Western food is also easy to find.

Money has been poured into the city's infrastructure, resulting in up-to-date communication and public utility services, and an excellent subway and bus system. The Seoul Metropolitan Government has planted trees, created green parks, and built sports facilities and cycleways along the banks of Hangang.

Despite being home to 10 million residents, Seoul is a safe and friendly city with a low crime rate. Seoulites work long hours, but also enjoy socialising and are generally more than kind to foreign visitors. If you look lost, someone is bound to offer to help you.

Popular excursions from Seoul include mountain hiking, taking a ferry to the unspoilt islands in the West Sea or touring the Demilitarized Zone (DMZ) 55km north of Seoul, a stark reminder of the harsh and dangerous division of the country. Reunification with the North in some form or other is the greatest challenge currently facing the South.

Seoul is the 600-year-old capital of a world-class economic powerhouse and is in every aspect of life and culture – architecture, religion, politics, film, literature, art, music, dance and fashion – a fascinating melting pot of old and new, East and West.

Facts about Seoul

HISTORY

Early Days

Seoul's history begins with the Three Kingdoms period (57 BC–AD 668), during which southern Korea was dominated by the Baekje and Silla dynasties, while the Goguryeo dynasty ruled north of the river Hangang. This period saw a remarkable flowering of art, architecture, literature and statecraft. Chinese influences were absorbed, reinterpreted and mixed with traditional Korean shamanist beliefs, with probably the single most important influence being Buddhism, which became the state religion of all three kingdoms.

The Three Kingdoms period ended when Silla allied itself with the Tang dynasty in China, conquered the other two kingdoms and unified the peninsula. Another renaissance then took place. Relics of Silla tombs, temples, pagodas, palaces and pleasure gardens can be found in Seoul's museums and in present-day Gyeongju, the former Silla capital.

Silla was itself overwhelmed in 918 and the Goryeo dynasty was established, but it suffered Mongol conquest in 1231. Economic devastation, the payment of tribute and the loss of Jejudo were the result. However, the dynasty continued until it was overthrown by one of its own generals, Yi Seong-gye, in 1392.

Royal Seoul

General Yi Seong-gye declared himself King Taejo and became the first of the long list of Joseon dynasty kings. King Taejo was a busy man. In 1394 he moved the capital to Hanyang, the site of modern-day Seoul, building large palaces and confiscating the property and wealth of the Buddhist temples and monasteries. He built Confucian shrines and schools, and established a new examination system for entry to government service. Within 10 years Seoul's population had grown to 100,000 and an 18km wall with eight huge gates had been built around the city. The remains of this wall are being renovated and can today be seen in the hills around Seoul.

Korean History at a Glance

Three Kingdoms period	57 BC–AD 668
Unified Silla dynasty	668–918
Goryeo dynasty	918–1392
Joseon (Yi) dynasty	1392–1910
Japanese rule	1910–45
Two Nations period	1945–present

The following 23 Joseon kings followed the same Confucian policies, which is why Seoul has only a handful of Buddhist temples today. The only other Joseon dynasty king regarded as great was Sejong, who ruled from 1418 to 1450. He was a scholar who strengthened the country's northern defences, introduced land and tax reforms, encouraged farmers to adopt new agricultural techniques and supervised scientific discoveries. He was the nearest to the Confucian ideal of a benevolent and wise ruler. It was during his reign that *hangeul,* a phonetic script for the Korean language, was introduced.

Invasions

In 1592 Toyotomi Hideyoshi, having united Japan, attacked Korea with 200,000 troops and, aided by superior technology, quickly conquered the country. However, Korea's Admiral Yi Sun-shin achieved brilliant naval successes against Japan with the help of a handful of ironclad 'turtle ships', known as *geobukseon,* that he helped to design. A large statue of him can be seen in central Seoul.

During this time, many of the palace buildings in Seoul were looted and destroyed, and craftspeople and cultural treasures were shipped off to Japan before their troops retreated home.

In 1636 the Manchus invaded. King Injo sent his family to Ganghwado, while he retreated to Namhansanseong, a fortress to the south of Seoul. He was soon forced to surrender and once again Seoul was ransacked by a powerful and aggressive neighbour. The Joseon kings generally accepted Chinese suzerainty, which meant vassal status for Korea but did offer some protection.

The Hermit Kingdom

In the mid-19th century, Regent Heungseon Daewongun (King Gojong's father) pursued an energetic policy of trying to restore royal power by rebuilding the palace Gyeongbokgung, shutting down Confucian schools and closing Korea to foreigners – a policy that led to the country being called the 'Hermit kingdom'.

The feudal system of *yangban* (aristocrats), serfs, slaves and outcast occupations (such as butchers and tanners) was still rigidly enforced, with detailed regulations enforcing dress, food, housing and behaviour codes. Despite a reform movement, the rulers sat in their Seoul palaces isolated from their own people and the rest of the world. Koreans who had converted to Catholicism via Jesuits from the Chinese imperial court in the late 1700s were persecuted and waves of executions in the 1860s took thousands of lives. Jeoldusan Martyrs' Shrine & Museum (Map 3) marks the site where 2000 Seoul martyrs were beheaded in 1866 for their faith.

Regent Heungseon Daewongun's policy ended in bankruptcy and failure in 1873. Japanese and Western traders forced their way into Korean ports, while China, Japan and Russia were the wolves at the door, each wary of the other and of growing American and European power. In 1896 King Gojong took refuge in the Russian Legation Building (Map 8) for more than a year after his wife, Queen Myeongseong (Queen Min), was assassinated in her bedroom in Gyeongbokgung by Japanese agents.

Japan fought against and defeated first China and then Russia, and gradually took over Korea, forcing King Gojong to sign treaties that were detrimental to the country's interests. Finally, in 1910 Japan annexed Korea and abolished the monarchy.

Japanese Control

On 1 March 1919, Sun Pyong-hui's Declaration of Independence was read out in Seoul's Tapgol Park and sparked off a nationwide revolt against Japanese rule. But all opposition was repressed, and many Korean patriots were tortured and executed in Seoul's Seodaemun Prison (Map 4), parts of which still stand today.

The Japanese invaded Korean fishing grounds, seized 'vacant' land, cut down forests and took over Seoul's Namdaemun market, and by 1911 more than 200,000 Japanese were living in Korea. Surprisingly, Christian missionaries were not persecuted and their influence spread, especially in Seoul, which became more Christian than Buddhist.

During WWII, thousands of Korean women were forced into prostitution as 'comfort women' and millions of men were conscripted into the Japanese army or forced to work in mines and factories in Korea, China and Japan; the Korean language was also banned. This Japanese policy of cultural genocide left scars that persist to this day.

Political Division & the Korean War

The abrupt end of Japanese rule in 1945 led to a deal between the Soviet Union, America and Britain to carve up Korea in a way similar to that carried out in Europe. The Soviets occupied the country north of the 38th parallel, while America and Britain governed the south. The Soviets did not permit elections in the north, preferring instead to install a communist officer by the name of Kim Il Sung, and so as the south elected its own government, the peninsula became politically divided.

Seoul was fought over four times between 1950 and 1951. On 25 June 1950 North Korea invaded the South, occupied Seoul two days later, and rapidly advanced into the rest of the country. A UN force drawn from America and 15 other countries then poured in to defend Busan. Following General MacArthur's daring seaborne landing at Incheon, Seoul was liberated on 25 September 1950 and the North Korean forces were

Reunification

Despite the collapse or reform of communist totalitarian states elsewhere in the world, secretive North Korea shows few signs of changing its hard-line policies. No one knows when the DMZ will disappear.

In 1997 President Kim Dae-jung announced that South Korea would embark upon a new diplomatic strategy in dealing with the North. This strategy incorporated three guiding principles, later to be labelled the 'Sunshine Policy': first, there would be zero tolerance of armed aggression; second, unification would not follow the German-style absorption method; and finally, inter-Korean reconciliation and cooperation would be actively promoted. This new strategy was based on the premise that change in the North would most likely come about in a 'sunny' environment of positive collaboration, rather than through a Cold War policy of containment and estrangement.

It rapidly produced a string of positive developments in the bilateral relationship, including increased dialogue on trade, tourism, family reunions and cultural exchanges. However, the process was not without hiccups, highlighted in particular by two brief but deadly naval engagements in the West Sea in June 1999 and June 2002. The latter incident dampened South Korea's World Cup soccer euphoria as four South Koreans died, one was missing presumed dead, 19 were injured and a patrol boat was sunk. Casualties on the North Korean side are unknown. But due to the strength of commitment by Kim Dae-jung, the Sunshine Policy was never derailed during his presidency, and current president Roh Moo-hyun, with a reformist, leftist reputation, is likely to pursue an even softer line towards the North.

One result of the thawing relationship was that in 1998 Hyundai started to run package tours to Kumgangsan in North Korea. Within 18 months 250,000 southerners had taken advantage of the offer to have a look at their northern relatives. Foreigners can also go on these three-day tours, which cost around W550,000. You stay on a cruise boat and go on guided tours around some picturesque areas of North Korea.

Then in February 2003 overland coach tours to Kumgangsan (known as Geumgangsan in the South) were started that crossed through the eastern end of the DMZ on a makeshift road. See the Organised Tours section of the Getting Around chapter for details.

Direct regular flights are being introduced for the first time between Yangyang in the South and Seondeok in the North. Seondeok is near one of the two nuclear reactors that are being built by an international consortium in return for North Korea abandoning its nuclear weapons programme. However, in 2002, work on building the reactors stopped due to signs that North Korea had not mothballed its nuclear weapon–making facilities.

As South Korea prospers and North Korea continues to suffer almost famine conditions, the cost of any future reunification grows every year. To raise the standard of living in the North to equal that of the South would be a far greater challenge than that faced by West Germany when it reunited with East Germany. Also, after living for so long under two completely different economic and political systems, the mind-set in the two halves of Korea is very different. Defectors from North to South usually have considerable trouble adapting to southern ways.

pushed back. But then in November 1950 the Chinese army attacked the South Korean and UN forces, and marched into Seoul on 3 January 1951. They were forced out again on 15 March and, after a long military stalemate, an armistice was signed in 1953 that continues in force today. No peace treaty was ever signed.

Asian Tiger

Despite the devastation of war, the South Korean economy developed very rapidly and in 1996 it joined the rich man's club, the Organisation for Economic Cooperation and Development (OECD). Economic progress has been matched by increasing democratisation following years of student and trade-union battles against a succession of military rulers. The election of democracy campaigner Kim Dae-jung as president in 1997 was a milestone on the way to a mature democracy.

South Korea has now recovered from the 1997 economic crisis, when the government was forced to borrow US$158,000 million from the International Monetary Fund (IMF). Painful economic reform and restructuring are continuing, but the cloud that is always on the horizon is their unpredictable and totalitarian neighbour in the north – the North Korean armed forces are just 55km north of Seoul. A visit to the Demilitarized Zone (DMZ) is a sobering experience, with all the paraphernalia of modern warfare ready to be used if necessary. Up to 37,000 American troops are still stationed in South Korea, and every fit Korean male has to serve 27 months in the armed forces. Any kind of reunification is going to be difficult and very expensive.

GEOGRAPHY

Seoul is in the northwestern corner of South Korea, 37° 30′ north of the equator. The city covers an area of 605 sq km and is 32km from Incheon, its airport and seaport on the West (Yellow) Sea. Bisected by Hangang, Seoul is surrounded by eight mountain peaks, although most of the city is below 100m elevation.

CLIMATE

Korea has four seasons and a notable feature is the summer and winter monsoons (seasonal winds). Seoul enjoys its best weather from September to November.

The autumn period is a time of little rain and mild temperatures. The winter monsoon is characterised by an icy Siberian wind blowing from the north making winter very cold, but at least it's dry; the worst of the cold is usually over by mid-March.

Spring temperatures are mild, but more prone to rain than autumn. Summer is not a particularly great time to be in Seoul, as the summer monsoon brings hot and muggy weather with lots of rain. Destructive typhoons are also a possibility from late June through to September.

Log on to W www.kma.go.kr for daily weather forecasts in English for Seoul and the rest of South Korea.

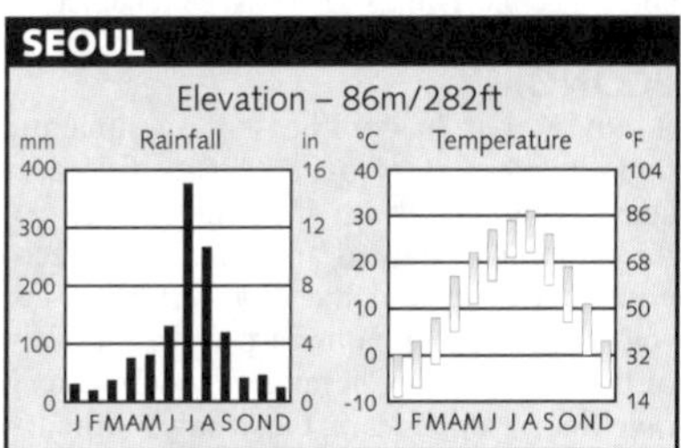

ECOLOGY & ENVIRONMENT

The Seoul Metropolitan Government has taken some praiseworthy steps to improve the city's environment. Millions of trees have been planted in recent years and Hangang is much cleaner than it used to be. Cycleways, sports facilities and parks have been developed along its banks.

The city is cleaner than most, but more and more cars squeeze onto the roads every year, increasing pollution levels and making life unpleasant for pedestrians. Plans for more traffic-free and traffic-quiet streets should be implemented soon in Insadong and elsewhere.

NATIONAL & PROVINCIAL PARKS

Just to the north of Seoul is Bukhansan National Park (Map 10), a stunning area of steep granite peaks and cliffs, which also includes a 16th-century fortress and a number of Buddhist temples. Only 25km southeast of Seoul is Namhansanseong, a provincial park that includes impressive 17th-century fortress walls that stretch for 9km, as well as fortress gates, Buddhist temples and a village of traditional restaurants. See the 'Mountain Hiking' special section for details on visiting these two attractive parks.

GOVERNMENT & POLITICS

Seoul has its own local government system, but real power resides in the Blue House (the president's residence and office north of Gyeongbokgung; Map 8) and the 273-member National Assembly on Yeouido (Map 5). The president is elected every five years while the National Assembly members serve a four-year term. Tours of both of the buildings are available – see the Things to See & Do chapter.

ECONOMY

South Korea has witnessed an amazing rags-to-riches story over the past five decades. Seoul has been the engine room of the nation's sustained and spectacular economic growth, and the city's universities, scientists and companies are at the forefront of the revolution. Chemicals, textiles, steel, machinery, ships, cars, electronics – the list of successful export industries led by Seoul-based *jaebol* (huge family-run corporations) is a long one. Even agriculture and fishing are vastly more productive than they used to be. South of Hangang is Teheran St, which is Seoul's Silicon Valley. Employees of the street's 1000 small Internet companies are said to work from 7am to 2am, and some offices are equipped with beds, wardrobes and even washing machines, as workers often don't go home.

Despite recent privatisations and deregulation, the central government is still in charge of nearly every aspect of the economy. The government, the banks, the stock exchange and the giant *jaebol* are all based in Seoul.

Seoul produces 23% of South Korea's GNP but holds 50% of the country's bank loans and deposits. The top 10 *jaebol* still control 60% of the economy, despite government efforts to force them to rationalise and sell off their non-core subsidiaries.

POPULATION & PEOPLE

Seoul's universities and job opportunities suck in people from all over the country. About 10.7 million people live in Seoul, but the figure increases to 18 million if you include its satellite suburbs. This means that 25% of Korea's population live in Seoul city and 40% live in Greater Seoul.

Birth rates are low, the population is getting older (life expectancy is 71 years for men, 79 years for women) and there is a shortage of young females – see the boxed text 'Where Have All the Young Girls Gone?'.

Korea is ethnically and linguistically homogeneous and, although the number of foreigners visiting and working in Seoul is increasing, expats still comprise a very small percentage of the population. However, the country's harmony and uniformity is often overstated, as family, clan, school, university, company, trade-union, religious, regional and social-class loyalties frequently cut across national unity.

Where Have All the Young Girls Gone?

In the future, not all young Korean men will be able to marry Korean brides, as a shortage of marriageable women is now facing South Korea. By the year 2010 it is estimated that there will be 128 single men at 'peak marriageable age' (27–30 years old) for every 100 single eligible women (24–27 years old). And those numbers get worse every year.

What is going wrong? Most young Korean families these days want only two children, and one of each gender is seen as ideal – two sons are acceptable but two daughters less so. Ultrasound scans can be used to discover the sex of any foetus and if female she will sometimes be aborted. It is illegal in South Korea for doctors to inform prospective parents of the sex of their foetus, but it does happen in some cases.

So why don't some Korean parents want daughters? The answer mostly stems from the strong residual neo-Confucianism in their social mores. It remains all-important that a man's family name be passed on to future generations and only males can properly perform the ancestor rituals that are still practised. Economic security in the golden years is another concern and some parents want a son to continue the family business. Parents traditionally tend to think of their daughters as given away to her husband's family and lost to her birth family when she gets married.

Theoretically, South Korea could 'import' young women from other countries, but most of Korea's neighbours have similar bride-shortage problems.

EDUCATION

From the Joseon dynasty government-service entrance exams to the present-day university entrance exams, an outstanding characteristic of Korean society has been an obsession with education. An old saying is that 'A person without education is like a beast wearing clothes'. These days one university degree is not enough and two or three is the norm, preferably including one from overseas.

One reason so many Koreans want to live in Seoul is because the best schools and universities are located there and always have been. Seoul now has more than 40 universities. To get into one of the top universities, high-school students go through examination hell, studying 14 hours a day and torturing their brains with multiple-choice questions on calculus, the intricacies of English grammar and numerous other topics. Almost from the cradle, mothers are preparing their offspring for those all-important exams that will determine their child's fate and status in life.

There is an inexhaustible desire for studying English – see the Work section later for information on teaching English in Seoul.

A Modern Tradition

Samulnori falls into the broad category of 'folk dance and music'. It is considered the definitive traditional Korean 'farmer's dance' and is popular with tourists who enjoy its party spirit, yet it has a very short history.

Samulnori was the name adopted by four musicians who formed a band in 1978. *Sa* means 'four', *mul* means 'musical instruments' and *nori* means 'playing'. The four musicians – Kim Young-bae, Choi Tae-hyun, Kim Duk-su and Lee Chong-dae – played four traditional Korean percussion instruments. Their instruments were, respectively, the *kkwaenggwari* (small gong), *ching* (large gong), *changgu* (hour-glass drum) and *puk* (large barrel drum).

Samulnori attempted to re-create an old tradition of folk music and dance in which wandering entertainers went from village to village to perform for local audiences, most of who were peasant farmers.

While the original Samulnori group no longer exists (Kim Young-bae died in 1985 and the other performers have gone their separate ways), the term *samulnori* has been adopted by other bands who continue to play the same traditional instruments.

ARTS

Dance

Traditional Korean folk dances take a wide variety of forms. The most popular ones include *seungmu* (drum dances), *talcum* (mask dances) and solo improvisational *salpuri* (shamanist dances).

The drum dancers perform in brightly coloured traditional clothing, twirling a very long tassel from a cap on their heads. Good coordination is required to dance, twirl and play a drum at the same time.

Elegant court dances accompanied by an orchestra are performed in front of Jongmyo every year on the first Sunday in May as part of the ceremony honouring the Joseon dynasty kings – see the 'Royal Seoul' special section later for details.

Sandaenori (a type of mask dance) has been an art form since at least the 12th century. The masks are made from the wood of the alder tree and convey social status as well as emotions, such as anger, sorrow, joy and laughter. Masks not only represent humans but also animals and supernatural beings. Troupes of mask dancers once went from village to village to entertain poor farmers. The performances often parodied the cruel ironies of life and satirised the privileged classes. Audience participation was common, and performances typically lasted for many hours.

Korea House *(Map 9; ☎ 2266 9101)* has daily one-hour traditional music and dance shows by leading performers for W29,000.

Log on to **W** www.korea.net and follow the link from the Culture section for an overview of modern dance in Seoul.

Music

Korean traditional music *(gugak)* is played on stringed instruments, most notably the *gayageum,* and on chimes, gongs, cymbals, drums, horns and flutes.

Traditional music can be subdivided into three categories – slow and serious court music *(jeongak),* music played and chanted in Buddhist temples, and folk music, which is usually fast and lively.

Traditional musical instruments can be seen in a museum at the Seoul Arts Centre – see the Entertainment chapter for details. You can also log on to **W** www.ncktpa.go.kr for information on 50 Korean percussion, woodwind and string instruments.

Radio Gugak broadcasts traditional Korean music to the Seoul area – see the Radio & TV section of the Facts for the Visitor chapter for details.

Western classical music is played in a number of concert halls in Seoul, and all the modern Western music styles also have their followers. Live-jazz bars are common, and Latin American, rock, punk, hip-hop, trance and a wide variety of other styles is played in the numerous dance clubs in the Hongik entertainment district. See the Entertainment chapter for more details.

Literature

In the 12th century, the monk Illyeon wrote *Samgukyusa* (Myths and Legends of the Three Kingdoms), the most important work of early Korean literature. During the Joseon dynasty, literature included many types of poetry based on Chinese models and written in Chinese characters even after the introduction of *hangeul* in the 15th century. *Hangeul* was a major boost to Korean literature, although outside of court circles most of the nation remained illiterate until the late 19th century.

In 1945 there was a sharp turn away from Chinese and Japanese influence of any kind, and Western influence, especially after the Korean War, increased dramatically. Existentialism was the guiding cultural philosophy. One of the best 20th-century Korean novelists is Ahn Cheong-hyo, who is bilingual and writes the same novels in both Korean and English. Two famous titles are *Silver Stallion,* about the Korean War, and *White Badge,* about Koreans fighting in the Vietnam War.

The Shadow of Arms by Hwang Suk-young is a powerful novel that explores Korean culture as it is experienced by a young boy living in the countryside. *A Dwarf Launches a Little Ball* (1976) by Cho Se-hui is a passionate and poetic novella about a family made homeless by urban redevelopment. The story is memorable in spite of the poor translation. *In the Shadow of the*

Korean Literature on the Web

English translations of short stories written by leading contemporary Korean writers are available free of charge on the Web. Poetry, folk tales, legends and even short novels can also be downloaded.

Log on to **W** www.korea.net and click on 'Culture' for access to eight short stories that provide a good introduction to modern Korean literature. Written in a variety of styles, the stories reflect many aspects of life in Seoul and elsewhere in Korea. Most of the stories are about love, friendship, alienation from society and the meaning of life, and the characters include an earnest rural schoolteacher, a student protestor, an insect collector, a schizophrenic, a lesbian and a bored housewife.

Where the Red Moon Rises by Bak Sang-u is an existentialist love story about two nameless writers and contains a twist at the end. *The Longhorn Beetle* by Lee Oe-su is a long short story contrasting two brothers – one a Zen Buddhist man of the mountains and the other a professional insect collector who loses his girlfriend and lands up in prison. *The Old Well* by O Jeung-hui is a well-written but uneventful story about a bored middle-aged housewife looking back over her unfulfilled life. *By the Sea* by Kim In-suk is about a diffident intellectual female writer and student protestor who reminisces about her brittle, on-off friendship with a very different kind of woman who is focussed on boyfriends and fashion.

From the Directory section of **W** www.korea.net there are links to websites such as Korean Literature Today, which has a library of Korean poetry, essays, novels and more short stories that have been translated into English. Other links are to websites that have collections of traditional folk tales and ancient legends.

Moons (1998) by Hong Nan-sook is the harrowing autobiography of the ex-wife of the eldest son of Moon Sun-myung (the leader of the Unification Church or 'Moonies'). It reveals how religion, wealth and drugs corrupted an autocratic Korean family.

Seoul is a city of poets and writing poetry has also been a popular tradition that goes back into the mists of time. Part of the Joseon government-service entrance exam *gwageo* consisted of writing a poem. Perhaps if this tradition was revived, it would produce more imaginative civil servants. Try *Faint Shadow of Love* (2002) by Kim Kwang-kyu and translated by Brother Anthony, which contains poems that are protests about ecological degradation and the sadness of middle-aged people who have lost the dreams and idealism of their youth. *Unforgettable Things* by So Chong-ju (translated by D McCann) is a wonderful collection of highly original poems that reflect his varied life and unusual philosophy.

Korea also has a huge number of folk tales that reflect Joseon society from the point of view of the peasants. Tales feature animals, clever children who trick their teachers and corrupt government officials, bad luck that turns out to be good luck and poor workers who suddenly become rich. The goblins are cute – tall and skinny, they come out at night and have magic mallets that can turn anything into gold. They generally reward good people and punish the bad, but being goblins, they can't always be trusted.

Architecture

The best examples of Korean traditional architecture are found in the palaces and temples. The style is characterised by massive wooden beams set on stone foundations, often built with notches instead of nails and thus easily dismantled and moved. Roofs are usually made from heavy clay tiles. The strikingly bold and colourful painted design under the eaves is called *daechong*. Seoul's great gates, Namdaemun and Dongdaemuns are also worth a mention. See the Things to See & Do chapter for details.

Namsangol Traditional Village (Map 9) and the Korean Folk Village near Suwon (see the Excursions chapter) show what traditional *hanok* houses looked like.

Modern skyscrapers made of concrete and glass dominate modern Seoul. The 63 Building (Map 5) on Yeouido, and Jongno Tower (Map 8) near Jonggak subway station (Line 1) are two of the more stylish ones.

Painting & Calligraphy

Chinese influence is paramount in traditional Korean painting. The basic tools (brush and water-based ink) are those of calligraphy, which influenced painting in both technique and theory. The brush line, which varies in thickness and tone, is the most important feature of Korean painting.

The function of traditional landscape painting was to be a substitute for nature. The painting is meant to surround the viewer and there is no fixed viewpoint as there is in traditional Western painting. Court ceremonies, portraits, flowers, birds and everyday scenes were also painted. Many paintings include one or more of the traditional symbols of longevity – the sun, water, rocks, mountains, clouds, pine trees, fungus, turtle, cranes and deer.

Buddhist art can be seen in Seoul temples, art galleries and museums. Modern Korean artists tend to follow Western trends, but with a Korean twist.

Calligraphy can be written in either traditional Chinese characters *(hanja)* or in *hangeul*. The Seoul Calligraphy Art Museum at the Seoul Arts Centre (Map 2) has examples of traditional and modern calligraphy; see the Other Art Galleries section of the Things to See & Do chapter for details.

Sculpture

Stone Buddhist statues and pagodas such as the one in Tapgol Park (Map 8) are common examples of ancient sculpture in Seoul. Cast bronze was also common for Buddhas and some marvellous examples can be seen in the National Museum (Map 8). Stone versions of shamanist spirit guardians also exist, although wooden ones are more common. Both types can be seen outside the National Folk Museum (Map 8) in Gyeongbokgung.

Over 200 modern sculptures by artists from around the world are on display in Olympic Park (Map 7). Every tall building in Seoul must, by law, have a sculpture out the front to beautify the streets and mystify passers-by, so keep an eye out for them.

Ceramics & Pottery

Archaeologists have unearthed Korean pottery that dates back some 10,000 years, although it wasn't until the early 12th century that Korean pottery-making reached its peak as amazingly skilled potters turned out wonderful celadon pottery with a green tinge. Today original celadon is much sought after and can fetch millions of dollars at auction. It's even on display at the British Museum.

The pottery business took a turn for the worse during the 13th-century Mongol invasion and the Koreans started to produce *buncheong* ware – less-refined pottery decorated with simple folk designs. But it was admired by the Japanese, and during the Imjin War whole families and villages of Korean potters were abducted and resettled in Japan to produce *buncheong* for their new masters. This was yet one more cause for Korean resentment against their island neighbours.

Cinema

The Korean film industry produces around 50 films a year, but in the past they were not very successful or popular with local audiences. A few art-house films about alienated and unhappy people were shown in foreign film festivals, but directors tended to come and go.

Then in the late 1990s, the industry became more professional and consumer-oriented. Protected by a quota system that forces each cinema to show Korean films on at least 146 days of the year, commercial success has been achieved with a string of gangster and comedy films. In 2000 Korean films attracted almost as many paying customers as imported Hollywood ones. See the boxed text 'Korean Films' in the Entertainment chapter for reviews of some Korean films that are worth seeing.

Theatre

Numerous small theatres in Daehangno put on local and imported dramas and a wide range of theatre is staged throughout Seoul, but it is all in Korean.

Korean Opera

Somewhat similar to Western opera is *changgeuk,* which can involve a large cast of characters. The theatre in Insadong's Insa Art Plaza (Map 8) specialises in this kind of traditional performance.

Another type of opera is *pansori,* which features a solo storyteller (usually female) singing in a strained voice to the beat of a drum, while emphasising dramatic moments with a flick of her fan.

SOCIETY & CONDUCT

Traditional Culture

Meeting the Koreans Korea is probably the most Confucian nation in Asia. At the heart of this doctrine are the so-called Five Relationships, which prescribe behaviour between ruler and subject, father and son, husband and wife, old and young, and between friends. Understanding this structuring of relationships is very important in making sense of Korean society.

All relationships require a placement in some sort of hierarchy so that everybody knows how to behave and speak with respect towards each other. The middle-aged male office worker jumping the queue to pay for a Coke at a 7-Eleven store does not even register your presence because you have not been introduced and he has nowhere to place you on the scale of relationships. An introduction and an exchange of business cards would immediately place you into a category that would demand certain behaviour from him.

Once contact has been established, everything changes. Courtesy is highly valued and most Koreans will go out of their way to be pleasant and helpful. And you should return the favour – be polite and smile even when bargaining over prices in the markets.

Social Hierarchy Korean relationships are complicated by the social hierarchy.

JULIET COOMBE

A smiling local couple wearing traditional *hanbok*.

JULIET COOMBE

Elderly men, sitting on park benches in Tapgol Park.

PATRICK HORTON

The city's parks are hubs of social activity and creativity

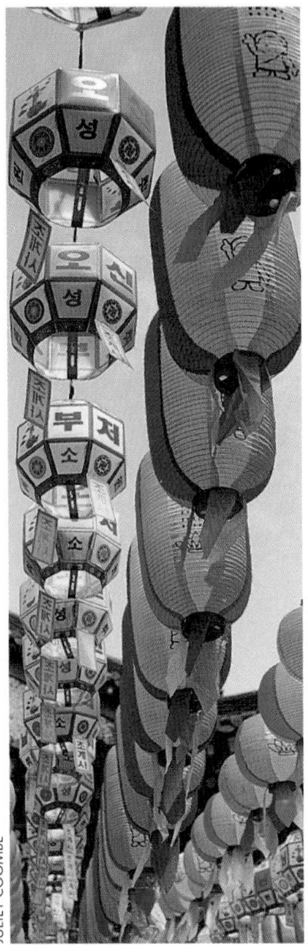

JULIET COOMBE

Festival lanterns at a temple

PATRICK HORTON

Put on a dramatic face with a tal mask, used in dance ceremonies

MARTIN VINCENT ROBINSON

Traditional drumming performance at Seoul Norimadang

Neo-Confucian ideals dictated that fathers, husbands, teachers, bosses and governments should be authoritarian rather than democratic, and this is changing only slowly. People with a high status may still act arrogantly towards those with lower status. Status is governed by many factors – for example, who is the older of the two? Who has the more prestigious job? Who attended the better university?

This notion of social status is one aspect of Korean culture that many foreigners (or those who prefer equality) find it difficult to accept. If you are working in Korea, your employer might make it all too clear that he or she is on the top of the social totem pole and you are at the bottom. But for short-term tourists, this is seldom a problem and since most Koreans are anxious to make a good impression, visitors are accorded considerable kindness and respect. Although even this depends on which country you are from – people from rich countries have a higher position in the social hierarchy than those from poorer countries.

Geomancy Based on Chinese feng shui, geomancy *(pungsu)* is the art of remaining in proper physical harmony with the universe. If a Korean finds that their business is failing, a geomancer might be consulted. The proposed solution might be to move the door of the business establishment to prevent good fortune disappearing out of the door, or to relocate an ancestor's grave because a restless, unhappy spirit can bring misfortune to the living.

The palaces of Seoul have all been correctly arranged according to the laws of geomancy, with mountains at the back and water in front. When the Japanese annexed Korea in 1910, they deliberately constructed their Capitol Building to obstruct the geomantic 'axis of power' on which the nation's fate depended.

In this day of modern high-rises and housing estates, most Koreans have had to push aside concerns about which direction their home or business is oriented towards. However, the positioning of a relative's grave is still taken very seriously.

Fortune-telling In the evening fortune-tellers set up their stalls on the pavements of Seoul. For a *saju* reading, inform the fortune-teller of the hour, day, date and year of your birth (if you know it), and after consulting a dog-eared little book he or she will predict your future. Another option is *gunghap,* when a couple give their birth details and the fortune-teller pronounces how compatible they are. These days most people do it for a bit of fun, but no doubt some take it seriously. Expect to pay W10,000 for *saju* and double that for *gunghap;* you'll also need an English-speaking Korean to translate.

Dos & Don'ts

Shoes Off In temples, private homes, Korean-style restaurants, guesthouses and *yeogwan* (small family-run hotels) you should take off your shoes and leave them by the front door. Wearing socks is more polite than bare feet, particularly in temples.

Losing Face It is important to bear in mind the Korean concept of *gibun* (face). Great efforts are made to smooth over potential problems, such as remarks that could lead to political or other disagreements. If you say something silly, there will be, at the most, an embarrassed laugh before someone steers the topic on to safer ground. Arguments or any situation that leads to one party having to back down will involve a loss of face, and this is a big no-no. The concept of face extends to the nation as well – Koreans generally consider it important that foreigners have a good impression of their country.

Keep it Neat In Korea you are judged by your appearance, more so than in the West. Travellers who dress like slobs will be treated with less respect than someone dressed casually but neatly. This is particularly apparent in Seoul, and out-of-towners always dress up to come to the capital city.

Greeting A short nod or bow is considered polite and respectful when greeting somebody or when departing, but don't overdo it.

A Gift for Giving

During my first month of teaching English in a junior high school in Korea I was showered with gifts such as free meals, free drinks, and free trips to the mountains, the seaside and a zoo. I wasn't allowed to pay for anything, and 'It's my treat' was the English phrase I heard most often.

Cans of health drinks, pens, rice cakes, fruit and choco pies kept appearing on my desk in the teacher's room. When a fellow teacher had a birthday, bought a new car or returned from a holiday they often bought everyone a small gift. One colleague had twins and bought all the teachers dog soup for lunch. When a foreign teacher in a nearby high school got sick, the teachers there collected W300,000 for him as well as filling his hospital room with drinks, fruit and presents.

At Chuseok (Thanksgiving Day) gift-giving reaches fever pitch and the shops are filled with mountains of gift packages. One foreign teacher had to hire a taxi to take all his Chuseok gifts back home from school. He was given 10kg of grapes, 10kg of pears, 1kg of *gimchi*, six pairs of socks, five tubes of toothpaste, a telephone card and a department store voucher.

Martin Robinson

Gift Giving It's customary to bring along a small gift when visiting somebody at their home. It can be almost anything – flowers, chocolates, fruit, a book, a bottle of liquor, tea or something from your home country. It's also appropriate to have your offering gift-wrapped.

When presented with a gift, your host may at first refuse it. This doesn't mean he or she doesn't want the gift – the idea is not to look greedy. You should insist that they take it, and they should accept it 'reluctantly'. For the same reason, the recipient of a gift is not supposed to open the package immediately, but rather put it aside and open it later. If you want to follow polite Korean custom, receive gifts using both hands.

Beckoning Don't use your forefinger to beckon someone. Put out your hand, palm down and flutter all your fingers.

Unlucky Number Most Korean hotels do not have a 4th floor because the word for 'four' *(sa)* sounds like the *hanja* for 'death'.

Embarrassed Smiles A driver almost runs over you then stops and gives you a big grin. Foreigners can get annoyed by this, but in fact the driver is not laughing at you – it's a sign of embarrassment, a form of apology and a gesture of sympathy.

RELIGION

There are four broad streams of influence in the Korean spiritual and ethical outlook: shamanism, which originated in central Asia; Buddhism, which entered Korea from China around the 4th century AD; Confucianism, a system of ethics of Chinese origin; and Christianity, which first made inroads into Korea in the 18th century.

Shamanism

Shamanism is not an organised religion; there are small shrines in the mountains, but it lacks a body of scriptures or written texts. Nevertheless, shamanism is still an important part of the Korean religious outlook.

Central to shamanism is the *mudang* (shaman) who nowadays is almost always female. Their role is to serve as the intermediary between the living and the spirit world. The mediating is carried out through a *gut,* a ceremony that includes ecstatic dancing, singing and drumming. Shamanist ceremonies are held for a variety of reasons: to cure illness, before setting out on a journey, to ward off financial problems, to send a deceased family member safely into the spirit world, or it might be held by a village on a regular basis to ensure the safety and harmony of its members and a good harvest.

Shamanism is often regarded as superstition these days, but it continues to be an active cultural force. Official records show that 40,000 *mudang* are registered in South Korea, but the actual figure could be closer to 100,000.

On Inwangsan, a wooded hillside in northwestern Seoul, is a shamanist village where *gut* ceremonies take place inside and outside a shrine, and offerings of food are made to the hungry spirits. See the Walking Tours section of the Things to See & Do chapter for details.

Buddhism

Buddhism in Korea belongs to the Mahayana school and, since its arrival in AD 370, has split into a number of schools of thought, the most famous of which is Seon, better known to the outside world by its Japanese name, Zen.

About 90% of Korean Buddhists belong to the Jogye sect, which has its headquarters in Jogyesa – a large temple located near Insadong. The sect claims to have 8000 monks and 5000 nuns, and is an amalgamation of two Korean schools of Buddhism: the Seon school, which relies on meditation and the contemplation of paradoxes to achieve sudden enlightenment; and the Gyo school, which concentrates on extensive scriptural study.

The small Taego sect distinguishes itself by permitting its monks to marry, a system installed by the Japanese during their occupation of Korea. The headquarters of the Taego sect is at Bongwonsa (Map 3).

Buddhism, a remarkably adaptable faith, has coexisted closely with shamanism. Many Buddhist temples have a *samseonggak* (three-spirit hall) on their grounds, which houses shamanist deities such as the Mountain God and the seven stars of the Big Dipper. Some Buddhist monks also carry out activities associated with shamanism, such as fortune-telling and the sale of good-luck charms.

Buddhism suffered a sharp decline after WWII. As South Korea's postwar economic boom got underway, Buddhism seemed to have little to offer – Koreans were not about to cast off their pursuit of worldly possessions to become a nation of fasting monks and nuns. But ironically, South Korea's success in achieving developed-nation status, coupled with a growing concern about the environment, is encouraging a revival of Buddhism. Visits to temples have increased, and a huge amount of money is flowing into temple reconstruction. It is estimated that approximately 25% of South Koreans are Buddhists, almost equal to the number of practising Christians.

Confucianism

Confucianism, properly speaking, is a system of ethics rather than a religion. Confucius (555–479 BC) lived in China during a time of great chaos and feudal rivalry known as the Warring States period. He emphasised devotion to parents and family, loyalty to friends, justice, peace, education, reform and humanitarianism. He also urged that respect and deference should be given to those in positions of authority – a philosophy exploited by Korea's Joseon ruling elite. He firmly believed that men are superior to women and that a woman's place was in the home.

His ideas led to the system of civil-service examinations, where one gains position through ability and merit, rather than from noble birth and connections. Confucius preached against corruption, war, torture and excessive taxation. He was the first teacher to open his school to all students on the basis of their willingness to learn rather than their noble birth and their ability to pay for tuition.

As Confucianism trickled into Korea, it evolved into Neo-Confucianism, which combined the sage's original ethical and political ideas with the quasi-religious practice of ancestor worship and the idea of the eldest male as spiritual head of the family.

Confucianism was viewed as being enlightened and radical when it first gained popularity, but during its 500 years as the state religion in Korea, it became authoritarian and conservative. It still lives on as a kind of ethical bedrock (at least subconsciously) in the minds of most Koreans, especially the elderly.

The main Confucian shrine is Taefongjon, on the campus of Sungkyunkwan University (Map 4), where traditional rites are occasionally held.

Christianity

Korea's first exposure to Christianity was via the Jesuits from the Chinese imperial court in the late 18th century. A Korean aristocrat was baptised in Beijing in 1784. When it was introduced to Korea, the Catholic faith took hold and spread quickly; so quickly, in fact, that it was perceived as a threat by the government and was vigorously suppressed, creating Korea's first Christian martyrs.

Christianity got a second chance in the 1880s, with the arrival of American Protestant missionaries who founded schools and hospitals and gained many followers.

Nowhere else in Asia, with the exception of the Philippines, have the efforts of Christian missionaries been so successful. About 25% of Koreans are Christian, but their influence is greater than their numbers because members of elite groups tend to be Christian.

The Catholic cathedral in Myeong-dong (Map 9) is a national symbol of democracy and human rights, and the outspoken Cardinal Kim is the conscience of the nation.

Chondogyo

This is a home-grown Korean religion containing Buddhist, Confucian and Christian elements that was started in 1860 by Cheoe Suun. Born in 1824, the son of an aristocratic family, Cheoe experienced a religious revelation and put his egalitarian ideas into practice by freeing a couple of his family's female slaves. The church was originally part of the Donghak (Eastern Learning) reform movement and embraced the idea of the equality of all human beings, a new concept in the Neo-Confucian order of the time.

The church is still going and followers believe that god is within and support humanist principles of peace and equality. The church headquarters, Suun Hall (Map 8), was built in 1921 near Insadong.

Facts for the Visitor

WHEN TO GO

Seoul has four very distinct seasons. The best time of year to visit is autumn, from September to November, when the weather is usually fine and Seoul's hillsides are ablaze with autumn colours. Spring, from April to May, is another beautiful season, with warm temperatures and cherry blossoms in late April. Winter is dry but bitterly cold, with January temperatures averaging -3°C. But white snow on the temple roofs is very picturesque and it is a good time to visit if you enjoy skiing or ice-skating. Try to avoid summer – late June to late July is the wet season, when Seoul receives some 60% of its annual rainfall, and August is unpleasantly hot and humid.

ORIENTATION

The main historical, sightseeing and accommodation part of Seoul is the downtown area, with Namsan and Seoul tower forming the southern perimeter. The tourist shopping and entertainment area of Itaewon is on the south side of Namsan. South of Itaewon, Hangang winds its way through the city. The small island of Yeouido, an important administrative centre, is situated in the river to the west.

The Gangnam district, south of the river, is where upwardly mobile citizens aspire to live. There are department stores and boutiques as well as many mid-range and top-end hotels. To the east is Jamsil, home to the giant COEX Mall, Lotte World and Olympic Park.

MAPS

The Korean National Tourism Organisation (KNTO) and Seoul City Council publish numerous free maps of Seoul. There is even a map showing all the public toilets. If you want some detailed hiking maps of the mountains around Seoul visit **Jungang Map Shop** *(Map 8; ☎ 730 9191)* near Insadong.

Just Fax Me the Map!

There is a good reason why most hotel business cards in Korea include a map on the reverse side – it's because addresses are almost impossible to find. One reason why fax machines have become so popular in Seoul is because Koreans often have to fax maps to each other to locate addresses.

In Korea, an 'address' exists in name only. In the entire country, there are almost no signs labelling street names. Indeed, most streets do not have names at all. Nor do houses have numbers on the outside, although every house does have an official number. Unfortunately, even these 'secret numbers' mean little – numbers are assigned to houses when they are built, so house No 27 could be next to house No 324, and so on. Many larger buildings have names – knowing the name of the building will often prove more useful than knowing the address.

A *gu* is an urban district only found in large cities like Seoul. A *dong* is a neighbourhood smaller than a *gu*. Seoul presently has 25 *gu* and 522 *dong*. Thus, an address like 104 Itaewon-dong, Yongsan-gu, means building No 104 in the Itaewon neighbourhood of the Yongsan district. However, you could wander around Itaewon for hours in search of this building with no hope of finding it, even with the help of a Korean friend. This is the time to make a phone call to the place you are looking for and get directions, or find a local police station, tourist information booth or – best of all – a fax machine.

The word for a large street or boulevard is *no* or *ro*. So Jongno means Jong St and Euljiro is Eulji St. Also worth knowing is that large boulevards are divided into sections called *ga*. Thus on the Seoul subway map there is a station at Euljiro 3-ga and Euljiro 4-ga – these are just different sections of Eulji St. A *gil* is a smaller street than a *no* or *ro* – Insadonggil is one such example.

Ondol

The best answer to Seoul's cold winters is the unique underfloor heating system known as *ondol*. Using *ondol* the entire floor is turned into a giant radiator. Traditionally, coal was burnt in an oven under a clay floor, but this style of *ondol* is very rare now. Modern apartments use hot water pumped through pipes in the floor. Not surprisingly, many Koreans abandon their beds for a traditional *yo* padded quilt on the floor during the winter months.

There is nothing quite so cosy, nor quite so Korean, as sleeping on a hot floor with snow on the ground outside. Unfortunately, sometimes the floors get a bit too hot and you wake up sweating in the middle of the night! Also don't leave your camera or films on an *ondol* floor in winter or they could get baked.

TOURIST OFFICES

Local Tourist Offices

KNTO operates an excellent **tourist information centre** *(Map 8; ☎ 757 0086; W www.knto.or.kr; open 9am-6pm daily Mar-Oct, 9am-5pm daily Nov-Feb)*, which has stacks of brochures as well as helpful and well-informed staff. Free Internet access, mobile phone rental, a café and a travel agent are also available. The auditorium shows Korean films with English subtitles free of charge on Tuesday at 4pm.

Another **information bureau** (Map 9) is situated in City Hall and it too offers free Internet access. Next door is **Seoul Information Centre** *(open 9am-10pm daily)*, and nearby are other tourist information booths situated inside and outside the palace Deoksugung. More than 30 **tourist information booths** are scattered around the tourist areas of Seoul and their number has been increasing every year.

A useful phone number to remember is ☎ 1330 (☎ 02-1330 if you are using a mobile phone), which provides information and help to tourists between 9am and 8pm daily.

Goodwill Guides *(W www.goodwillguide.com)* is an organisation that provides volunteer guides for foreign tourists. You pay only for your guide's expenses, such as transportation, admission tickets and food. Apply at least two weeks in advance. There are 3000 registered guides, but not all of them are reliable and turn up at the agreed place and time.

If you have problems with a particular hotel, guesthouse, restaurant, shop or taxi, contact the **KNTO Tourist Complaints Centre** *(☎ 735 0101, fax 777 0102; e tourcom@mail.knto.or.kr; PO Box 1879, Seoul 110-618)*.

KNTO Tourist Offices Abroad

For a complete list of the addresses of all KNTO overseas offices in 12 countries, see the KNTO website at W www.knto.or.kr (hit the Homepage link at the bottom of the first screen).

TRAVEL AGENTS

Top Travel *(Map 8; ☎ 720 8056, fax 722 0329; 5th floor, YMCA Bldg)* is recommended by many travellers and has a large number of English-speaking staff who deal with foreign customers.

KISES *(Map 8; ☎ 733 9494, fax 732 9568; YMCA Bldg)* is the STA Travel agent in Seoul.

Other travel agents advertise fares in the English-language newspapers.

DOCUMENTS

Visas

With a confirmed onward ticket, visitors from nearly all West European countries, New Zealand, Australia and around 30 other countries receive 90-day permits on arrival. Visitors from the USA and a handful of countries receive 30-day permits, 60-day permits are granted to citizens of Italy and Portugal, while Canadians receive a six-month permit.

About 30 countries – including the Russian Federation, China, India, the Philippines and Nigeria – do not qualify for visa exemptions. Citizens from these countries must apply for a tourist visa, which allows a stay of 90 days.

You cannot extend your stay beyond 90 days except in cases like a medical emergency; if you overstay the fine starts at W100,000. Phone ☎ 650 6341 for immigration advice for foreigners or log on to W www.moj.go.kr or W www.mofat.go.kr to find out more.

To get to the main **immigration office** *(Map 8; ☎ 650 6231)*, take Line 5 to Omokgyo subway station, leave by Exit 7 and it is a 10-minute walk. The downtown office (Map 8) may be able to help.

Applications for a work visa can be made inside Korea and are processed in as little as a week, but you must leave the country to pick up the visa. Most applicants fly to Fukuoka in Japan where it usually takes two days to process the visa. You can also apply for a one-year work visa before entering Korea but it can take a few weeks to process. Take note that the visa authorities will want to see originals (not photocopies) of your educational qualifications.

You don't need to leave Korea to renew a work visa as long as you carry on working for the same employer. But if you change employers you must apply for a new visa and pick it up from outside Korea.

If you don't want to forfeit your work or study visa, you must apply at your local immigration office for a re-entry visa before making any trips outside South Korea. The fee is W30,000 for a single re-entry or W50,000 for a multiple re-entry visa.

If you are working or studying in Korea on a long-term visa, it is necessary to apply for an alien registration card within 90 days of arrival. This is done at your local immigration office and requires fingerprints.

Driving Licence

It takes time to adapt to Korean driving methods, especially in Seoul, and the country has a bad road-accident record. Driving is not recommended – you'll spend most of your time lost, stuck in a traffic jam or trying to find a parking space. Public transport is a much better option and taxis are cheap, too.

You can use an International Driving Permit for a year, but you must obtain one in your home country before you come, as they are not available in Korea. After one year you must apply for a Korean licence. You will have to take an eye test, but otherwise it is a relatively straightforward process as long as you have a driving licence from your home country. However, if you are not from countries such as the USA, Canada, UK, France or Germany, you will need a certificate from your embassy stating that you are licensed to drive in your home country – check with your embassy or local driving licence centre for details.

There are four driving licence centres in Seoul and you must go to the one that serves the area where you live:

Dobong Office (☎ 934 7000) North Seoul
Gangnam Office (☎ 555 0855) South Seoul
Gangseo Office (☎ 666 4500) West Seoul
Seobu Office (☎ 374 6811) East Seoul

If you intend to drive, bring copies (or preferably originals) of your vehicle insurance documents from your home country. Being able to prove that you have a good insurance history should give you a discount on your insurance in Korea.

Travel Insurance

A travel insurance policy to cover theft, loss and medical problems is a good idea. Some policies offer lower and higher medical-expense options; the higher ones are chiefly for countries such as the USA, which have extremely high medical costs. There is a wide variety of policies available, so check the small print.

EMBASSIES & CONSULATES

South Korean Diplomatic Missions

Australia (☎ 02-6273 3044) 113 Empire Circuit, Yarralumla, ACT 2600
Canada (☎ 613-244 5010, W www.emb-korea.ottawa.on.ca) 150 Boteler St, Ottawa, Ontario K1N 5A6
China (☎ 10-6532 0290) 3, 4th Ave East, Sanlitun, Chaoyang District, Beijing 100600
France (☎ 01-47 53 01 01) 125 Rue de Grenelle, 75007 Paris
Germany (☎ 30-260 65432, W www.koreaemb.de) Kurfurstenstrasse 72-74, 10787 Berlin
Hong Kong (☎ 2529 4141) 5th floor, Far East Finance Centre, 16 Harcourt Rd, Central
Ireland (☎ 01-608 800) 20 Clyde Rd, Ballsbridge, Dublin 4

Japan (☎ 03-3452 7611) 1-2-5 Minami-Azabu, 1-chome, Minato-ku, Tokyo 106
Netherlands (☎ 070-358 6076) Verlengde Tolweg 8, 2517 JV, The Hague
New Zealand (☎ 04-473 9073) 11th floor, ASB Bank Tower Bldg, 2 Hunter St, Wellington
Philippines (☎ 02-811 6139) 10th floor, The Pacific Star, Makati Ave, Makati, Metro Manila
Russian Federation (☎ 095-956 1474) Ul Spiridonobka Dom 14, Moscow
Singapore (☎ 256 1188) 101 Thomson Rd, United Square 10-03, Singapore 307591
Taiwan (Visa Office, ☎ 02-2758 8320) Room 1506, 333 Keelung Rd, Section 1, Taipei
Thailand (☎ 02-247 7537) 23 Thirmruammit Rd, Ratchadapisek, Huay Kwang, Bangkok 10320
UK (☎ 020-7227 5500) 60 Buckingham Gate, London SW1E 6AJ
USA (☎ 202-939 5600, W www.koreaembassyusa.org) 2450 Massachusetts Ave NW, Washington DC 20008

Diplomatic Missions in Seoul

About 75% of Seoul's foreign missions are in an area southeast of Itaewon known as 'UN Village'. Log on to a site such as W www.embassyworld.com for contact details on embassies worldwide. Embassies in Seoul include:

Australia (Map 8; ☎ 2003 0100, W www.australia.or.kr) 11th floor, Kyobo Bldg, Jongno 1-ga, Jongno-gu
Canada (Map 9; ☎ 3455 6000, W www.korea.gc.ca) 10th floor, Kolon Bldg, 45 Mugyo-dong, Jung-gu
China (Map 9; ☎ 319 5101) 83 Myeong-dong 2-ga, Jung-gu
France (Map 4; ☎ 312 3272, W ambassade.france.or.kr) 30 Hap-dong, Seodaemun-gu
Germany (Map 6; ☎ 748 4114) 308-5 Dongbinggo-dong, Yongsan-gu
Ireland (Map 9; ☎ 774 6455, W www.irelandhouse-korea.com) 15th floor, Daehan Fire & Marine Insurance Bldg, 51-1 Namchang-dong, Jung-gu
Japan (Map 8; ☎ 2170 5200, W www.kr.emb-japan.go.jp) 18-11 Junghak-dong, Jongno-gu
Netherlands (Map 8; ☎ 737 9514, W www.nlembassy.or.kr) 14th floor, Kyobo Bldg, Jongno 1-ga, Jongno-gu
New Zealand (Map 8; ☎ 730 7794) 18th floor, Kyobo Bldg, Jongno 1-ga, Jongno-gu
Philippines (☎ 577 6147) 9th floor, Diplomatic Centre, 1376-1 Seocho-dong, Seocho-gu
Russian Federation (Map 7; ☎ 552 7096) 1001-13 Daechi-dong, Gangnam-gu

Your Own Embassy

It's important to realise what your own embassy – the embassy of the country of which you are a citizen – can and can't do to help you if you get into trouble. Generally speaking, it won't be much help in emergencies if the trouble you're in is remotely your own fault. Remember that you are bound by the laws of the country you are in. Your embassy will not be sympathetic if you end up in jail after committing a crime locally, even if such actions are legal in your own country.

In genuine emergencies you might get some assistance, but only if other channels have been exhausted. For example, if you need to get home urgently, a free ticket home is exceedingly unlikely – the embassy would expect you to have insurance. If you have all your money and documents stolen, it might assist with getting a new passport, but a loan for onward travel is out of the question.

Some embassies used to keep letters for travellers or have a small reading room with home newspapers, but these days a mail-holding service is rare and even newspapers tend to be out of date.

Singapore (Map 9; ☎ 744 2464) 19th floor, Samsung Taepyeongno Bldg, 310 Taepyeongno 2-ga, Jung-gu
Taiwan (Map 8; ☎ 399 2767) Visa Office, 6th floor, Gwanghwamun Bldg, Jongno-gu
UK (Map 9; ☎ 3210 5500, W www.britishembassy.or.kr) 4 Jeong-dong, Jung-gu
USA (Map 8; ☎ 397 4114, W usembassy.state.gov/seoul) 82 Sejongno, Jongno-gu

CUSTOMS

You must declare all plants, fresh fruit and vegetables that you bring into South Korea; meat is not allowed into the country. If you have more than US$10,000 in cash and travellers cheques, this should be declared and you may have to fill in a form. Gifts worth more than US$400 should also be declared.

Leaving the country, the duty-free allowance is 1L of liquor, 200 cigarettes and 59ml (2 ounces) of perfume. Antiques of national importance are not allowed to be exported, so if you are thinking of buying a very expensive genuine antique, check first with the **Cultural Properties Appraisal Office** *(☎ 662 0106)*. Log on to Ⓦ www.customs.go.kr if you need further information.

MONEY

Currency

The South Korean unit of currency is the won (W), with W10, W50, W100 and W500 coins. Notes come in denominations of W1000, W5000 and W10,000. The highest-value note is worth less than US$9 at the current exchange rate, so you may need to carry around a thick wad of notes.

Exchange Rates

country	unit		won (W)
Australia	A$1	=	W742
Canada	C$1	=	W843
China	RMB1	=	W150
euro zone	€1	=	W1337
Hong Kong	HK$1	=	W160
Japan	¥100	=	W1050
New Zealand	NZ$1	=	W685
Taiwan	NT$1	=	W35
UK	UK£1	=	W1970
USA	US$1	=	W1242

The won tends to be volatile so log on to Ⓦ www.keb.co.kr for up-to-date exchange rates.

Exchanging Money

You can use US dollars on American military bases, including the United Service Organizations (USO, the entertainment arm of the US military), at Panmunjeom on the Demilitarized Zone (DMZ) tour, at duty-free shops and in some tourist shops in Itaewon, but otherwise you will need Korean won. Duty-free shops also accept Japanese yen and some other foreign currencies.

Many banks in Seoul offer foreign-exchange services and there are a few licensed moneychangers, particularly in Itaewon, that keep longer hours than the banks and provide a faster service. However, as with shops and hotels that offer to exchange money, compare their rates and commissions with the banks before using their services.

US dollars are easiest to exchange but the banks accept any major currency. If you have trouble exchanging a currency, try the Korean Exchange Bank. Traveller's cheques usually have a slightly better exchange rate than cash. Exchanging money is easier in Seoul than elsewhere, so if you plan to make trips beyond the capital it's a good idea to exchange plenty of won before you go.

Don't forget to reconvert your surplus won into another currency before you leave the country, as exchanging won outside Korea is a major problem. If you need to reconvert more than US$2000 worth of won at Incheon airport, you will need to show receipts for the money.

ATMs Korean automated teller machines (ATMs) are a little strange. If you have a foreign credit card, you need to find an ATM with a 'Global' sign and the logo of your credit card company. Some of the Global ATMs have all their instructions in Korean, so you may need help. ATMs can be found outside banks and post offices, and inside deluxe hotels, subway stations, convenience stores and department stores.

Restrictions on the amount you can withdraw vary from machine to machine. It can be as low as W100,000 or W300,000 per day, but most ATMs have a W700,000 limit.

Most ATMs only operate between 9am and 10pm. Also be aware that if you use an ATM after 10pm or even outside banking hours you may be charged a higher commission. The reason for these restrictions seems to be to protect small local banks that cannot afford to introduce ATMs.

Itaewon subway station (Map 11; Line 6) has a Global ATM that has instructions in English, is open 24 hours and has a withdrawal limit of W300,000.

Credit Cards More and more hotels, shops and restaurants accept foreign credit cards, such as **American Express** *(☎ 552 7600)*, **Diners Club** *(☎ 3498 6100)*, **Visa** *(☎ 524 9827)*, **MasterCard** *(☎ 730 1221)* and **JCB** *(☎ 755 4977)*. Visa has a **customer service office** *(Map 9; ☎ 755 4071; open 10am-5pm daily)* opposite the Royal Hotel in Myeong-dong.

International Transfers Sending money overseas by telegraphic transfer is straightforward as long as the total amount is less than US$10,000.

Bank Accounts

It is easy enough for foreign residents with an alien registration card to open a bank account at one of the big banks – just find a clerk who can speak English and have your passport and alien registration card with you.

Costs

Seoul is a big city in a developed country, but prices are reasonable and you can get by on a low budget. Public transport, basic meals, admission prices and accommodation are all relatively cheap, although luxury hotels and famous restaurants are expensive. The exchange rate is a key factor and the stronger the won is, the more expensive Seoul is for foreign visitors.

Some typical costs are:

accommodation	cost (W)
dormitory bed	15,000
budget hotel room	25,000
luxury hotel room	350,000

food & drink	cost (W)
convenience-store ice cream	500
bottle of water	600
apple	1000
loaf of bread	1500
convenience-store sandwich	1500
local beer in a bar	3000
food-court lunch	6000
steak dinner	25,000
top-class dinner	50,000

other	cost (W)
local phone call	50
newspaper	600
palace entry ticket	700
cinema ticket	7000
traditional dinner and show at Korea House	80,000

transport	cost (W)
subway or bus ticket	700
1.5km taxi ride	2000
1.5km deluxe taxi ride	4000
flight to Jejudo	72,000

Tipping & Bargaining

Tipping is not necessary in Seoul, although a compulsory 10% service charge is added to the bill at top-end hotels and restaurants.

Most budget *yeogwan* (small family-run hotels) have fixed prices, but you can always try and bargain the price down if you are staying a week or more – some even offer special monthly rates. It is usually easier to bargain down the price of mid-range and top-end hotels, depending on the season and their occupancy rate.

In the traditional markets, it is common to make an offer 30% lower than the initial price asked for by the salesperson. But always bargain politely, as getting into an argument won't achieve anything. 'Smiling the price down' is the best method.

VAT & Refunds

Goods purchased in South Korea are subject to a 10% value-added tax (VAT), which is usually included in the selling price. It is possible to get some of this tax refunded if you are not a Korean resident and take the goods out of the country. Korea Refund and Global Refund are two schemes that you can take advantage of – see the Shopping chapter for more details.

Mid-range and top-end hotels usually add 10% VAT to all their bills as well as a 10% service charge; this comes as a 21% surcharge when you pay your bill.

POST & COMMUNICATIONS

Post

Domestic postal rates are W140 for a postcard, W170 for a letter, W1170 for a registered letter and W1500 for a package weighing less than 2kg. Local mail is usually delivered in two days or so.

International letter and parcel rates vary according to region but are reasonable. Postcards cost W350, aerograms cost W400, airmail letters cost from W420 to W500 and a 1kg parcel varies from W13,000 to W36,000. Don't seal your package if you want to take advantage of the lower rate that applies to sending printed paper. Larger post offices have a quality packing service that costs from W2000 to W5500.

You can find the poste restante counter on the 3rd floor of Central Post Office (Map 9).

Telephone

Despite the popularity of mobile phones, there are still plenty of public telephones in Seoul, especially at subway stations.

Some public phones accept only W10, W50 and W100 coins and can be used for local calls. Other phones accept phone cards and can be used for local or long-distance calls. Phones that can make international calls have a sign to that effect. The cost of a local call is W50 for three minutes; calls to mobile phones cost W300 a minute.

When using local-call phones, you will often find that the phone has been left off the hook. The reason is that the phones do not give change and it's the local custom to let someone else use your unused credit. If you can find a phone off the hook just press the green button and dial your number for a free call.

There is a 30% discount on long-distance local and international calls made between 9pm and 8am Monday to Saturday, and all day on Sunday and public holidays.

Useful Phone Numbers The *Korean Yellow Pages* is published every year in English and you can obtain a free copy if you visit one of its offices; you can also pay W4000 and have it delivered. For details log on to W www.yellowpages.co.kr.

The following are some numbers you may require; see also Emergency Numbers on page 28.

English Directory Assistance	☎ 080-211 0114
Focus 24-Hour Emergency Service	☎ 798 7592
	☎ 797 8212
International SOS Service	☎ 790 7561
Tourist Advice & Help	☎ 1330
Tourist Complaint Service	☎ 735 0101

Telephone Cards Telephone cards usually give you a 10% bonus and can be bought at many small shops. There are two types of cards so if your card does not fit in one type of phone, try a different-looking one. A few phones accept credit cards.

City & Provincial Area Codes

Both Korea's provinces and large cities have their own area codes. South Korea's country code is ☎ 82. Do not dial the first zero if calling from outside Korea.

Busan	☎ 051
Chungcheongnam-do	☎ 041
Chungcheongbuk-do	☎ 043
Daegu	☎ 053
Daejeon	☎ 042
Gangwon-do	☎ 033
Gwangju	☎ 062
Gyeonggi-do	☎ 031
Gyeongsangbuk-do	☎ 054
Gyeongsangnam-do	☎ 055
Incheon	☎ 032
Jeju-do	☎ 064
Jeollabuk-do	☎ 063
Jeollanam-do	☎ 061
Seoul	☎ 02
Ulsan	☎ 052

International Calls KT (☎ 001), Dacom (☎ 002) and Onse (☎ 008) offer direct calls overseas and you can make international calls from many KT telephone booths. Much cheaper international rates are offered by other providers whose call-back telephone cards are available in Itaewon. American Access offers calls to USA or Canada for 8.7c a minute at any time of day, while calls to Germany cost 12c and Australia costs 16.6c a minute. Eagles is another option in this competitive market. You could also log on to W www.kallback.com and W www.newworldtele.com for further information.

Lonely Planet's ekno global communication service provides low-cost international calls – for local calls you're usually better off with a local phone card. ekno also offers free messaging services, email, travel information and an online travel vault, where you can securely store all your important documents. You can join online at W www.ekno.lonelyplanet.com, where you will find the local access numbers for the 24-hour customer-service centre.

Emergency Numbers

Ambulance	☎ 119
Fire Brigade	☎ 119
Police	☎ 112

Note that operators are unlikely to be able to understand or speak English.

Mobile Phone Rental Mobile phones can be rented at Incheon International Airport and the KNTO tourist information centre (Map 8). Charges are around W20,000 for the initial rental and then W2000 to W3000 a day. Incoming calls are free and outgoing domestic calls cost around W350 a minute.

Fax

If you want to send a fax, first ask at your guesthouse, *yeogwan* or hotel, but if they can't help you, try the nearest convenience store or photocopy shop.

Email & Internet Access

There are cheap Internet cafés on almost every street of Seoul that charge around W1000 per hour; look out for the 'PC' signs. As they are popular with Internet gaming fans, some are open 24 hours but only charge from 10pm to 8am.

A complete list of free Internet venues would be extremely long but would include KNTO, City Hall, Itaewon subway station tourist information bureau, Incheon airport and Megaweb at the COEX Mall. Many guesthouses, cafés and even fashion boutiques offer free Internet access to their customers.

Internet Service Providers (ISPs) can offer you an English-language home page and continuous access for around W35,000 a month.

DIGITAL RESOURCES

There is no better place than **w** www.lonelyplanet.com to find news updates on Korea as well as the latest traveller's reports and suggestions.

The well-funded and well-organised KNTO runs an excellent site at **w** www.knto.or.kr – which has lots of information, an active bulletin board and useful links to other sites.

Seoul Metropolitan Government has a website for foreign tourists at **w** www.visitseoul.net. Also check out **w** www.seoulnow.net, **w** www.metro.seoul.kr, **w** www.lifeinkorea.com and **w** www.theseoultimes.com, which have useful information on all aspects of living in Seoul. The Seoul Times site includes roommate and homestay offers and details about Korean-language classes.

The *Korean Yellow Pages* publishes an English version at **w** www.yellowpages.co.kr that also has tourist information.

The newspaper websites **w** www.koreaherald.co.kr, **w** www.koreatimes.co.kr and **w** english.chosun.com have news, 'What's On' sections and article archives.

The website of the government-run Korean Information Service **w** www.korea.net covers Korean society, culture and arts, as well as politics and economics. The site also has links to translations of Korean poems, legends, folk tales and short stories.

Reviews of many interesting Korean films can be found at **w** www.koreanfilm.org. The local film industry produces a wide range of quality films that are successfully competing against imported Hollywood blockbusters.

For information on current and upcoming arts and culture events in Seoul log on to **w** event.kf.or.kr.

The chat site **w** www.kexpat.com has 200 members who are mainly foreigners in Seoul or other parts of Korea. It has links to other useful sites with information on different aspects of life in Korea.

BOOKS

Large local bookshops have sections devoted to English-language books on Korea. Books covering culture, cooking, history, Korean language and photography are common, but you can also find translations of Korean novels, short stories and poems. For Korean fiction and biography, see the Literature section in the Facts about Seoul chapter.

Lonely Planet publishes a *Korean phrasebook* – helpful in a city where English is not widely spoken or understood – and *Korea* – for travel throughout the country, including North Korea.

Korea Old and New: A History (1990) by various authors is objective, informative and readable. *Hanok – Traditional Korean Houses* (1999) is an illustrated history of house design in Korea. *Spirit of the Mountains* (1999) by David Mason is a thorough and well-presented study of shamanist rituals and beliefs. *Hanbok: The Art of Korean Clothing* (1999) by Sunny Yang is another well-illustrated book with lots of information. *Contemporary Dance Scenes of Korea* (2001) is a comprehensive, chronological book on the modern dance scene based in Seoul, which has become much more active recently.

Expatriate Handbook: Seoul, Korea (1996) by Jacqueline de Ville-Colby is an A-to-Z guide to Seoul for foreign residents.

Let's Eat Korean Food (1997) by Betsy O'Brien is a short introduction to Korean food with recipes. *Seoul Food Finder* (2002) by A & J Salmon has in-depth reviews of 140 Seoul restaurants. Although written in expatriate style, it is a useful guide to the more expensive restaurants.

A Field Guide to the Birds of Korea by various authors is comprehensive and reliable.

NEWSPAPERS & MAGAZINES

Korea has two locally published English-language newspapers: the *Korea Times* (W500) and the *Korea Herald* (W600). They are published Monday through Saturday, and it's difficult to tell them apart; both fill most of their pages with news agency reports and local business and political news. However, they do employ some young writers who file entertaining stories on local festivals, restaurants, cafés, nightclubs and out-of-the-way tourist attractions. At present the Friday editions have 'What's On' listings and articles. Their websites at **W** www.koreaherald.co.kr and **W** www.koreatimes.co.kr are an excellent source of 'What's On' listings and other useful information for visitors.

A third locally produced newspaper is the English edition of the *Joong Ang Ilbo,* which is an insert in the *International Herald Tribune*. Again, its website **W** joongangdaily.joins.com is probably more useful than the actual newspaper.

Chosun Ilbo and *Donga Ilbo* do not have printed editions but maintain websites at **W** english.chosun.com and **W** english.donga.com.

American magazines can be bought at the cover price plus a 50c shipping charge at the USO (Map 4), a 10-minute walk from Namyeong subway station (Line 1).

Various locally produced free English magazines are available from the KNTO or tourist offices. *Seoul Classified* has articles of interest to expatriates, as well as restaurant, job and accommodation advertisements. *Seoul Scope* is a monthly arts, events and entertainment magazine in English that can be found free of charge at the KNTO office.

Koreana is a magazine on all things Korean and can be found in both foreign and local libraries. *Korea Now* is published by the Korean Information Service and covers politics, business, society and the arts. Some of the current issue as well as past articles can be read online by logging on to **W** kn.koreaherald.co.kr.

RADIO & TV

There are five Korean-language TV networks: KBS1, KBS2, MBC, SBC and EBS. They often show American films that are invariably dubbed into Korean, but many TVs have a button you can press to hear the original English version. EBS is an education channel.

AFN is an English-language TV station run by the US military. It shows mainly popular American shows and action films. Log on to **W** afnkorea.com for the weekly schedule. AFN also provides radio broadcasts on 1530AM and 102.7FM, which focus on country music and American sporting events.

Arirang is a government-subsidised TV station that broadcasts educational programmes in both Korean and English. It is only available on cable and programme listings can be found at **W** www.arirang.co.kr. Also on cable are CNN, film, documentary, home shopping, golf, music video, cartoon, *baduk* (go) and Buddhist programmes. Satellite TV is also available.

Radio Gugak is a digital, government-funded station that broadcasts to the Seoul area for 22 hours a day (off-air from 3am-5am). It broadcasts all kinds of Traditional Korean music on 99.1FM. You can also listen by logging on to **W** www.gugakfm.co.kr and clicking on 'on-air'.

VIDEO & DVD SYSTEMS

South Korea has adopted the NTSC video standard used in the USA, Canada, Japan and Taiwan, but is incompatible with the PAL standard (used in New Zealand, Australia, Hong Kong, the UK and most of Europe) and Secam (used in France and Germany).

Video rental shops are numerous, especially in residential areas, and rental fees are cheap. It is worth checking that the video you want to rent has not been dubbed into Korean. Many *yeogwan* offer a library of videos that their guests can borrow for free, but you may not like their choice of titles.

If you are buying DVDs check that you can play them in your home country. DVDs can be watched in a DVD *bang* (room) for W7000 per person, or you can hire DVDs of Korean films with English subtitles from **Seoul Selection Bookshop** *(Map 8; ☎ 734 9564)* for W2000.

PHOTOGRAPHY & VIDEO

The big-name brands of print film are readily available in Seoul at reasonable prices. Processing facilities are of international standard and are not expensive. Slide film is more difficult to find as there is not much demand for it.

All the major camera and video brands are available as well as the local brands, such as Samsung, who are challenging the Japanese manufacturers. Yongsan Electronics Market (Map 6) and Techno Mart (Map 7) are the best places to buy all kinds of camera and video equipment. See the Shopping chapter for details.

Most people do not mind being photographed, but market traders and monks in particular should always be asked first as they may not want to be photographed. Taking photographs of shamanist shrines, offerings and rituals on Inwangsan without asking first is extremely offensive behaviour. In the DMZ you can usually take photos, but always follow the advice of your guide or you might spark off World War III.

TIME

South Korea has one time zone; the time in Seoul is Greenwich Mean Time (GMT) plus nine hours. When it is noon in Seoul it is 7pm the previous day in San Francisco, 10pm the previous day in New York, 3am in London and 1pm in Sydney. Korea does not have a daylight saving period.

ELECTRICITY

South Korea is on the 220V standard at 60Hz and uses two round pins with no earth. However, a few old buildings and *yeogwan* may still be wired for 110V and have two flat pins.

WEIGHTS & MEASURES

Nowadays Korea uses the international metric system for just about everything. The only exceptions are real estate, which is measured in *pyeong* (3.3 sq m) and the food markets, which still use traditional square wooden boxes such as *doe* to measure dried goods. *Ho* is a measurement for paintings, which used to be priced according to their size rather than their quality.

LAUNDRY

Guesthouses usually provide a washing machine free of use, and most *yeogwan* and all hotels provide a laundry service. Laundrettes, which charge around W4000, do exist but there are very few of them. Dry-cleaning shops are more common.

TOILETS

Seoul is one of the few cities in the world with plenty of clean, modern and well-signposted public toilets. Virtually all toilets are free of charge, and some are decorated with flowers and pictures. The cleaning staff do an excellent job.

All the major tourist attractions, parks, subway, train and bus stations have public toilet facilities. The small shopping, café and restaurant district of Insadong has no less than eight public toilets dotted around the area. Even when you go hiking in the mountains you will find lots of toilets.

The Asian-style squat toilets are losing their battle with the European-style ones with seats, but there are still a few around. Face the hooded end when you squat.

Carry tissues around with you as not all of the rest rooms supply toilet paper.

LEFT LUGGAGE

Incheon International Airport has a left-luggage storeroom and most subway stations have storage lockers, although most of them are too small to take a full-size backpack. The lockers cost W1000 a day and are easy to use.

To store luggage:
(1) Press the red button
(2) Press the number of the locker you want to use (empty ones have a key in the door)
(3) Insert the money
(4) Put your luggage in the locker, lock it and take the key with you

To retrieve luggage:
(1) Press the green button
(2) Press the number of your locker
(3) Pay any extra money owing
(4) Unlock the locker and take out your luggage

HEALTH

Opinions are divided as to whether you should drink the tap water in Seoul, but most locals drink filtered or bottled water, which is widely available and inexpensive.

Seoul is a healthy city with standards of sanitation and medical care that are equal to that of Western countries. There are two health systems – one is Western style and the other is based on traditional Asian principles and makes use of herbal remedies and acupuncture.

Many medicines are not available over the counter from pharmacies, so if you need a doctor's prescription try the **International Clinic** *(Map 11; ☎ 790 0857, fax 798 7480; W www.internationalclinic.co.kr; open 9am-noon & 2pm-6pm Mon-Fri, 9am-noon & 2pm-3pm Sat)*, which is in the Hannam Building on Itaewon's main street.

Fortunately a number of top hospitals have international clinics and sections where staff speak English. The one usually recommended is the international clinic at **Severance Hospital** *(Map 3; ☎ 361 6540; W www.severance.or.kr; open 9.30am-noon & 2.30pm-5pm Mon-Fri, 9.30am-noon Sat)* in Yonsei University. Yonsei also has a College of Dentistry. The nearest subway station is Sinchon (Line 2), but it is quite a walk, so if you are sick you had better take a taxi.

Another international clinic with an excellent reputation and English-speaking staff is at **Asan Hospital** *(Map 7; ☎ 222 5001, emergencies ☎ 2224 5001; open 9am-4pm Mon-Fri, 9am-11am Sat)*. The nearest subway station is Seongnae (Line 2, Exit 1) but again it is a 1km walk to the hospital, so take a taxi if you're really sick.

Another famous (but crowded) medical facility is **Seoul National University Hospital** *(Map 12; ☎ 760 2114)*, which is in Daehangno near Hyehwa subway station (Line 4). South of the Han river are **Gangnam St Mary's Hospital** *(Map 6; ☎ 590 1114)*, which is near Seocho subway station (Line 2), **Gangnam Hospital** *(Map 7; ☎ 3480 6114)*, near Samseong subway station (Line 2), and **Anse Hospital** *(Map 6; ☎ 541 1541)*, which is south of Apgujeong subway station (Line 3).

There are also oriental medicine hospitals that follow more holistic practices. **Kyunghee Oriental Hospital** *(Map 10; ☎ 958 8111; W www.khmc.or.kr)* in Dongdaemun-gu is a famous one that offers acupuncture and other treatments.

It is customary in Korea for a relative or friend to stay with a patient who is in hospital, often overnight in the case of a serious illness. They are there to help with the nursing work.

Pharmacies

Visit a pharmacy for minor illnesses, but you will need a doctor's prescription for most medicines. Pharmacists usually know some English but it may help them if you write down your symptoms or the medicine you want on a piece of paper. Pharmacists in Itaewon are more likely to be able to communicate in English than elsewhere, and there is a doctor's clinic for foreigners that is conveniently situated on the main street.

Some brand-name medications, special sunscreens, deodorants, dental floss and other health products can be difficult to obtain so stock up on them before you arrive in Seoul.

WOMEN TRAVELLERS

Seoul is one of the safest cities in the world for women, but the usual precautions should be taken. Walking alone at night is probably not a sensible idea in any big city.

Confucianism ruled Korea for six centuries and still lingers in the 21st century despite all the modernisation, urbanisation and Westernisation that has occurred over the past hundred years. In the Joseon era, Korea was a very male-dominated society and women were expected to obey first their father, then their husband, and if widowed, their eldest son. Upon marriage, daughters left their birth family, and most of the parents' wealth was inherited by the eldest son. Women visitors should therefore expect some interesting discussions with people who still have a Confucian view of a woman's role.

Another legacy from the past is that higher standards are expected of women than men, so it is generally regarded as bad manners for women to smoke, shout, display affection or reveal too much of themselves in public.

GAY & LESBIAN TRAVELLERS

Korea has never passed any laws that overtly discriminate against homosexuals. But this should not be taken as a sign of tolerance or acceptance. Korean law does not mention homosexuality because it is considered so bizarre and unnatural that it is unmentionable in public. Many older Koreans insist that there are no gays in Korea. Recent attempts by gays and lesbians to come out of the closet have met with hostility even in Seoul.

Virtually all Korean gays and lesbians keep their sexual orientation a secret from their family, work colleagues and friends. There are a few gay and lesbian clubs, bars and saunas, but they keep a low profile. Despite some discussion on the issue (see the boxed text 'Seoul's Bravest Man'), it is generally a taboo topic, especially for the older generation. Gay and lesbian travellers who publicise the fact can expect some hostile reactions.

Log on to **W** www.utopia-asia.com for up-to-date information on gay and lesbian issues and listings of bars and events in Seoul and elsewhere in the region.

DISABLED TRAVELLERS

In the past, Korea has not been geared to cater for disabled people, as disabled Koreans tended to stay at home or in their neighbourhood area and there were few disabled foreign tourists. But in Seoul this is changing, and the subway stations in particular have been making a huge effort to become more disabled-friendly. Many

Seoul's Bravest Man

Hong Seok-chun was a presenter of children's programmes on TV until 2000 when he became the first well-known Korean to admit publicly that he was gay. He was sacked, but was later given another TV job.

Facing up to the widespread hostility to gays, he is continuing his lonely battle to change deep-rooted traditional attitudes. 'Gays are not aliens from outer space, but are ordinary people like your regular friends and family members. I expect our society will develop into a more generous society that will embrace these minorities with a warm heart.'

But the reality is that virtually all Korean gays are still in the closet and have to be secretive. Their situation is like that of gays in the US army with its policy of 'Don't ask, don't tell, don't harass'.

Presumably there are millions of gay Korean men and women, but most are married, have children and keep it to themselves. That situation is unlikely to improve in the near future despite Hong Seok-chun's efforts to make homosexuality more acceptable.

subway stations now have lifts and elevators, and many new toilets for the disabled have also been built.

Tourist attractions, especially government-run ones, offer generous discounts or even free entry for disabled people and a helper.

A useful brochure is the *Accessible Seoul* map, which is available from tourist information offices. More information is available at **W** www.easyaccess.or.kr.

SENIOR TRAVELLERS

Some government-run tourist attractions offer discounts to senior citizens over 65, but you will need a passport or some other ID. Other organisations generally restrict discounts to local residents but it is always worth asking.

Respect for the elderly is one of the more admirable legacies of Confucianism so middle-aged and elderly visitors can expect young people to offer them seats on buses and subway trains.

USEFUL ORGANISATIONS

Lost & Found

If you leave something behind on a subway train, contact the relevant Lost & Found Office:

Lines 1 & 2 City Hall station (Map 9; ☎ 753 2408)
Guro station (Map 2; ☎ 869 0089)
Seoul Station (Map 9; ☎ 755 7108)
Lines 3 & 4 Chungmuro station (Map 9; ☎ 2271 1170)
Lines 5 & 8 Wangsimni station (Map 4; ☎ 2298 6767)
Lines 6 & 7 Taereung station (Map 10; ☎ 949 6767)
Bundang Line Suseo station (Map 7; ☎ 2226 6881)
Incheon Line Bupyeongsamgeori station (☎ 032-451 3650)

You can also log on to **W** www.seoulsubway.co.kr where lost and found items are posted.

If you lose something in the street, it is always worth reporting it to the nearest neighbourhood police station in case someone has handed it in there. The police also run a useful website **W** www.lost114.com which has long lists of items that have been handed in. In general Seoul residents are very honest, so it is worth trying to find whatever it is that you have lost.

Incheon International Airport has its own lost and found office – see the Getting Around chapter for details.

Foreigners Services

Foreigners Community Service *(Focus; ☎ 798 7529, fax 793 8370; **W** www.focusonseoul.com; open 9am-1pm Mon-Fri)* provides advice regarding health, legal and accommodation matters. Run by the Lutheran Church in Yongsan, it has volunteer lawyers who provide free legal advice for foreigners.

United Service Organizations *(USO; Map 4; ☎ 724 7003; **W** www.uso.org/korea; open 8am-5.30pm Mon-Fri, 8am-5pm Sat)* is the US military's entertainment wing. It organises numerous interesting tours and excursions that civilians of any nationality can go on. See the Organised Tours section of the Getting Around chapter for more details. It also runs a cheap US-style diner, sells US magazines at the cover price plus 50c and provides space to a travel agent called **Apple Tours** *(☎ 793 3478, fax 798 0698; **e** appleuso@yahoo.com)*. This is not the cheapest travel agent, but it organises short package tours and staff speak English.

Royal Asiatic Society Korea Branch *(Map 8; ☎ 763 9483, fax 766 3796; **W** www.raskorea.org; open 10am-noon & 2pm-5pm Mon-Fri)* was founded in 1900 and is still going strong with over 1000 local members. Free lectures open to all are organised twice a month and excellent weekend tours go to all parts of Korea; nonmembers pay 20% more than members. Membership costs W40,000 for a calendar year or W20,000 after 1 July. The office is a five-minute walk north of Jongno 5-ga subway (Line 1, Exit 2) in the Korean Christian Building, and has an interesting range of English-language books on Korea that are not available elsewhere.

Seoul International Women's Association *(**W** www.siwapage.com)* is an active group that organises weekly outings, monthly meetings, coffee mornings and other activities. Membership is W40,000 a year.

Translation Services

Hankuk University of Foreign Studies *(Map 10; ☎ 961 4114, fax 963 8780)*, the Graduate

School of Translation & Interpretation at **Ewha Women's University** *(Map 3; ☎ 3277 3662, fax 3277 3705)* and **Korea Herald Translations** *(Map 9; ☎ 778 2028, fax 778 1575; w www.pantrans.net)* are three options from the thousands of services available.

Religious Services

English-language Christian services are listed in the Saturday edition of the *Korea Times*. The **Lotus Lantern International Buddhist Centre** *(Map 8; ☎ 735 5347, fax 720 7849; w www.lotuslantern.net)* holds ceremonies in English every Sunday at 6.30pm. The **Korean Muslim Mosque** (Map 11) in Itaewon has prayers in English and Arabic every Friday at 1pm.

LIBRARIES

The **National Library** *(Map 6; ☎ 535 4142, 590 0586; w www.nl.go.kr; open 9am-6pm Mar-Oct, 9am-5pm Nov-Feb; closed 2nd & 4th Mon each month)* has a wide selection of English books, newspapers and magazines.

The **USIS Library** *(Map 4; ☎ 732 2601)*, opposite the USO, is run by the United States Information Service and is one of the best English-language libraries in Seoul. Non-military visitors cannot check out books but you can read them in the library. You might need your passport to gain entry.

British Council *(Map 8; ☎ 3702 0656; w www.bckorea.or.kr; open 8.30am-6pm Mon, Tues & Fri, 8.30am-7.30pm Wed & Thur, 10am-4pm Sat)* has a selection of newspapers, magazines, CD ROMs, DVDs, reference books and lots of videos of British films. Membership is W30,000 a year, or pay W2000 to watch a video or use the Internet.

The **Arts Library** *(Map 2; ☎ 760 4677; w www.sac.or.kr; open 10am-6pm Mon-Fri, 10am-5pm Sat Mar-Oct, 10am-5pm Mon-Sat Nov-Feb)* at the Seoul Arts Centre has many English-language books on the arts.

Universities and Seoul city districts have their own libraries, such as **Namsan Public Library** *(Map 9; ☎ 754 7579; open 7am-9pm Tues-Sun)*, but most books are in Korean. Major bookshops encourage their use as libraries by providing chairs and you can usually read there undisturbed.

UNIVERSITIES & FOREIGN SCHOOLS

Universities

Seoul is home to more than 50 universities, including many of the top ones. The Sinchon area (Map 3) is surrounded by four high-status universities – **Hongik**, **Sogang**, **Yonsei** and **Ewha Women's University** – and is flooded with the kind of shops, cafés, restaurants, bars, clubs and other entertainment facilities that appeal to students.

Some of the famous older universities have historic buildings that are worth a look as well as notable museums. Just inside the grounds, Ewha Women's University has Joseon-era and modern items on display in its art gallery and museum, while **Sejong University** (Map 2), opposite Children's Grand Park, has a large collection of folk items in its museum. These museums close during university holidays.

Sungkyunkwan University (Map 2) was the National Confucian Academy during the Joseon era, and the main Confucian shrine, Munmyo, is within the grounds. Confucian ceremonies are held there occasionally.

Foreign Schools

Seoul has a selection of schools catering for the children of resident or expatriate workers. There are schools that use English, Chinese, Japanese, French and German as the medium of instruction.

Seoul Foreign School *(Map 3; ☎ 330 3100, fax 335 1857; w www.sfs.or.kr)*, in Seodaemun-gu, is the largest with over 1000 pupils and takes all ages from pre-school to high-school level; it usually has a waiting list.

Seoul International School *(☎ 2233 4551; w www.sis-lhs.gyeonggi.kr)*, in Songpa-gu, takes all ages from elementary to high-school level and has many American students.

A **Montessori School** *(☎ 795 8418, fax 795 8439; e eclc@chollean.net)* is in the UN Village in Yongsan-gu and takes children from 30 months to six years old.

Log on to w www.metro.seoul.com for a list of foreign schools.

DANGERS & ANNOYANCES

Seoul is one of the safest cities in the world, except when it comes to traffic safety standards. Drivers tend to be impatient and careless, and many of them, particularly bus drivers, routinely go through red lights, so don't be the first person to cross over any pedestrian crossing. Vehicles rarely stop at pedestrian crossings that are not protected by traffic lights so it's better not to use them. Crossing any road except at traffic lights is not a sensible idea, and jaywalking is illegal.

Drunks in Seoul are better behaved than elsewhere. The swaying packs of late-night revellers usually pose more of a threat to themselves than to other people. Of course there is always an exception, so arguing with a drunk should be avoided whatever the provocation.

Visitors are often surprised to see police in full riot gear, carrying large shields and long batons, streaming out of police buses that have their windows covered in protective wire. Student (and sometimes trade-union) demonstrations do occasionally turn violent, although this is far less common nowadays as a democratic system of government has been introduced. Needless to say, it is wise to keep well out of the way of any confrontations that may occur.

LEGAL MATTERS

The Korean police tend to be easy-going with foreigners and most legal problems either involve visa violations or illegal drugs. In the case of visa transgressions, the penalty is normally a fine and possible expulsion from the country. As for using or selling narcotics, think twice: you could spend a few years researching the living conditions in a South Korean prison.

BUSINESS HOURS

For most government and private offices, business hours are from 9am to 6pm Monday to Friday, and from 9am to 1pm on Saturday. Government offices usually close an hour earlier from November to February. However, the five-day week is gradually being introduced, so fewer offices will be open on Saturday mornings.

Banking hours are from 9.30am to 4pm Monday to Friday. Post offices are open from 9am to 6pm Monday to Friday from March to October, and 9am to 5pm November to February. On alternate Saturdays they open from 9am to noon but this could soon end.

Department stores traditionally open from 10.30am to 7.30pm daily with one day off a week. Nowadays some open every day and a few open until late evening. New youth-oriented shopping malls tend to open late and some are open all night. Small shops often stay open until midnight even in suburban areas, and many convenience stores are open 24 hours.

Restaurants are usually open from noon to 9pm or 10pm. Cinemas are traditionally open from 11am with the last show ending at 11pm, but a few run later.

There is plenty for night owls to do in Seoul – some saunas, markets, malls, convenience stores, cinemas and restaurants open all night, while many bars and nightclubs stay open until dawn. Partying, watching movies or shopping until 5am means you can catch an early subway train home and save on the taxi fare.

PUBLIC HOLIDAYS

Nine Korean public holidays are set according to the solar calendar and three according to the lunar calendar, meaning that they fall on different days each year. Some public holidays – Arbour Day, Children's Day and Memorial Day – may be moved to Saturday when a five-day working week is introduced.

New Year's Day 1 January
Lunar New Year Begins 22 January 2004, 8 February 2005
Independence Movement Day 1 March
Arbour Day 5 April
Children's Day 5 May
Buddha's Birthday 26 May 2004, 15 May 2005
Memorial Day 6 June
Constitution Day 17 July
Liberation Day 15 August
Chuseok (Thanksgiving) Begins 11 September 2003, 28 September 2004, 17 September 2005
National Foundation Day 3 October
Christmas Day 25 December

SPECIAL EVENTS

Festivals of all kinds have proliferated in Seoul in recent years. There is an animated film festival, fringe theatre festival, drum festival, dance festival, folk arts festival, ceramics festival, taekwondo festival, *gimchi* festival and even a mud festival. See the KNTO office *(Map 8; ☎ 757 0086)* or **W** www.knto.or.kr for dates and a festival programme.

January/February

Lunar New Year Begins 22 January 2004, 8 February 2005. You can expect Korea to grind to a halt during this three-day holiday when Koreans return to their hometown, visit relatives, and eat rice cakes and other special goodies. Traditionally, babies are one year old when they are born, and then would turn two at their first lunar new year, which was everyone's birthday.

Valentine's Day This day has been split into two, so there is a day for females to give presents to their loved ones (February 14th) and another day for the males to reciprocate (March 14th), known as White Day. On 11 November (11/11) lovers exchange stick-shaped candies, and on Christmas Eve every young person tries to find a date for an evening meal. So Korean lovers have four days to celebrate! It's good for the candy manufacturers and shops.

March

Independence Movement Day 1 March. This is the anniversary of the day in 1919 when a protest movement against Japanese rule began following a public meeting in Tapgol Park. Demonstrations spread all over the country but were ruthlessly suppressed. You'll see lots of flags flying from people's apartments on this day.

April

Cherry Blossom Festival The date depends on nature and the weather. On warm days, eating and drinking under the blossoms in Yeouido's Cherry Blossom Park is the best way to celebrate this festival. On the southeastern side of Yeouido is a park full of cherry trees.

May

Parents Day 8 May. On this day countless red carnations are sold and children buy flowers or other gifts for their parents.

Teachers Day 15 May. On this day even strict teachers receive presents from their grateful students.

Buddha's Birthday 26 May 2004, 15 May 2005. The birth of Buddha has been celebrated in Korea for over 1000 years with a lantern festival, and so temples are decorated with brightly coloured lanterns. The Sunday before Buddha's birthday, Seoul celebrates with a huge evening parade by 100,000 Buddhists from Tapgol Park to Jogyesa.

June

Dano Festival 22 June 2004, 11 June 2005. Held according to the lunar calendar, this festival features shamanist rituals and dances.

August

Liberation Day 15 August. This celebrates the day that the Japanese surrendered to the Allied forces in 1945, marking the end of their 35-year rule of Korea.

September

Chuseok (Thanksgiving) Begins 11 September 2003, 28 September 2004, 17 September 2005. This is the Harvest Moon Festival, a three-day holiday when families get together, eat crescent-shaped rice cakes and visit their ancestors' graves.

October

Armed Services Day 1 October. Military parades take place on this day.

National Foundation Day 3 October. The legendary Dangun, regarded as the founder of the Korean nation, was born on this day in 2333 BC. He was the product of a union between the son of God and a bear who ate garlic and mugwort and turned into a beautiful woman. He ruled for 1000 years and when he died he became the mountain god.

Hangeul Day 9 October. This festival began in 1926 during the period of Japanese occupation as a means of maintaining Korea's cultural identity.

Seoul Citizen's Day 28 October. To celebrate this day a big programme of events is organised by the Seoul Metropolitan Government.

WORK

South Korea in general, and Seoul in particular, is a popular place for English teachers to find work. The job pays around W30,000 per hour and income tax is low. English teachers can expect to teach 30 hours per week and earn around W2 million a month, with a furnished apartment, medical insurance, return flights, paid holiday and completion bonus all being part of a one-year package.

Most English teachers work in a *hagwon* (private language school) but others work in government schools or universities. Private tutoring, company classes and even teaching via the telephone are also possible. Teaching hours in a *hagwon* are usually in the evening and at the weekend.

A degree in any subject is sufficient as long as English is your native language. However, it is a good idea to obtain some kind of English teaching certificate before you arrive as this increases your options and you should be able to get a better job.

Some *hagwon* owners are less than ideal employers so check out the warnings on the websites following before committing yourself. One point to keep in mind is that if you change employers, you will need to go through the procedure of obtaining a new work visa, which requires you to leave the country.

The English-language newspapers have a few job advertisements but there are hundreds of English teaching jobs on the Internet. A very useful website for English teachers is w www.englishspectrum.com, which has lots of job offers as well as useful tips on teaching techniques, information on living and working in Korea, and a bulletin board with accommodation offers. The website w www.kotesol.org is organised by a group of English teachers who run conferences and has links to other sites of interest. Also try w www.eslcafe.com, w www.eslhub.com or the job section of w www.yellowpages.co.kr. Koreans have an insatiable appetite for studying English so finding an English teaching job should not be too difficult.

Volunteer Work

WWOOF – Willing Workers on Organic Farms (*☎ 723 4458, fax 723 9996; KPO Box 1516, Seoul 110-601; w www.wwoofkorea.com*) has about 40 farms and market gardens in its scheme in Korea. Volunteers work for four to five hours per day in return for their board and food, and most of the hosts speak some English. The minimum period of stay is a few days and the maximum is by mutual agreement between volunteers and their host. Joining costs W15,000 and you will receive a list of farms that you can apply to.

Volunteer teachers are needed to teach English to some of the 26,000 children in Korean orphanages. Log on to w www.yheesun.com for information about becoming a volunteer teacher for a couple of hours per week.

Getting There & Away

AIR

Departure Tax

A domestic departure tax of W3000 is included in domestic ticket prices. International departure tax is included in your ticket.

Other Parts of South Korea

South Korea has only two domestic carriers – **Korean Air** (☎ *1588 2001;* **W** *www.koreanair.com)* and **Asiana Airlines** (☎ *1588 8000;* **W** *www.flyasiana.com)*. Fares charged by both companies are virtually identical on domestic routes, although fares are cheaper from Monday to Thursday and you're also more likely to get a seat. Flights on public holidays are expensive and often booked out, so avoid travel on these days if possible. There are discounts for students and children. Foreigners should carry their passports for ID purposes on all domestic flights.

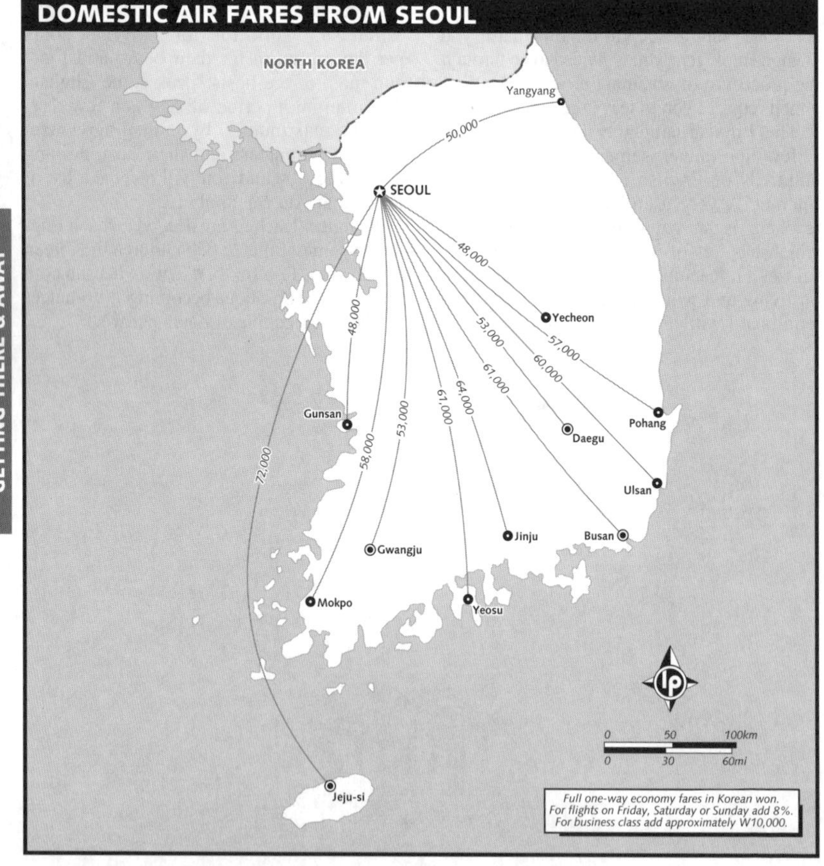

The longest flight (Seoul–Jeju-si) takes just over an hour. See the Domestic Air Fares from Seoul map for details of basic fares.

The USA

From the east coast, Delta Airlines, Korean Air and United Airlines all have return flights from New York to Seoul for around US$1100. Some flights go via Los Angeles or Tokyo.

From the west coast, direct flights from Los Angeles to Seoul on Korean Air or Asiana Airlines, or via Tokyo on United Airlines, start at around US$900.

Check out **STA Travel** *(☎ 800-781-4040; W www.statravel.com)* for cheap fares.

Flights from Seoul to New York begin at W790,000, while flights to Los Angeles start at around W690,000.

Canada

Direct return flights from Toronto to Seoul on Korean Air cost C$2310, or you can go via Tokyo on United Airlines for around C$2250. From Vancouver the price goes down to C$1450, but you have to go via Seattle and Tokyo.

Travel Cuts *(☎ 1-866-246-9762; W www.travelcuts.com)* is one of the largest discount travel agents in Canada, with offices in more than 10 cities. The website has no fares to Asia at present, but you can find the addresses and phone numbers of its offices.

Flights departing from Seoul to Toronto start at W934,000 and to Vancouver start at W720,000.

Australia

Return flights from Sydney to Seoul start at A$1010 on Vietnam Airlines, while Malaysia Airlines and Philippine Airlines charge A$1170. Qantas Airways and Korean Air both have fares at A$1210.

Two well-known travel agents in Australia are **Flight Centre** *(☎ 133 133; W www.flightcentre.com.au)* and **STA Travel** *(☎ 1300 733 035; W www.statravel.com.au)*, which have offices all round the country.

Flights from Seoul to Sydney, Brisbane or Cairns start from around W750,000.

New Zealand

Malaysia Airlines is often the cheapest carrier between New Zealand and Seoul, with fares around NZ$1460. Garuda Indonesia and Singapore Airlines charge NZ$1520 and NZ$1560 respectively. Korean Air has a NZ$1690 fare while Qantas Airways charges NZ$1720.

Travel Smart *(☎ 0800 622 000; W www.travelforless.co.nz)*, **Flight Centre** *(☎ 0800 243 544; W www.flightcentre.co.nz)* and **STA Travel** *(☎ 0508 782 872; W www.statravel.co.nz)* are travel agents with offices in the main cities.

Flights from Seoul to New Zealand start at W750,000.

The UK

In the UK, discount travel agents are known as 'bucket shops'. The cheapest return flights to Seoul from London start at UK£440 via Frankfurt with Lufthansa Airlines, but this is a winter fare. Air France has a UK£550 fare via Paris, and British Airways charges UK£700 via Frankfurt. Some relatively unknown airlines also offer cheap fares.

London has hundreds of discount travel agents, a few of which include **Trailfinders** *(W www.trailfinders.co.uk)* and **STA Travel** *(☎ 0870 160 0599; W www.statravel.co.uk)*. You can also log on to **ebookers.com** *(W www.ebookers.com)* and **WorldPlus** *(W www.worldplus.co.uk)* to check up-to-date prices. The latter company specialises in flights to the Far East.

Direct flights from Seoul to London start at W850,000, but are usually cheaper via Osaka at around W630,000.

Continental Europe

The cheapest return flight from Frankfurt to Seoul can go as low as €670 on Aeroflot Airlines. Korean Air charges €780, KLM Airlines €820 and British Airways €840. Air France has the cheapest student/youth fare at €640. Check **STA Travel** *(☎ 01805-456 422; W www.statravel.de)* for up-to-date fare details. Direct flights from Seoul to Frankfurt cost around W850,000.

Return fares from Amsterdam start at €745. For travel advice, try **NBBS Reizen** *(☎ 020 620 5071; W www.nbbs.nl)*, which has branches in most cities. Flights from Seoul to Amsterdam usually cost around W850,000.

The cheapest return fares from Paris are around €1410 on Air France. Try **Usit Connect Voyages** *(☎ 01 42 44 1400; W www.usitconnections.fr)* or **OTU Voyages** *(☎ 01 40 29 1212; W www.otu.fr)*, reliable travel agencies with branches nationwide. Flights from Seoul to Paris are generally around W850,000.

Return fares from Rome cost around €650. Contact **CTS Viaggi** *(☎ 06 462 0431; W www.cts.it)* for bookings. Flights from Seoul to Rome cost around W850,000.

Return fares from Zurich start at €810. Try **SSR** *(☎ 022 818 0202; W www.ssr.ch)* or **Nouvelles Frontieres** *(☎ 022 906 8080; W www.nouvellesfrontieres.com)* to book tickets. Flights from Seoul are around W850,000.

Japan

Japanese tourists make up the majority of foreign visitors to Seoul and increasing numbers of Koreans are flying to Japanese cities, sometimes just for the weekend.

There are direct nonstop flights from 19 Japanese cities to Seoul, but flights from Tokyo are usually the cheapest, starting at around ¥35,000 on Northwest Airlines. For stays of a month or more the cost rises to around ¥45,000 on Asiana Airlines, United Airlines or Northwest Airlines. Fares tend to go up and down with the seasons; fares in Golden Week and in August cost up to twice the price of low-season fares.

Airline Details

Airline	Code	Office (☎)	Airport (☎)
Aeroflot	SU	551 0321	744 8672
Air Canada	AC	779 5654	744 0898
Air China	CA	774 6886	744 3250
Air France	AF	3788 0400	744 4900
Air New Zealand	NZ	723 1114	–
All Nippon Airways	NH	752 5500	744 3200
American Airlines	AA	1588 8000	744 3282
Asiana Airlines	OZ	774 4000	744 2626
British Airways	BA	774 5511	–
Cathay Pacific Airways	CX	311 2800	744 6777
China Eastern	MU	518 0330	744 3780
Continental Airlines	CS	724 7088	–
Garuda Indonesia	GA	773 2092	744 1990
Japan Airlines	JL	757 1711	744 3600
Japan Air System	JD	752 9090	744 3300
KLM Royal Dutch Airlines	KL	733 7878	744 6700
Korean Air	KE	1588 2001	742 5175
Lufthansa Airlines	LH	3420 0400	744 3411
Malaysia Airlines	MH	777 7761	744 3500
Northwest Airlines	NW	732 1700	744 6300
Qantas Airways	QF	777 6871	744 3282
Singapore Airlines	SQ	755 1226	744 6500
Thai Airways International	TG	3707 0011	744 3571
United Airlines	UA	757 1691	744 6666

Remember to dial the prefix ☎ 032 for Incheon airport numbers when calling from Seoul.

Across Traveller's Bureau *(☎ 03-3374 8721)*, **STA Travel** *(☎ 03-5391 2922; W www.statravel.co.jp)* and **Just Travel** *(☎ 03-3207 8311)* have English-speaking staff who can help you find discounted fares. Also check classified advertisements in the *Japan Times* newspaper or on its website W www.japantimes.co.jp, as well as in the *Tokyo Journal* monthly magazine.

Flights from Seoul to Tokyo, Osaka and Fukuoka start at W250,000, but flights to Hiroshima (W330,000), Nagoya (W350,000), Niigata (W400,000), Sendai (W450,000) and Sapporo (W450,000) cost more.

Mainland China

Flights from Beijing to Seoul start at around RMB3400, while flights from Shanghai cost around RMB6000. There are also flights from Shenyang, Dalian, Guangzhou, Qingdao, Yantai and Tianjin.

Flights from Seoul to Beijing start at W250,000, to Shenyang, Qingdao and Tianjin cost W320,000, while those to Shanghai are W360,000.

Hong Kong

Flights from Hong Kong to Seoul start at HK$3680 on Korean Air.

To book flights try **Phoenix Travel Services** *(☎ 2722 7378, fax 2369 8884)* in the Tsimshatsui district of Hong Kong, which receives good reviews from travellers. Other reliable agencies in the same area are **Shoestring Travel** *(☎ 2773 2306, fax 2721 2085)* and **Traveller Services** *(☎ 2375 2222, fax 2375 2233)*. Check the classifieds in the English-language newspapers for a guide to current prices.

Flights from Seoul to Hong Kong start at W305,000.

Singapore

Flights to Seoul start at S$950 on Korean Air.

STA Travel *(☎ 737 7188; W www.statravel.com.sg)* has offices in Singapore, and other travel agents publish special offers in the classified columns of the *Straits Times*.

Flights from Seoul to Singapore cost W360,000.

BUS

There are no international buses to or from Seoul, but thousands of long-distance buses will take you to just about every small town in South Korea. Most major roads have a special bus lane that reduces delays due to heavy traffic and buses are so frequent that it's not necessary to buy a ticket in advance, except perhaps on holidays and weekends. Superior-class buses have more leg room but cost 50% more than ordinary buses. Night-time buses that travel after 10pm have a 10% surcharge and are generally superior class.

Buses go to far more places than the trains, but are not so comfortable or safe; for travelling long distances to major cities the trains are the better option.

Comparing the three forms of transport, Seoul to Busan costs W18,900 by ordinary bus and W28,350 by superior-class bus and takes 5½ hours, while the *mugunghwa*-class (limited express) train costs W22,900 and takes five hours. Flying costs W61,000 and only takes an hour, but you also have to travel to and from the airports.

Seoul Express Bus Terminal

Take subway Line 3 or 7 to get to the Express Bus Terminal station. The terminal is in two separate buildings.

The **Honam Terminal** (Map 6) is part of the Central City Mall, which includes the Korea City Air Terminal (KCAT), Shinsegae department store and the JW Marriott Hotel, as well as shops and restaurants. Buses leave from here for the southwestern provinces of Jeollabuk-do and Jeollanam-do, and travel to many small towns as well as to the major ones.

The **Gyeongbu-Yeongdong Terminal** (Map 6) is surrounded by shops and restaurants, and a large market complex occupies the floors above – clothes, linen and flower shops are spread over eight floors. Buses leave from here for towns in the eastern provinces.

Other Bus Terminals

The **Tong-Seoul Bus Terminal** (Map 7) serves major cities plus towns in the eastern provinces. Buses from the **Nambu Bus Terminal** (Map 6) go to 70 towns that are

Bus Schedules

Honam Terminal Sample Bus Schedules:

destination	first/last bus	frequency (mins)	fare (W)	travel time (hrs)
Mokpo	5.30am/midnight	40	16,000	5
Gwangju	5.30am/1am	10	14,000	4
Jeonju	5.30am/midnight	10	10,500	3¼

Gyeongbu-Yeongdong Terminal Sample Bus Schedules:

destination	first/last bus	frequency (mins)	fare (W)	travel time (hrs)
Busan	24-hour service	15	18,400	5¼
Daegu	24-hour service	10	13,100	4
Daejeon	5.50am/9.55pm	10	7000	2
Icheon (for ceramics village)	6am/9.20pm	30	3300	1
Yongin (for Everland)	6.30am/9.30pm	25	1900	1

southwest of Seoul or in the south central region of South Korea. **Seobu Bus Terminal** (Map 2) is home to buses that run to the small communities northwest of Seoul. **Sinchon Bus Terminal** (Map 3) has buses to Ganghwado, a historical island northwest of Seoul.

TRAIN

Seoul is at the hub of an extensive domestic rail network operated by **Korea National Railroad** *(☎ 1544 7788; ⓦ www.korail.go.kr)*. The railway ticketing system is computerised and tickets can be bought up to one month in advance at many travel agents as well as at train stations.

Foreigners can buy a 'KR pass' at overseas travel agents – try STA Travel, which sell them in 15 countries – or from the Korea National Railroad website, which contains full details on the pass and other Seoul rail services. The KR pass offers unlimited rail travel for three/five/seven/10 consecutive days at a cost of US$48/72/91/106, or you can select travel days within a one-month period. Couples or larger groups are entitled to a 10% discount and students aged under 25 receive a 20% discount.

There are three classes of trains. The fastest and most luxurious are *saemaeul* trains, but they only stop in major towns. *Mugunghwa* trains are also comfortable and fast, while *tongil* trains are cheap, stop at every station and only run on certain routes. *Saemaeul* class is nearly 50% more expensive than *mugunghwa* class, which is 80% more expensive than *tongil* class.

First-class seats (not available on *tongil* trains) are 30% extra. Tickets are discounted 15% from Tuesday to Thursday and standing tickets are discounted 15% to 30% depending on the length of the journey. If you hold a standing ticket you are allowed to sit on any empty seats.

A bullet train service is planned to begin between Seoul and Busan in 2008, which will reduce the journey time between Seoul and Busan from four hours to two hours.

There are also on-going talks about reopening rail links between North and South Korea, but this depends on the agreement of the North Korean government. If the link ever does get up and running, it would open the way to the development of a Seoul–London and even a Seoul–Singapore rail link but this is just a dream at the present time.

BULLET TAXI

These long-distance share taxis are useful if you miss the last bus or train. Negotiate a price before you set off. As their name suggests, the drivers tend to drive fast.

Sample Train Fares

destination	saemaeul (W)	mugunghwa (W)	tongil (W)
Busan	33,600	22,900	12,800
Mokpo	31,400	21,400	12,000
Daegu	24,500	16,700	9300
Daejon	12,600	8600	4800

BOAT

Other Parts of South Korea

Ferries travel to Jejudo (W42,000, 14 hours) from Yeonan Pier in the South Korean port of Incheon. Ferries from Yeonan Pier also service the many islands that are scattered in the West Sea. See the Incheon section of the Excursions chapter for details.

To get to Yeonan Pier, take subway Line 1 to Incheon station and then catch bus No 12 or 24, or take a taxi (W4000).

Japan

Ferries link the South Korean city of Busan with Shimonoseki and Hakata (Fukuoka) in Japan. Combined rail/ferry tickets cost W290,300 for Seoul–Busan–Shimonoseki–Tokyo, and W202,600 for Seoul–Busan–Fukuoka–Osaka. Tickets can be bought at Seoul Station (Map 9).

China

Regular ferries connect Incheon's International Terminal with seven cities in China – Shanghai, Tianjin, Qingdao, Weihai, Dalian, Dandong and Yantai. Fares start at around W115,000 but the cheapest fare to distant Shanghai is W135,000. Prices double for the more comfortable cabins. You can usually buy a visa for China on the boat for about US$20. A through-ticket is available that includes a ferry trip and train journeys in Korea and China – see **w** www.korail.go.kr for details.

Getting Around

KOREA CITY AIR TERMINAL

You can check-in your luggage and go through customs and immigration procedures at the Korea City Air Terminal *(KCAT; w www.kcat.co.kr; open approx 5am-10pm daily)* and non-stop limousine buses run every 10 minutes to Incheon airport (W11,000) or Gimpo airport (W6000). If you want to use the service, check the opening hours and make sure that your airline has a check-in desk there. Allow at least 90 minutes to get from KCAT to the airport.

The terminal has two locations – one is in the **COEX Mall** *(Map 7; ☎ 551 0077)*, while the other is in the **Central City Mall** (Map 6) and only serves international Korean Air passengers.

INCHEON INTERNATIONAL AIRPORT

This spacious modern airport, 52km west of Seoul, opened in March 2001, cost US$4.5 billion and relegated Gimpo airport to handling domestic flights. However, a few Korea Air and Asiana Airlines flights to Jejudo and Busan do leave from the small domestic section at Incheon airport.

The airport has been built on reclaimed land between two islands in the West Sea off Incheon city and is connected by a road bridge to the mainland. The subway train link to Seoul won't be completed until around 2006.

The 1st floor is for arrivals. There are **car-rental counters**, **tourist information offices** and 20 **foreign currency exchanges** *(open 6am-10pm daily)*. Mobile phones can be rented at the **KT office** *(open 6.30am-9.30pm daily)* and **LG Telecom** *(open 6.30am-10pm daily)*. **Bus information** and **tickets** are available, and frequent buses leave for destinations around South Korea from just outside the airport building.

The 2nd floor has a **business centre** and the **KT plaza** *(open 7am-9pm daily)*, next to the **post office** *(open 9am-6pm daily)*, which offers free Internet access for 30 minutes.

The 3rd floor is for departures and has plenty of opportunities for retail therapy in the **duty-free shops**. **Restaurants**, fast-food outlets, cafés and bars charge reasonable prices. The **left-luggage office** *(open 7am-9.30pm daily)* rents backpacks for W3000 a day. The **lost & found office** *(☎ 741 3114; e find119@airport.or.kr; open 7am-10.30pm daily)* is the place to contact if something goes missing. **Banks** in the shopping area beyond immigration control enable you to exchange any won before leaving the country.

If you want to obtain a **tax refund** on goods you bought at a shop that participates in one of the tax refund schemes, you must show the goods and receipt to one of the customs officers behind the check-in counters. After you've gone through immigration control, show the stamped receipt at the refund counter to receive your money.

The 4th floor is hard to find but has Korean and Japanese **restaurants**, a cheap **snack bar** (pumpkin porridge and ginseng tea for W5000) and a **games arcade**. Try **Café Royal** *(American breakfast W12,000, continental breakfast W9300)*.

The basement contains an **ice-cream parlour**, a **supermarket** and **restaurants** that offer a range of meals for under W10,000. If you have time to kill, you can enjoy a game of **ten-pin bowling**; games are W3000, shoe hire is W1000. Men can pay W9500 for a session at the **fitness club** *(open 6am-10pm daily)*, or try out the **sauna** *(open 24hrs)* for W6500 during the day and W13,000 at night. **Massages** are also available here for W30,000. You can sleep in the sauna all night if you don't mind a hard bed and pillow. If you need medical or dental treatment, contact the **Medical Centre** *(☎ 743 3115, emergency ☎ 743 3119; open 9.30am-5.30pm Mon-Fri, 9.30am-3pm Sat)*.

Accommodation

The **Air Garden Transit Hotel** *(☎ 743 3000, fax 743 3001; w www.airgardenhotel.com; 6-hr standard rooms/deluxe rooms/suites W40,000/*

City Limousine Bus Schedule

bus (destination)	route
600 (Jamsil)	Incheon airport, Gimpo airport, Gonghangno, Heukseok-dong, Seoul Express Bus Terminal, Bongeunsaro, Samseong station, Lotte World
601 (Dongdaemun)	Incheon airport, Yanghwa Bridge, Hapjeong-dong, Sinchon, City Hall, Jongno
602 (Cheongnyangni)	Incheon airport, Hapjeong station, Gwanghwamun, Dongdaemun, Cheongnyangni
603 (Guro)	Incheon airport, Gimpo airport, Mokdong Ogeori, Jinmyeong School, Galsan School, Guro station
604 (Geumcheon-gu Office)	Incheon airport, Gimpo airport, Nambu Cargo Terminal, Gaerong station, Novotel Hotel, Geumcheon-gu Office
605 (City Hall)	Incheon airport, Gangbyeon Express Way, Mapo, Gongdeok-dong, Seoul Station, City Hall, Gwanghwamun, Chungjeongno
606 (Jamsil)	Incheon airport, Olympic Expressway, Seoul Express Bus Terminal, Apgujeong-dong, Samseong station, Lotte World
607 (Songjeong station)	Incheon airport, Gimpo airport, Songjeong station
608 (Yeongdeungpo station)	Incheon airport, Gimpo airport, Dangsan station, Yeongdeungpo station
609 (Daechi station)	Incheon airport, Seoul Express Bus Terminal, Gangnam station, Yangjae station, Dogok-dong, Daechi-dong

50,000/70,000) is rather like a love motel and rents out 90 non-smoking rooms on a short-term basis. Add 21% for tax and service and W12,000 for double occupancy. Located inside the airport, it is only available to transit passengers. Facilities include lounges, Western and Korean meals, a business centre and a games room.

To/From Incheon Airport

There are two types of buses that run from Incheon airport to Seoul: the City limousine buses cost W6000 and run along a variety of routes from around 5am to 11pm. The KAL limousine 25-seat buses cost W11,000 and drop passengers off at 18 major hotels in Seoul. Buses usually run every 15 minutes. Travelling on these buses to downtown Seoul takes around 90 minutes depending on traffic conditions in the city. Frequent buses also run every 10 minutes to Gimpo airport along a special airport road, which takes about 30 minutes and costs W4000 on the City limousine buses or W6000 on the KAL ones. If no airport bus travels where you want to go, ask the bus driver to drop you near a subway station. For up-to-date information on the airport and the buses log on to W www.airport.or.kr.

Intercity buses also run from the airport to cities such as Jeonju, Wonju, Taean, Gwangju, Daejon, Cheongju, Chuncheon and towns in Gyeonggi-do.

Regular taxis charge around W40,000 to downtown Seoul while a deluxe taxi could cost W60,000. From midnight to 4am taxis charge 20% extra.

GIMPO DOMESTIC AIRPORT

Since the opening of the Incheon International Airport, Gimpo airport *(W gimpo.airport.co.kr)*, 18km west of Seoul city centre, handles only domestic flights. The 1st floor is for arrivals, the 2nd floor is for checking in, the 3rd floor is for departures and the Sejong Restaurant is on the 4th floor. The **tourist information booth** *(open 9am-10pm daily)* offers free Internet access. Facilities in the airport include souvenir shops, a food court, fast-food outlets, a café and a convenience store.

KAL Limousine Bus Schedule

bus (destination)	route
KAL1 (City Hall)	Incheon airport, KAL, Chosun Hotel, Lotte Hotel, Plaza Hotel, Koreana Hotel, Gimpo airport, Incheon airport
KAL1 (City Hall)	Incheon airport, Gimpo airport, KAL, Chosun Hotel, Plaza Hotel, Koreana Hotel, Incheon airport
KAL2 (Namsan)	Incheon airport, Seoul Station, Hilton Hotel, Shilla Hotel, Hyatt Hotel, Seoul Station, Holiday Inn, Gimpo airport, Incheon airport
KAL2 (Namsan)	Incheon airport, Gimpo airport, Ambassador Hotel, Shilla Hotel, Tower Hotel, Hyatt Hotel, Hilton Hotel, Seoul Station, Holiday Inn, Incheon airport
KAL3 (Gangnam)	Incheon airport, Ritz Carlton Hotel, Palace Hotel, Gimpo airport, Incheon airport
KAL3 (Gangnam)	Incheon airport, Gimpo airport, Renaissance Hotel, Grand Intercontinental Hotel, COEX Intercontinental Hotel, Novotel Hotel, Ritz Carlton Hotel, Palace Hotel, Incheon airport
KAL4 (Jamsil)	Incheon airport, Sheraton Walker Hill Hotel, Dong-Seoul Bus Terminal, Lotte World, Gimpo airport, Incheon airport
KAL4 (Jamsil)	Incheon airport, Gimpo airport, Lotte World, Dong-Seoul Bus Terminal, Sheraton Walker Hill Hotel, Incheon airport
Direct (Gimpo airport)	Incheon airport, Gimpo airport
Direct (KCAT)	Incheon airport, KCAT
Direct (Seoul Express Bus Terminal)	Incheon airport, Seoul Express Bus Terminal
Direct (Seoul Station)	Incheon airport, Seoul Station, Itaewon, Incheon airport, 63 Building, Itaewon Hotel, Crown Hotel
KCAT	Incheon airport, Gimpo airport, KCAT
Dobong & Nowon	Incheon airport, Gimpo airport, Naebu Expressway, Gireum station, Dongduk Women's University, Taereung station, Hagye station, Junggye station, Nowon station, Chang-dong station, Sofia, Banghak Sageori

The KAL limousine buses run on two routes – one goes downtown via Gimpo airport and returns direct to Incheon, while the other goes direct to downtown and returns to Incheon via Gimpo. But since going to Gimpo involves only a short diversion, it doesn't make much difference to the journey time.

The best way to travel the 18km between Gimpo airport and downtown Seoul is to take subway Line 5, which costs W800. There are also buses and taxis.

SUBWAY

Seoul's subway system (W *www.seoulsubway.co.kr, www.smrt.co.kr*) is modern, fast, frequent, clean, safe and cheap, but try to avoid rush hour. Trains run every few minutes from around 5.30am to 11.30pm, but there are plans to run trains an hour later. In central Seoul the average time between stations is two minutes, so it takes about 20 minutes to go 10 stops.

Many subway stations have lifts or stair lifts for wheelchairs. Neighbourhood maps help you to decide which of the many exits to take, but north can be in any position, which makes the maps confusing. The stations all have clean modern toilets, but you need to carry around your own toilet paper. Luggage lockers are widely available, although most are too small to take a full-size backpack. Every station is well signed in English and the whole system is very user-friendly.

Hawkers walk up and down the carriages selling a variety of small goods, such as rubber gloves, razors and CD players. The occasional handicapped beggar also wanders down the aisle with a begging bowl and a cassette playing hymns.

The basic one-way subway fare is only W700 and this covers most of the Seoul area. Hour-long trips cost up to W1000. The best plan is to buy a W10,000 stored-value card which gives you W11,000 worth of travel. Another type of travel card called *gyotongkadeu* can be used on buses as well as the subway; you can buy them from kiosks near major bus stops and must pay a small deposit on the card.

The **Korea Pass Card** (☎ *1566-7331;* W *koreapasscard.com)* is a convenient pre-paid card that can be used on the subway and buses. It also works as a telephone card and credit card, and offers discounts on some tourist attractions and services. You can buy the cards in denominations ranging from W50,000 to W500,000 at the Hotel Information desk in Incheon airport, at the Korean National Tourism Organisation (KNTO) and at deluxe downtown hotels such as Lotte and Radisson Plaza.

BUS

It is usually more convenient to travel by subway, but Seoul also has a comprehensive and cheap city bus system that operates from around 5.30am to midnight. Most buses have their major destinations written in English on the outside and they usually have a taped announcement of the names of each stop in English, but most bus drivers don't understand any English.

The basic fare on ordinary buses is W700; express buses cost W1300 and deluxe express buses cost W1400. You put the money in the box with a glass top and the driver will give you change if necessary. The *Seoul Bus Guide Map* contains useful information on major bus routes.

CAR

Driving a vehicle is something to avoid in Seoul because of the traffic jams, the lack of street names, directional signs and parking places, and the unpredictability of other road users. Public transport is so cheap and convenient that few tourists get behind a steering wheel. However, renting a car to tour around outside Seoul is more sensible, but a lack of signs in English can be a problem and drivers have to pay tolls to use the expressways. You must be over 21 years of age and have an International Driving Permit in order to rent a car. Prices start at W36,000 for six hours, W46,000 for 10 hours and W64,000 for 24 hours. Another option is to rent both a car and a driver but the driver will cost W100,000 or more. The best place to hire a car would be Incheon airport; see what **Kumho-Hertz** (W *www.kumhorent.com)* has to offer.

TAXI

Regular taxis are a good deal and are cheaper than the bus or subway for three people who want to make a short trip. Regular taxis cost W1600 for the first 2km and then W100 for every 168m or 41 seconds afterwards. A 20% surcharge is payable between midnight and 4am. Deluxe taxis *(mobeom)* cost W4000 for the first 3km and then W200 for every 205m or 50 seconds, and don't have a late-night surcharge.

Taxis outside Seoul charge less – W1500 in Gyeonggi-do or W1300 in Incheon for the first 2km.

Few drivers can speak English, but some taxis have a free interpretation service – you speak on the phone to a translator who then talks to the taxi driver. Tipping is not a Korean custom and is not necessary.

BICYCLE

See Cycling in the Things to See & Do chapter for cycle trips around Seoul.

WALKING

Walking around downtown Seoul is no particular problem, although going down and up underpasses to cross major roads is tiresome. Also, care needs to be taken on pedestrian crossings – even ones protected by traffic lights. Outside the downtown area, places of interest are far apart and so taking the subway is a better policy than walking. See the Walking Tours section of the Things to See & Do chapter for some interesting walks.

ORGANISED TOURS

There are lots of tours to choose from in Seoul. If you join a tour, make sure there is an English-speaking guide. Most Korean tours include lunch and shopping stops. Log on to **W** www.startravel.co.kr for examples of tours and prices, or visit the KNTO office for leaflets and information on what tours are available.

Tours to Icheon Ceramics Village and Ganghwado are a good idea, as both these areas are difficult to look around using public transport. See the Excursions chapter for more information.

The **Royal Asiatic Society Korea Branch** (*☎ 763 9483, fax 766 3796;* **W** *www.raskorea.org*) organises over 90 different tours to all parts of South Korea, usually at weekends. Non-members are welcome and all tours are led by English speakers who are experts in their field. Tour costs vary from W6000 to W60,000.

The **United Service Organizations** (*USO; ☎ 724 7003, fax 723 4106;* **W** *www.uso.org/korea*) organises tours for American troops but civilians are welcome to join in. Twice a week the USO runs tours to Panmunjeom, the Demilitarized Zone (DMZ) and an Infiltration Tunnel for US$40, not including lunch. The tours start at 7.30am and finish at 3pm. See the Panmunjeom & the DMZ section of the Excursions chapter for more details. The USO also runs all-day Gwanghwado tours for US$22 from 8.30am to 4.30pm, as well as skiing and white-water rafting excursions.

TrekKorea (*☎ 540 0840, fax 540 0656;* **W** *www.trekkorea.com*) runs rafting, caving, mountain-biking, horse-riding, camping and hiking tours. Tours that last one or two days cost W60,000.

Exciting Korea (*☎ 725 1237, fax 725 1238;* **W** *www.excitingkorea.com*) runs inexpensive tours around Korea on the weekend and mid-week that cost W30,000 to W50,000. The tours consist of minibus-sized groups of Koreans and foreigners.

iculture Tours (*☎ 878 3977, fax 871 3464;* **W** *www.iculturetour.com*) organises two-day martial-arts tours (*sunmudo, hapkido, taekkyon, kunmodo, gumdo* and taekwondo) from W160,000. It also runs historical and cultural tours.

Overland tours to North Korea have been operated by Hyundai Asan since February 2003. Coaches leave from the northeastern province of Gangwon-do in South Korea, cross over the highly fortified DMZ and drive for an hour through North Korea to Geumgangsan (spelt Kumgangsan in North Korea), a famous scenic area of towering mountain peaks, granite pinnacles and waterfalls. No visas are required – just two passport-size photographs. If you share a dormitory (six persons), a three-day/two-night tour costs W230,000, while the same tour costs W350,000 per person if you share a double room at Haegeumgang Hotel. The tour includes a coastal route as well as two hikes (Guryongyeon and Manmulsang), a hot-spring bath, a circus or cultural performance and souvenir shops. Phone ☎ 3669 3000 for more information or find a travel agent that handles these tours.

Seoul City Tour Bus

Especially designed for tourists, these comfortable buses run along various routes linking Seoul's top tourist attractions north of Hangang and on Yeouido. Buses run every 30 minutes between 9am and 7pm. Ticket holders are also entitled to discounts on some tourist attractions on the route. Log on to **W** www.seoulcitytourbus.com for more details. The Tour Bus is excellent if you have only a few days and want to see everything as quickly as possible.

A one-day ticket costs a very reasonable W10,000, while a two-day ticket is only W15,000. You can buy the tickets on the bus.

Royal Palaces of Seoul

Royal Palaces of Seoul

BILL WASSMAN

DENNIS JOHNSON

Title Page: The main hal
and courtyard of the
historic Changdeokgung
(Photograph by Jeff Yates

Top: Gyeongbokgung

Bottom: Gyeonghoeru
pavilion once served as a
banquet hall in
Gyeongbokgung

Although their size and splendour have been greatly reduced by wars, fires and Japanese colonial policy, Seoul's royal palace compounds contain a variety of restored buildings that offer visitors glimpses of Korea's fascinating feudal past. Traditional Korean palaces followed Confucian ideas of simplicity, so don't expect the opulent decor of Western palaces. The palaces were mini towns surrounded by high walls and resemble monastery complexes. Restoration and rebuilding work is going on all the time as the government seeks to recreate the palaces as they were during the Joseon dynasty. It's a huge, ambitious scheme that will take decades to complete.

The large palaces used to be a maze of corridors and courtyards, buildings and walls, ponds and gardens, thronged with government officials and scholars, eunuchs and concubines, soldiers, servants and slaves. The grand formal buildings, where government business was carried on, contrasted with the smaller, more informal living quarters where men and women were separated according to strict Confucian principles and lived separate lives.

In the warmer months, free historical re-enactments and concerts are held in the palace grounds. Check with the **KNTO** *(Map 8; ☎ 757 0086; W www.knto.or.kr)* or log on to W www.ocp.go.kr for more information on the palace buildings.

The palaces are popular places for wedding photos and videos that are usually taken weeks before the wedding, that way they are bound to be perfect. Don't expect a quiet historical atmosphere either – you are quite likely to be swamped by excited children on a school trip all eager to show off their English-language skills.

Gyeongbokgung 경복궁

Palace of Shining Happiness

Originally built by King Taejo, the founder of the Joseon dynasty, this palace *(Map 8; ☎ 762 8262; adult/age 7-24 W700/300; open 9am-5pm Wed-Mon Mar-Oct, 9am-4pm Wed-Mon Nov-Feb)* served as the principal palace until 1592 when it was burnt down during the Japanese invasions.

The grandest palace in Seoul lay in ruins for nearly 300 years until Heungseon Daewongun, regent and father of King Gojong, began to rebuild it in 1865. Unfortunately the rebuilding project bankrupted the government, which was forced to seek loans from its old enemy, Japan. However, King Gojong moved in during 1868.

Nearly 30 years later, on 8 October 1895, his wife, Queen Myeongseong (Queen Min), and some of her ladies-in-waiting were killed in her bedroom by Japanese assassins. They burnt her body and only one finger survived the fire. The building where she was killed no longer exists, but the spot where she was murdered is marked. Four months later King Gojong fled from the palace to the sanctuary of the nearby Russian legation. He was smuggled out by a eunuch and a maid in a curtained palanquin. After a year in the Russian legation he moved to Deoksugung, still close to the protective foreign legations.

During Japanese colonial rule, 300 of the 330 buildings in the palace were either destroyed or moved to other parts of Seoul. Two amazing large-scale models in the National Museum show the palace before and after Japanese rule. But for its wanton destruction the palace would be one of Asia's greatest tourist attractions and comparable to Beijing's Forbidden City. The project to restore the palace to its former glory will continue until at least 2020.

The outstanding 48-columned Gyeonghoeru pavilion and the imposing Genjeongjeon, with its spacious flagstone courtyard and surrounding corridors, illustrate the splendour of the Joseon dynasty; while the attractive lily pond, the island pavilion of Hyangwonjeong, the rock garden and the decorative brickwork of the residential quarters show the more relaxed side of life in those feudal, Confucian times.

See the Things to See & Do chapter for details on the National Folk Museum and the National Museum housed in buildings in the palace's spacious grounds.

To get to Gyeongbokgung, take subway Line 3 to Gyeongbokgung station and leave by Exit 5.

Deoksugung 덕수궁

Palace of Virtuous Longevity

This aristocratic villa *(Map 9; ☎ 771 9952; adult/age 7-24 W700/300; open 9am-6pm Tues-Sun Mar-Oct, 9am-5.30pm Tues-Sun Nov-Feb)* became a palace in 1593 when King Seojo moved here because all of Seoul's other palaces had been destroyed during the Japanese invasions. Despite two kings being crowned here, it became a secondary palace.

In 1897 King Gojong moved into Deoksugung after leaving the nearby Russian legation. Although he was forced to abdicate 10 years later by the Japanese, he carried on living here in some style until he died in 1919. He'd lost his kingdom but he kept his harem, and his son, Sunjong, reigned as a puppet emperor with his Japanese wife until 1910 when he too was forced to abdicate – the Joseon dynasty was ended after more than 600 years.

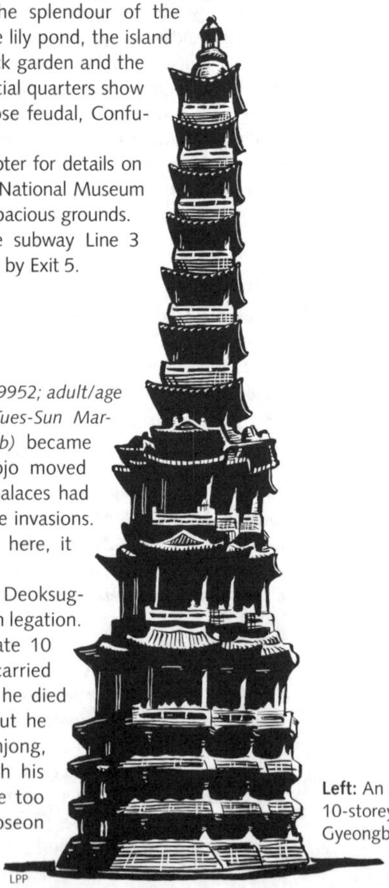

LPP

Left: An elaborate 10-storey pagoda at Gyeongbokgung

The Palace Eunuchs

The eunuchs played a vital role in the strange life inside Seoul's royal palaces. They were the personal servants and bodyguards of the king and royal family and protectors of the king's large harem, those pampered but unfortunate ladies who were imprisoned for life within the palace walls.

Usually born into low-class households, they were offered to the king by their families, and unlike eunuchs in other countries, they often married and adopted boys who in turn became eunuchs themselves.

They were an odd mixture of slave and high official. They dressed and bathed the king, cleaned his room and watched over him every moment of the day and night. In theory they were meant to direct all their energies to serving their sacred master with no thought of selfish, personal desires, just as a monk was supposed to serve only Buddha. But coming from poor backgrounds and being uneducated, they were invariably greedy for money and status, and were one cause of the court intrigues and corruption that resulted in the downfall of the Joseon dynasty. The eunuchs had access to the king 24 hours a day and so were a major but secret influence on all his decisions and policies.

The palace contains gardens and ponds and an extraordinary mixture of architectural structures. They include a grand audience hall in traditional Korean style, a Western-style tea pavilion where King Gojong drank the soothing beverage while discussing politics, economics, philosophy and poetry with his visitors, and two early-20th-century neoclassical buildings that house the Royal Museum and the National Museum of Contemporary Art (Annex) – see the Things to See & Do chapter for details on the museums. The unusual stone animals around the wooden audience hall are *haetae* – mythical creatures that are believed to eat fire, hence guarding against it.

Another large building, Jungmyeongjeon, used to be inside the grounds but is now outside it. There are plans to turn it into a museum. The 1905 treaty with Japan was signed here under which Korea lost its independence.

A tourist information bureau is located inside the palace grounds. Nearby you can dress up as a Joseon-dynasty soldier or general, and try your hand at a traditional stick-throwing game.

To get to Deoksugung, take subway Line 1 (Exit 2 or 3) or Line 2 (Exit 12) to City Hall station.

Changing of the Royal Guard

This colourful and musical spectacle takes place outside Daehanmun, Deoksugung's impressive entrance gate. It brings to life the pageantry of the Joseon dynasty that ruled Korea for over 500 years. The initial ceremony starts at 2pm, and the guards are changed at 2.15pm, 2.45pm and 3.15pm Tuesday to Sunday from March to December.

Changdeokgung 창덕궁

Palace of Illustrious Virtue

This Unesco World Heritage palace complex *(Map 8; ☎ 762 8262; adult/age 7-24 W2200/1100)* can only be visited on a tour. Originally constructed between 1405 and 1412, the buildings have often burnt down and been rebuilt. It was Seoul's main centre of power from 1618 to 1896.

On the tour you can see Seoul's oldest stone bridge (built in 1411), the throne hall, the blue-tiled royal office, and Naksonjae (originally built by King Honjong for one of his concubines, Lady Kim), which was home to descendants of the royal family until 1989. In this year the Japanese wife of King Gojong's son Yi Un (his mother started life as a maid and progressed to being a royal concubine) died here.

Cadillac and Daimler cars that were used by the last Joseon king, Sunjong, are also on display. But the highlight is the wonderful Biwon (Secret Garden), where the library, poem-writing pavilions, square lily ponds and park-like setting create a perfectly tranquil rural atmosphere. This is the place in Seoul where you can sense the ghosts of Joseon kings and their rigid Confucian world of duty and study. Here the kings could indulge in their love of nature and scholastic argument.

To get to Changdeokgung, take subway Line 3 to Anguk station and leave by Exit 3. Tours with English-speaking guides run from Tuesday to Sunday at 11.30am, 1pm and 3.30pm, and take 90 minutes.

Changgyeonggung & Jongmyo 창경궁, 종묘

Palace of Flourishing Gladness

Originally built in the early 15th century during King Sejong's reign, the buildings of Changgyeonggung *(Map 8; ☎ 762 4868; adult/age 7-24 W700/300; open 9am-5pm Wed-Mon Mar-Oct, 9am-4.30pm Wed-Mon Nov-Feb)* are modest in size. The oldest structure, the throne hall, dates from 1616, while the splendid botanic garden glasshouse is almost a century old.

In olden days Joseon kings used to plant and harvest rice at the location of today's scenic pond. They did this to keep in touch with the nation's agricultural roots.

LPP

Left: Changdeokgung, originally built as an annexe to Gyeongbokgung.

The King & the Confucian Social Order

The apex of the Confucian Joseon system was the king, who had absolute power although he was expected to be benevolent towards his people. Neo-Confucianism was the ruling ideology that lasted over 500 years from 1392 to 1910, and it strengthened the rigid class and caste system that was inherited from the previous dynasties.

Traditional Korean society was divided into four hereditary groups. At the top were the *yangban* (aristocrats), most of whom were landowners. They collected rent for themselves and taxes for the government, both of which the peasant farmers usually paid with crops or textiles. The *yangban* enforced the laws vigorously with floggings.

The important *yangban* lived in Seoul and disdained military and business occupations but admired teachers, scholars and artists – attitudes that still exist today. They rarely paid taxes or did military service. The symbols of their rank included a tiled house and black hats of woven horsehair.

To become an important government official they had to learn the Chinese language and memorize key Confucian texts. Then they could pass the all-important government exams, the narrow gateway to a good job, wealth and high status. Unfortunately the top-level *yangban* often joined factions based on family and regional groups. For long periods of Joseon history, weak kings were dominated by feuding *yangban* factions who threw off their Confucian restraints and indulged in assassinations and massacres.

The next social group were the *chungin*, the middle people, who were high-ranking soldiers, merchants or local magistrates. The merchants were few since the government taxed many products and generally controlled and restricted the economy. One troublesome group in this class were the numerous offspring of the *yangban* and their concubines.

The *sangmin* (common people) were the largest group, consisting of the peasant farmers, free labourers and fishermen. They spent their lives working hard for little or no reward. Forced to pay high levels of rent and tax (perhaps 50% of what they produced), they were also subject to regular military conscription and forced labour on government projects such as building fortresses or palaces. The peasants often led a miserable, downtrodden life enlivened by the occasional festival or bout of *makgeolli* (milky-white rice brew) drinking.

The peasants were hardly better off than the *chonmin* or low-born who were at the lowest level of society. The *chonmin's* largest element was the 30% of the population who were slaves. Many slaves were owned by the king, and the rest were privately owned and worked on farms or in *yangban* households. Many artisans were slaves so these occupations had a low status. Government slaves were officially freed in 1801, but slavery was not finally abolished until 1894.

Workers in certain occupations were called *paeckchong* and were totally despised. The lowest of the low were butchers and tanners who were forced to live in segregated hamlets outside the ordinary towns and villages. In the 1920s butchers were still campaigning against discrimination and for the right of their children to attend schools.

The Joseon kings administered this feudal system until military weakness and economic backwardness allowed Japan to take over the country and abolish the monarchy in 1910.

Changgyeonggung suffered the ultimate indignity during the Japanese occupation of being turned into a zoo.

The Joseon-dynasty civil-service examination is re-enacted here every October. An hour-long re-enactment of 21-year-old King Sejong's coronation in 1418 also takes place here while the main palace is being renovated.

Walk over the footbridge to Jongmyo *(Map 8; ☎ 765 0195; adult/age 7-24 W700/300; open 9am-5pm Wed-Mon Mar-Oct, 9am-4.30pm Wed-Mon Nov-Feb),* the shrine where the spirit tablets of the Joseon kings and queens are kept. They are housed in small rooms in two long buildings surrounded by woodland. The main hall was originally built in 1395, while Yeongneyeongjeon dates from 1421.

Usually the rooms are locked, but on the first Sunday in May the peaceful atmosphere is shattered by the crowds who come to watch the royal procession and a seven-hour Confucian ritual performed by the many living descendants of the royal family, who pay homage at the shrine to their ancestors. The royal spirits are welcomed and praised, fed with offerings of cooked meat and rice wine, entertained with solemn music and dance, and then respectfully farewelled. During the Joseon dynasty the ritual was carried out five times a year. Nowadays it usually starts at 3pm at Yeongneyeongjeon, with the royal procession at 5pm and the ceremony at the main hall starting around 8pm.

To get to Jongmyo take subway Line 1, 3 or 5 to Jongno 3-ga and leave by Exit 11. From Jongmyo you can walk over the footbridge to visit Changgyeonggung. If you visit both these places at the same time and use the footbridge between them, there is no admission fee to Changgyeonggung.

Unhyeongung 운현궁

Cloud Hanging Over the Valley Palace

This palace *(Map 8; ☎ 766 9098; admission W700; open 9am-7pm Tues-Sun Mar-Oct, 9am-5pm Tues-Sun Nov-Feb)* was the home of Heungseon Daewongun – the stern and stony father of King Gojong, whose policies included massacring Catholics and the exclusion of foreigners. Gojong was born and raised here until he ascended the throne in 1863 at the age of 12. Unhyeongung's buildings are smaller than the other palaces but are well preserved and the decorative brickwork is attractive. The small but charming rooms are furnished in *yangban* (aristocratic) style, which gives the buildings a more historical atmosphere.

A re-enactment of the marriage of King Gojong to Queen Myeongseong (Queen Min) is held here, where the actual event took place in 1867. He was 15, she 16, and the Confucian wedding ceremony had six stages and took months to complete. The re-enactment lasts only an hour, but the music and costumes are authentic and the solemn ritual recalls the ethos of a slower age where nothing much changed as the centuries flowed by.

To get to Unhyeongung, take subway Line 3 to Anguk station and leave by Exit 4.

Gyeonghuigung 경희궁

Palace of Shining Celebration

Built in 1616, Gyeonghuigung (Map 8) used to consist of 100 buildings but was completely dismantled by the Japanese during their colonial rule. The area is a now a park where a few buildings – Sungjeongjeon, the audience hall, and behind it Jujeongjeon, the living quarters – have been reconstructed, but are not usually open to the public. The impressive entrance gate has moved around Seoul, including a spell outside Hotel Shilla, before it returned here in 1988.

Royal Tombs 궁중릉

The spirit tablets of the Joseon kings and queens are in Jongmyo, but their impressive tombs are scattered all over Seoul. The tomb of King Seonjeong (ruled 1469–94), his second wife, Queen Jeonghyeonwanghu, and his second son, King Jungjeong (ruled 1506–44), are in wooded **Samneung Park** *(Map 7; admission W400; open 9am-5.30pm Tues-Sun Mar-Oct, 9am-4.30pm Tues-Sun Nov-Feb)*, a 15-minute walk from the COEX Mall, south of Hangang. King Seonjeong is remembered as being prolific in both authoring and fathering (he had 28 children by 10 concubines), while Jungjeong ruled for a long time but was a weak king. The tombs follow the Chinese fashion and are guarded by larger-than-life stone statues of warriors and smaller statues of horses, tigers and imaginary animals that look like sheep.

To get to the Samneung Park royal tombs, take subway Line 2 to Seolleung station and leave by Exit 8. Turn left at the first road and left again at the park fence. The ticket booth is less than 10 minutes' walk from the subway station.

Seonnong-je 선농제

Royal Sacrificial Rite

For centuries the Joseon kings went to the altar Seonnongdan (Map 4) at Seonnong-je to pray for a good harvest. A cow was killed and everyone present was served *seonnongtang* beef soup, named after the altar. The name changed to *seolleongtang* but it remains a popular soup today.

A re-enactment of the event takes place in April and begins with a royal procession to the altar where food offerings are laid out in special brass containers. Musicians in red robes play traditional instruments and a singer chants the same words used in the original Joseon rituals. After the Confucian ceremony everyone eats *seolleongtang* and drinks *makgeolli* (milky-white fermented rice wine) free of charge.

To get to Seonnongdan, take subway Line 1 to Jegi-dong station, leave by Exit 1 and walk to the information board where you turn right. Then fork right along the tree-lined street, and the altar is a few minutes' walk up the hill on the right. Normally there is nothing to see at the site except for the stone altars and a stone statue, but the re-enactment is definitely worth attending.

Things to See & Do

HISTORICAL SEOUL

Cheongwadae 청와대

The Blue House

The Blue House *(Map 8; ☎ 737 5800; W www.president.go.kr)* is Korea's answer to America's White House – the presidential residence. In truth though, the famous blue-tiled building (completed in 1991) is full of offices, and the president and first lady live elsewhere.

Back in 1968 a squad of 31 North Korean commandos was caught just 500m from the Blue House – their mission was to assassinate President Park Jung-hee. The threat from the North has diminished but still remains, so security is tight.

To access Cheongwadae, visitors must join a free Korean-language guided tour that lasts 80 minutes and shows you the palatial grounds but not inside any important buildings. Tours are available in April, May, September and October on Friday and Saturday from 9am to 5pm. Also included in the tour is **Chilgung** – small shrines that contain the spirit tablets of seven royal concubines whose sons became kings in the Joseon dynasty.

Take subway Line 3 to Gyeongbokgung station, leave by Exit 5 and walk to Gwanghwamun, the palace's main gate. Here you'll find a ticket booth where you need to show your passport to receive your tour ticket. A tour bus takes you the short distance from the car park to Cheongwadae.

Seodaemun Prison 독리봉원서대문전시장

Seodaemun Prison *(Map 4; ☎ 363 9750; adult/child W1000/550; open 9.30am-6pm Tues-Sun Mar-Oct, 9.30am-5pm Tues-Sun Nov-Feb)* is a stark reminder of the sufferings of Korean independence fighters who challenged Japanese colonial rule between 1910 and 1945. The entrance gate and watchtower, the execution room, punishment cells and seven of the original 15 buildings are on view.

You can walk between long lines of cells where the prisoners were held and see photo-graphs and videos of the harsh life inside the high red walls. Overcrowding, poor food, beatings, torture and interrogation caused many deaths. The small building where executions took place is poignant and the interrogation rooms are nightmarish.

Highlights

- Exploring the royal palaces, such as Gyeongbokgung and Deoksugung, to soak up the atmosphere of the feudal royal court
- Touring the Seoul Museum of History, the National Folk Museum and Namsangol Traditional Village to experience traditional life and culture
- Visiting the War Memorial Museum and Seodaemun Prison, which provide an excellent introduction to Seoul's complex and tragic history
- Attending the royal ancestral rites festival at Jongmyo, as well as other historical re-enactments that reveal an Asian society with its own very distinctive style
- Meditating, eating temple food and taking part in a tea ceremony with Buddhist monks at Jogyesa or Bongeunsa
- Walking up Namsan to Seoul Tower or up Inwangsan to the shamanist shrine – both provide great views of Seoul
- Cycling along the banks of Hangang to Olympic Park or to the World Cup Stadium Parks
- Hiking around the huge fortresses Bukhansanseong and Namhansanseong that were built in the forest-covered mountains around Seoul
- And for the kids, spending a day in a Disney-style amusement park at Lotte World

Next to the prison is **Dongnimmun Park**, which features an impressive Western-style granite archway built by the Independence Club in 1898. It stands at the place where envoys from Chinese emperors used to be officially welcomed to Seoul. This ritual symbolised Chinese suzerainty over Korea, which ended when King Gojong declared himself emperor in 1897.

To get here, take subway Line 3 to Dongnimmun station and leave by Exit 5.

Namsangol Traditional Village 남산골한옥마을

This small village *(Map 9; w fpcp.or.kr; admission free; open 9am-7pm Wed-Mon May-Sept, 9am-6pm Wed-Mon Oct-Apr)*, situated at the foot of Namsan, contains five different *yangban* houses from the Joseon dynasty, furnished in period style. They look similar to each other, although there are subtle differences. Empress Sunjeong (who married Korea's last emperor in 1906 when she was 12 years old) was brought up in one of the houses, which were transported here from different parts of Seoul. The architecture and furniture is generally austere and plain, reflecting the Confucian tastes of the Joseon-dynasty aristocracy.

A pleasant **park** and **Time Capsule Square** adjoins the village. A time capsule containing 600 items was buried in the square in 1994 and will be opened in 2394.

Free traditional performances take place on Saturday and Sunday afternoons between April and October, and usually start at 2pm. Craft workers can be seen at work every day, and one traditional house has been converted into a restaurant. Although the menu is limited, the historical atmosphere makes it an interesting place for lunch.

To get here, take subway Line 3 or 4 to Chungmuro station and leave by Exit 3.

Insadong 인사동

Insadong (Map 8) is one of the few parts of Seoul that has retained an atmosphere of the past. The narrow alleyways are packed with more than 50 art galleries, as well as traditional teashops and small restaurants selling a wide range of Korean food. Craft shops sell fans, handmade paper boxes, masks, lacquerware, pottery and antiques. Munch on a traditional snack bought from a street stall, and buy a *tojang* (name seal), a handmade cup or a second-hand book – the choice is endless. You can even buy a souvenir from North Korea. This picturesque area is being made traffic free, which will add to its charm.

Tapgol Park 탑골공원

'Tapgol' means 'pagoda' and this park (Map 8) is named after the 10-tier, 12m-high marble pagoda that can be found here. It is all that remains of the temple buildings and monuments of Wongaksa that were destroyed in 1515. The pagoda, constructed in the 1470s, is decorated with beautiful Buddhist carvings. But sadly, in order to protect the monument, it has been encased in a metal and glass structure that takes away most of its ancient beauty and charm.

Opened in 1897, Tapgol was Seoul's first Western-style public park and is famous for its role in Korean resistance to Japanese rule. Mounted on a pedestal in the park is a statue of Son Pyong-hui (1861–1922), leader of the independence movement. On 1 March 1919, Son Pyong-hui and 32 other Korean dissidents drew up a declaration of independence, which was read aloud in the park two days later – the entire contents have reproduced on a brass plaque.

The declaration unleashed a torrent of anti-Japanese feeling and the *sam-il* (1 March movement) was born. Countrywide protests against Japanese rule broke out but were ruthlessly suppressed. The Japanese authorities admitted that hundreds of protestors were killed and 12,000 were arrested, but Korean nationalists put the figures much higher. Murals in the park depict scenes from the anti-Japanese protests.

Namdaemun 남대문

Great South Gate

The Great South Gate (Sungnyemun; Map 9) of Seoul fortress was originally constructed in 1398, rebuilt in 1447 and has been renovated often since then.

Designated as National Treasure No 1, it's an impressive sight, especially when floodlit at night, and is a reminder of the once mighty Joseon dynasty. The famous day-and-night Namdaemun market that starts at the gate is equally historic, and street traders have been selling food and household goods here for centuries. For details on the market see the Shopping chapter.

Dongdaemun 동대문

Great East Gate

Seoul's other surviving fortress gate, Dongdaemun (Heunginjimun; Map 4), dates back to the 14th century, but the existing structure was built in 1869 and was renovated after being severely damaged during the Korean War. Dongdaemun market starts at this gate, a mixture of indoor arcades, outdoor street stalls and modern high-rise shopping malls that makes this day-and-night shopping area one of the biggest and busiest in Asia. For more details see the Shopping chapter.

Bosingak 보신각

Situated in Jongno (Bell St), Seoul's main street during the Joseon period, this pavilion (Map 8) houses a modern version of the city bell originally forged in 1468. The bell is rung only at New Year, when crowds gather here to celebrate.

In Joseon times the great bell was struck 33 times at dawn (one for each of the 33 heavens in Buddhism) and 28 times at sunset (for the 28 stars that determine human destiny). The striking of the bell signalled the opening and closing of the city gates. The evening bell also signalled a male curfew within the city, which provided an opportunity for aristocratic women, who were limited to their homes during the day, to go out into the streets. At midnight the bell was struck once to announce a full curfew until dawn.

Admiral Yi Sun-shin's Statue 이순신장군동상

This statue (Map 8) is one of the landmarks in the downtown area. Yi Sun-shin (1545–98) was born in Seoul and he designed a new type of warship that was clad in metal. Called *geobukseon* (turtle ships), the ad-miral used them to help him achieve a series of stunning victories over the much larger Japanese navy that attacked Korea at the end of the 16th century.

BUDDHIST TEMPLES

Jogyesa 조계사

The largest Buddhist shrine (Map 8) in Seoul was built here in 1938, but the design followed the Joseon-dynasty style. Murals of scenes from Buddha's life and the carved floral latticework doors are two attractive features of the shrine. You can also follow the tradition of lighting a candle or incense stick and then walking around the seven-tiered pagoda to make a wish.

Jogyesa is the headquarters of the Jogye sect, the largest Buddhist sect in Korea, which emphasises Zen-style meditation and the study of Buddhist scriptures as the best way to achieve enlightenment.

Located in the belfry are the four musical instruments that can be found in all Korean Buddhist temples. There is a large drum to summon earthbound creatures, a wooden fish-shaped gong to summon aquatic beings, a cloud-shaped metal gong to summon airborne creatures and a large bronze bell to summon underground creatures. Around the temple are shops that sell Buddhist beads, candles, incense, music, artwork, hats and clothing.

The temple runs programmes where visitors can join the monks for a typical vegetarian meal, meditation, a tea ceremony and other activities. See Korean Buddhist Temple Programmes under Activities later in this chapter for details.

Bongeunsa 봉은사

Just north of the COEX Mall, Bongeunsa temple (Map 7) was originally founded in AD 794, but was rebuilt in 1498 when restrictions on Buddhists were eased. The oldest building still standing, constructed in 1856, is a library that contains 150-year-old woodblocks with Buddhist scriptures and art carved into them.

Try to visit the temple between 10am and noon when the library is open to visitors (it's closed at other times to preserve the woodblocks). The calligraphy on the front of the library was written by one of Korea's most famous calligraphers, Kim Jeong-hui, who completed it just days before his death. The temple also contains a 23m stone statue of the Future Buddha.

Ask at the entrance gate if there is an English-speaking volunteer guide who's available. Bongeunsa also runs temple-stay programmes where visitors can experience different aspects of a monk's lifestyle first-hand. See Korean Buddhist Temple Programmes under Activities later in this chapter for details.

Bongwonsa 봉원사

Situated northeast of Yonsei University and in front of Ansan (296m), this temple (Map 3) can trace its history back to 1748. The main shrine was destroyed during the Korean War but was rebuilt in 1966. It is the headquarters of the Taego sect of Buddhism, which was established during Japanese rule. Taego's monks are allowed to marry.

The temple is not very near a subway station. To get there, take a bus from Sinchon bus terminal (just ask for 'Bongwonsa'), which is a few minutes' walk southeast of Sinchon subway station (Line 2).

CHRISTIAN CHURCHES

Myeong-dong Catholic Cathedral 명동성당

This cathedral (Map 9) is an elegant brick Renaissance-style building that was constructed in 1898. It provided a sanctuary for student and trade-union protestors during the long period of military rule after the Korean War, and is an important national symbol of democracy and human rights.

Anglican Church 대한성공회대성당

This imposing Renaissance-style church (Map 9), built in the shape of a cross with Korean-style tiles on the roof, is a good example of architectural fusion. Only a few minutes' walk from Deoksugung, it is worth a look. Work began in 1922, but the full design wasn't completed until 1996.

MUSEUMS

War Memorial Museum 전쟁기념관

This large and interesting museum *(Map 6; ☎ 709 3139; W www.warmemo.co.kr; adult/child W3000/2000; open 9.30am-6pm Tues-Sun Mar-Oct, 9.30am-5pm Tues-Sun Nov-Feb)* documents the many attacks on Korea by Mongols, Chinese, Japanese and other groups. Korea has a turbulent and tragic history, and it's a miracle that the country survived.

Upstairs are exhibits giving a detailed description of the Korean War using newsreels, photographs, maps and artefacts of the period. Also covered is Korea's involvement in the Vietnam War, where 4000 Koreans died. The Combat Experience Room shows you the reality of modern warfare. Outside the museum are 150 items of military hardware ranging from artillery to bombers.

Every Friday from March to December at 2pm a performance by a military band and marching parade culminates in an awesome display of military precision and weapon twirling by the honour guard of the army, navy and air force. The Women's Army Corps and soldiers in Joseon-dynasty uniform also take part.

To get here, take subway Line 4 or 6 to Samgakji station and leave by Exit 12.

National Museum 국립중앙박물관

This museum *(Map 8; W www.museum.go.kr; admission W700; open 9am-6pm Tues-Sun Mar-Oct, 9am-5pm Tues-Sun Nov-Feb)* focuses on pre-Joseon artefacts. One highlight is the collection of ancient Goryeo celadon with its classical yet varied designs. It is more refined than the Buncheong pottery that came later and has rougher designs that look more like folk art. Buncheong appealed to the Japanese so much that in the late 16th century, during their invasion of Korea, the Japanese shipped whole villages of Korean potters to Japan and forced them to work there.

The giant metal Buddhas in the museum are also impressive and the detailed models of the nearby palace, Gyeongbokgung, before and after Japanese colonial rule show the extent of the damage it suffered. Interesting videos (with English subtitles) on Korean pottery and other subjects are shown on the hour.

There are plans to move the National Museum in 2005 to a huge new building that is being constructed in Yongsan Park (Map 6), and when that happens the current National Museum will become the Joseon Palace Museum.

Royal Museum 궁중유물전시관

This museum *(Map 9; admission free with entry to Deoksugung; open 9am-6pm Tues-Sun Mar-Oct, 9am-5.30pm Tues-Sun Nov-Feb)* is housed in the east wing of the neoclassical building at the far end of the Deoksugung palace compound. The 1st floor used to be occupied by palace staff and servants, the 2nd floor was for official meetings, and the 3rd floor was the private apartment for the king and queen.

A varied collection of royal items is on display, including clothing, food, kitchenware, furniture and works of art. Highlights include pocket-sized sundials, an eight-section screen showing King Jeongjo's procession to his father's tomb, and a *choheon* – an unusual one-wheeled sedan chair pushed by up to nine servants and used by government officials.

A few of the items on display have been returned by Japan, and efforts are continuing to retrieve more Korean treasures that were taken to Japan during the colonial period.

National Folk Museum 국립민속박물관

This museum *(Map 8; W www.nfm.go.kr; admission free with entry to Gyeongbokgung; 9am-5pm Wed-Mon Mar-Oct, 9am-4pm Wed-Mon Nov-Feb)* is in a traditional-style building that was constructed in 1972 inside the grounds of Gyeongbokgung. Outside are shamanist stone statues and wooden posts that used to guard the entrances to villages.

The exhibits inside contrast the lifestyle of aristocrats with that of ordinary people during the Joseon period. The clothing, games, rituals, handicrafts, food, housing and occupations of that era are displayed to show visitors what life was like in times gone by. Aristocratic women wore exquisitely embroidered silk shoes, while peasant women wore wooden clogs or straw sandals. Aristocratic men wore black horsehair hats that ordinary folk were not allowed to wear. Most husbands saw their wives for the first time on their wedding day, and slaves were bought and sold at prices fixed by the government.

An English-language audio guide costs W3000 and provides brief but helpful comments.

The museum also runs classes teaching foreigners how to make fans, pottery, *hanji* boxes and *gimchi*. See Traditional Culture under Courses later for details.

Seoul Museum of History 서울역사박물관

Seoul Museum of History *(Map 8; ☎ 724 0114; W www.museum.seoul.kr; adult W550; open 9am-6pm Tues-Sun Mar-Oct; 9am-5pm Tues-Sun Nov-Feb)* was opened in 2002. It focuses on Seoul during the Joseon period, and the style of presentation encourages individual exploration. In those days, Seoul was called Hanyang or Hanseongbu and was confined to the northern side of Hangang.

In the Joseon period aristocratic ladies hardly ever left their houses, and when they did they had to hide their faces behind a headscarf. When high officials were being carried along in sedan chairs ordinary people had to prostrate themselves as they went past.

Only brief descriptions of the items on display are given, so the English-language tour at 2.30pm is a good idea. The museum also organises special exhibitions that change regularly; check the website for details.

Jeoldusan Martyrs' Shrine & Museum 절두산순교성지

Jeoldusan means 'Beheading Hill' and is the place (Map 3) where up to 2000 Korean Catholics were executed in 1866 following a decree signed by Regent Heungseon

Daewongun, King Gojong's father, to kill all Catholics. The victims' bodies were thrown into Hangang and only 40 of their names are known.

The small museum *(☎ 323 1950; admission W500; open 9am-5pm Tues-Sun)* has relics of the martyrs and displays depicting the early Catholic converts who faced waves of government persecution. In church, nobles and ordinary people sat together as equals in the sight of God, which challenged the rigid hierarchical system of the Joseon dynasty.

The chapel is open every day, with Mass at 10am and 3pm. A volunteer guide may be available.

Take subway Line 2 or 6 to Hapjeong station and leave by Exit 7. Go left at the second turning and walk along the covered railway line, following the small brown signs. It's a 10-minute walk to the museum and memorial.

Agriculture Museum 농업박물관

The Agriculture Museum *(Map 9; ☎ 397 5673; admission free; open 9.30am-5.30pm daily except public holidays)* has three floors of traditional farm equipment and handicrafts plus the inevitable *gimchi* section. Don't miss the giant mousetraps.

Military Academy & Army Museums 륙군사관학교

Tours of this elite academy (Map 10) cost W3000 and take place at 10am, 1pm and 3pm on Saturday and Sunday; the Saturday 10am tour includes a military parade. Ancient weapons and the North Korean and Vietcong exhibits are the highlights. 'Win through learning' is the academy motto and could be the motto of the entire country.

To get here, take subway Line 6 to Hwarangdae station and leave by Exit 4. After walking for five minutes, fork left and then, opposite the entrance to Seoul Women's University, cross the road and turn right, following the sign to the academy. Take your passport for ID purposes. A restaurant next to the ticket office on the 2nd floor of the blue-tiled building sells *donkkaseu* (pork cutlet and salad) for W3000 and other inexpensive meals.

Amsa-dong Prehistoric Settlement Site 암사선시주거지

This open air museum *(Map 2; ☎ 3426 3867; admission free; open 10am-5pm daily)* features restored prehistoric huts at a site where human settlement dates back to 3000 BC.

To get here, take subway Line 8 to Amsa station and walk 1km due north to the site, which is on the south bank of Hangang.

Other Museums

Sejong University Museum *(Map 2; ☎ 3408 3076; admission free; open 10am-3pm Tues-Fri, closed university holidays)*, opposite the entrance to Children's Grand Park, has a large display of folk items spread over five floors in a Baekje-dynasty pagoda-style building.

Ewha Women's University Museum *(Map 3; ☎ 3277 3151; admission free; open 9.30am-5pm Mon-Sat, closed university holidays)* has Joseon-dynasty artefacts on display together with an **art gallery** that exhibits work by female artists.

The Bank of Korea (Map 9) in Myeong-dong has a **Currency Museum** and nearby is the **Postal Museum**, which is housed in the Central Post Office (Map 9).

ART GALLERIES

Seoul Museum of Art 서울시립미술관

This art gallery *(Map 9; ☎ 2124 8800; adult/student W2000/1000; open 10am- 7pm Tues-Sun Mar-Oct, 10am-6pm Tues-Sun Nov-Feb)* was only recently opened in 2002. It is considered one of the best and puts on interesting and varied exhibitions that reflect every style of modern art in Seoul. The displays change regularly. Its ultra-modern and bright galleries hide behind the brick-and-stone facade of the 1927 Supreme Court Building.

National Museum of Contemporary Art 국립현대미술관

This large and impressive art gallery *(Map 2; ☎ 2188 6000; W www.moca.go.kr; adult/child W700/free; open 9am-6pm Tues-Sun Mar-Oct, 9am-5pm Tues-Sun Nov-Feb)* is

Closed on Monday

Many palaces, museums and other tourist sites close on Monday. Gyeongbokgung (Map 8) and Changgyeonggung (Map 8) are the only palaces open on Monday, along with Namsangol Traditional Village (Map 9). Otherwise, the amusement parks are open every day, as are the aquariums in the 63 Building on Yeouido and the COEX Mall. Markets are open on Monday but the three fashion malls (Migliore, Freya Town and Doota) in Dongdaemun market are closed. Hiking or cycling are other options on Monday.

spread over three floors and also has sculptures out in the garden. You are unlikely to miss one exhibit – a huge pagoda-shaped video installation that is 18m high and uses 1000 flickering screens to make a comment on our increasingly electronic universe. It's the work of Paik Nam-jun, a video artist with an international reputation, and is entitled 'The More the Better'.

Free films are shown on Saturday during August, concerts are performed in July, and music and dance performances can be seen in October.

To get here, take subway Line 4 to Seoul Grand Park station and leave by Exit 4. A free shuttle bus goes to the gallery every 20 minutes. Otherwise you can walk there in 20 minutes – walk up to the entrance of Seoul Grand Park and then turn left.

National Museum of Contemporary Art (Annexe) 국립현대미술관

This art gallery *(Map 9; ☎ 779 5310; admission W2000; open 9am-6pm Tues-Sun Mar-Oct, 9am-5.30pm Tues-Sun Nov-Feb)* is in the west wing of the neoclassical building in Deoksugung. With four large galleries on two levels, the exhibitions vary but concentrate on pre-1960 modern art. Tea or coffee in the café is W2000.

Hoam Art Museum 호암아트갤러리

For information on this major art gallery, see Everland in the Excursions chapter.

Other Art Galleries

The **Rodin Gallery** *(Map 9; ☎ 2259 7781; W www.rodin.co.kr; adult/student W4000/2000; open 10am-6pm Tues-Sun)* has two large sculptures by Rodin on permanent display in a glass pyramid-shaped structure and changing exhibitions in other galleries.

The **Sejong Centre for the Performing Arts** *(Map 8; ☎ 399 1773; W www.sejongpac.or.kr; open 10am-7pm daily)* and **Hangaram Design Art Museum** *(☎ 580 1540; W www.designgallery.or.kr; admission W2000; open 10am-6pm daily, closed 1st Mon of each month)* in the Seoul Arts Centre (Map 2) both have worthwhile and changing art exhibitions.

The **Seoul Calligraphy Art Museum** at the Seoul Arts Centre (Map 2) has 10 galleries and is the best place in Seoul to see examples of traditional and modern calligraphy.

Numerous small art galleries covering all styles of art can be seen in **Insadong** (Map 8). The street running along the eastern side of Gyeongbokgung (Map 8) also contains a number of well-known galleries – see the Between the Palaces Walk later in this chapter.

HIGH-RISE SEOUL

Seoul Tower & Namsan 서울타워

The views from the top of Namsan are great and the night view is especially memorable. **Seoul Tower** (Map 9), which was completed in 1975, has a range of restaurants, shops and tourist attractions. Taking the lift to the **observation deck** at the top of the tower costs W4000.

The **Global Folk Museum** *(☎ 773 9590; adult/student/child W3000/2500/2000; open 9.30am-10pm daily)* is full of curiosities such as African masks, chastity belts and the world's largest silver coin. Nearby are two attractions for children – **Fairy Land** and a **3-D Animation Cinema** – which cost the same as the Global Folk Museum. Discounts are offered if you visit all three places.

Restaurants include one that sells delicious pumpkin porridge, the well-known semi-vegetarian **Pulhyanggi** *(☎ 539 3390;*

set lunch/dinner from W20,000/32,000) and a **revolving restaurant** at the top of the tower that receives mixed reviews from travellers.

The **signal beacons** are similar to those that were built on Namsan during the Joseon period so that messages could be sent from the capital to all parts of the country. A series of hill-top beacons provided fast, long-distance communication in a prepostal service, pretelephone era.

See Walking Tours later in this chapter for more information on Namsan.

COEX Mall 코엑스몰

This huge underground mall *(Map 7; W www.coexmall.com)* includes numerous shops, three food courts, the Hyundai Department Store (which has its own food court), restaurants, the COEX Conference Centre & Exhibition Hall, the World Trade Tower, Asem Tower, the City Air Terminal (KCAT), two luxury hotels, a multiplex cinema with 17 screens, and a nightclub.

COEX Aquarium *(☎ 6002 6200; W www.coexaqua.co.kr; adult/high-school student/child W14,500/12,000/9500; open 10am-8pm Sun-Fri, 10am-9pm Sat)* is the largest in Korea, with 40,000 fish and other sea creatures in 90 tanks. You can see live coral, evil-looking piranhas, sharks, turtles and rays swimming around a huge tank. Exquisitely beautiful small creatures such as pulsating jellyfish, glass fish and sea horses are also on display. Visiting the aquarium is also cheaper than scuba diving.

Next door is **Deep Blue** *(☎ 6002 6199; seafood meals W30,000-50,000; open noon-10pm daily)*, where one wall of this classy Western-style restaurant is taken up by an aquarium tank so diners can watch sharks, rays, gropers, turtles and fish of all shapes and colours float by. It creates a special atmosphere and the prices reflect this – salmon and seafood set meals are W52,000 and a Caesar salad is W14,000. You can also just order tea or coffee for W6000.

Megabox *(open 9am-midnight daily)* is a popular 17-screen multiplex cinema with over 4000 seats that shows films on large screens and uses the latest digital sound systems.

Next door is **Megaweb** *(open 10am-11pm daily)*, which has a free fun zone funded by Korea Telecom (KT), although it may not be free for very long. Besides watching DVDs and using the one-hour Internet service, you can beat the hell out of a drum kit in a sound-proof room for 10 minutes, and even record your own CD – all for free. The CD recording is *noraebang*-style singing to a backing track with the words (in English) appearing on a screen.

Bandi & Luni's *(☎ 6002 6002; open 10.30am-9pm daily)* bookshop has one of the best selections of English-language books and magazines in Seoul.

The **Gimchi Museum** *(admission W3000; open 10am-5pm Tues-Sat, 1pm-5pm Sun)* is only for real fans of this peppery pickled cabbage.

Yeouido 여의도

This island (Map 5) in Hangang is around 3km long and 2km wide and is a mixture of pleasant parks and high-rise buildings, such as the gold-tinted 63 Building. Skyscrapers house the headquarters of many media, finance and insurance companies, as well as local *jaebol* – huge family-run corporations with diversified business interests. The Stock Exchange and the National Assembly buildings are also on the island.

The **Hangang Parks** and **Yeouido Park** are popular places on warm weekends, with cyclists and rollerbladers. Families come for a picnic while others take advantage of the outdoor **swimming pool** *(adult/child W2500/1500; open for swimming 9am-6pm daily Jul & Aug, for ice-skating Dec-Feb)*, as well as other sports facilities. Bicycles can be hired – see the Cycling section later in this chapter. Surprisingly, Yeouido Park once used to be an asphalt aircraft landing strip, but no sign of its past remains.

At the western end of the island is the **National Assembly** *(☎ 788 3804)*, which was completed in 1975. Free tours take only 15 minutes although they can take longer if the country's 273 elected representatives are in session. Full meetings are held in February, April and June, and from September to December.

The **Korea Stock Exchange** *(☎ 3774 9246; admission free; open 9am-noon & 1pm-5pm Mon-Fri)* is near Yeouido subway station, but as stocks and shares are now bought and sold by clicking a mouse, there is nothing to watch. However, in the old trading room on the 2nd floor you can see a video in English and look round an exhibition on the stock exchange's importance to the local economy.

At the eastern tip of the island is the **63 Building** *(W www.63city.co.kr)*, the tallest skyscraper in Korea, which took five years to build and opened in 1985. On B1 floor is an **aquarium** *(☎ 789-5663; adult/child W9000/7200)* that features seal and sea-lion shows, and an **Imax large screen cinema** *(☎ 789-5663; adult/child W7000/5000)* with headphones that provide a commentary in English. The **observation deck** *(adult/child W6000/4400)* is on the 60th floor. You can see all three attractions for W18,000.

The 56th to 59th floors have Western, Chinese and Japanese **restaurants** with a view, while down on the 4th floor is a Korean restaurant and lower still are the fast-food franchises. Also in the basement is **Plaza Fountain Buffet**, a famous restaurant that offers a cosmopolitan buffet (W35,000 to W40,000) on tables grouped around a 'dancing' fountain.

The **Han River Pleasure Boats** *(☎ 785 4411)* provide enjoyable one-hour trips along the river – one-way and return trips both cost W7000 (adults) and W3500 (children). There are four ferry piers – Yeouido (Map 5), Yanghwa (Map 2), Ttukseom (Map 7) and Jamsil (Map 7). One option is to take the 15km cruise from Yeouido pier to Jamsil pier and then walk the 15 minutes to Sincheon subway station (Line 2). Alternatively, you can come back on the ferry for the same price. The boats operate all year round, and run every hour from 11am to 8pm in July and August, and every one to two hours in other months.

Along the southeastern side of the island is **Cherry Blossom Park**, which follows the channel that separates Yeouido from the southern part of the city. It's popular in mid-April when the cherry trees blossom, but is nothing special during the rest of the year.

To get to Yeouido take subway Line 5 to either Yeouido station in the middle of the island or to Yeouinaru station in the north.

Seoul for Children

There are interesting **aquariums** to explore at the COEX Mall (Map 7) and the 63 Building (Map 5) on Yeouido. Everland has a world-class aquatic centre, as well as a popular Disney-style amusement park and a **motor racing track**. Seoul Grand Park and Children's Grand Park (Map 2) both have large **zoos**. The former has a dolphin and seal show, while the latter has a chimpanzee and seal show. Both also have **amusement parks** with lots of thrill rides as well as other facilities. Lotte World (Map 7) is a mainly indoor amusement park with restaurants, a folk museum, 3-D films, thrill rides, concerts and musical parades. In the same area is an **ice-skating rink**, a **swimming pool** with slides, **cinemas**, shops and **ten-pin bowling**.

In winter there is skiing, snowboarding and sledding at **ski resorts** near Seoul. In summer children can swim at the beaches on the islands scattered in the West Sea off Incheon or in swimming pools in the parks along Hangang.

The latest children's clothing fashions are on sale at Namdaemun and Dongdaemun **markets**, while Freya Town in Dongdaemun has an entire floor of toys and a 24-hour multiplex cinema. Nor is there any shortage of **ice creams** – Baskin Robbins outlets and convenience stores are so numerous that you are never more than 100m from a frozen treat. **Western fast food** and pizza places are as plentiful as back home. Also plentiful are video **game rooms**, Internet game rooms and *noraebang* (karaoke rooms). You can hire **rollerblades** in Jangchung Park (Map 9) or **bicycles** on Yeouido (Map 5).

Finally, how about a souvenir featuring **Mashimaro**, Korea's temperamental cartoon rabbit, who hits heads with what looks like a toilet plunger?

AMUSEMENT PARKS & ZOOS

Lotte World 롯데월드

Lotte World *(Map 7; W www.lotteworld.com)* is a huge complex that includes Lotte World hotel, Lotte department store, a shopping mall, and numerous restaurants and fast-food outlets.

Lotte World's famous **indoor ice-skating rink** *(☎ 411 2000)* costs W9200 for adults (W8000 for children) before 7pm and W7700 (W6500 for children) after 7pm; skates can be rented for W3200. A game at the 26-lane **bowling alley** *(open morning until midnight)* costs W2700 plus W1200 to rent bowling shoes. A paddle in the large indoor **swimming pool** *(open to the public 1pm-7pm daily)* costs W6500 and the water slide costs W500 per go. You can even learn scuba diving in a special pool – ask for details at the scuba-diving counters opposite the swimming pool ticket office.

The **Folk Museum** *(adult/child W4500/2000; open 9.30am-11pm daily)* is on the 3rd floor. Using imaginative techniques like moving waxworks, dioramas and scale models, it brings to life how ordinary people lived in the past.

But the main attraction is **Lotte World Adventure & Magic Island** *(open 9.30am-11pm daily; adult/child W18,000/12,000, Big-5 ticket W24,000/17,000; after 5pm adult/child W12,000/8000, Big-5 ticket W18,000/12,000)*. It's a Korean version of Disneyland, complete with a monorail train, live musical entertainment, 3-D films, and a laser show at 9pm each day. You can swing in the Viking Ship, ride in simulators, whiz through water, and go round and round and up and down on other thrill rides. On the Gyro Drop you fall 70m in two seconds – the scarier the ride, the longer the queue will be. The main Lotte World Adventure section is indoors, while the Magic Island is outside in the middle of a lake.

To get to Lotte World take subway Line 2 or 8 to Jamsil station.

Seoul Grand Park 서울대공원

This excellent zoo *(☎ 500 7114; W grandpark.seoul.go.kr; adult/student/child W1500/1200/700; open 9am-7pm daily Apr-Sept, 9am-6pm daily Oct-Mar)* is set among the forested hillsides south of Seoul. A river runs through the park and families picnic along its shady banks. You can hike along a number of marked trails that are 2km to 6km long.

The zoo is home to a long list of exotic creatures, including the popular African ones. A huge aviary contains cranes, swans, pelicans and other large birds, and an indoor botanic garden houses a forest of cacti, numerous orchids and carnivorous pitcher plants. Ants and swimming beetles are on display in a 'miniature creature' exhibit. An entertaining dolphin and seal show costs only W500 and starts at 11.30am, 1.30pm and 3pm.

Next door is **Seoul Land** *(☎ 504 0011; adult/student W5000/3500, all-inclusive ticket W25,000/13,000; open 9am-7pm daily Apr-Sept, 9am-6pm daily Oct-Mar)*, a large amusement park with a roller coaster, shot drop and bungy swing among the many adrenalin rides.

To get to Seoul Grand Park, take subway Line 4 to Seoul Grand Park station, which is 45 minutes away from City Hall. Leave by Exit 2 and then either walk (10 minutes) or take a mini-train (W500) to the entrance. Another option is to take the sky lift (adult/child W3000/1500) to the far end of Grand Park and then walk back through the zoo.

Children's Grand Park 어린이대공원

This park *(Map 2; adult/student W900/500; open 9am-7pm daily)* has a large zoo and an indoor botanic garden. The natural surroundings make it an ideal place for a picnic, although there is no shortage of restaurants, snack bars and food stalls. Concerts and art events are organised, and on some days children can have their picture drawn by talented young artists for free. A chimpanzee and sea-lion show, a circus, an outdoor swimming pool (open July and August) and funfair thrill rides are all part of the park, but cost extra.

Seoul Dream Land 서울드림랜드

This is yet another amusement park *(Map 10; ☎ 982 6800; adult/child W2000/1000;*

open 9am-7.30pm daily Mar-Oct, 9am-6pm daily Nov-Feb) with the usual thrill rides. There's also a swimming pool and a miniature golf course.

To get here, head north on subway Line 4 to Miasamgeori station and take a taxi the 1.5km to the amusement park.

PARKS

Unlike many other Asian cities, Seoul is well endowed with parks. Even in the central city area you are never far from some greenery, with plenty of it inside the palace compounds in particular.

Yongsan Park 용산가족공원

This park (Map 6), to the south of Itaewon, was the former golf course for the Yongsan military base. It then became a quiet natural area of ponds and trees that made it a favourite place for family picnics, but now it is the site of the new seven-storey National Museum, which is due to open in 2005.

To get here, take subway Line 1 or 4 to Ichon station.

Olympic Park 오림픽공원

This park (Map 7) has a large open green area with a lake that is home to pheasants, ducks and geese. A Baekje-dynasty earth fortification, **Mongchontoseong** runs through part of the park. The small **Mongchontoseong Museum** *(admission free; open 10am-5pm Tues-Sun)* houses Baekje-dynasty relics found in the area. The objects on display include impressive golden crowns and jewellery.

Two hundred large **modern sculptures** are scattered around other parts of the park. Designed and made by artists from around the world, the collection was started during the 1988 Seoul Olympics, but has been growing ever since. Most of the artwork is puzzling even after you have read the artists' descriptions of their work.

The **Olympic Museum** *(☎ 410 1052; W seoulolympicmuseum.com; adult/child W5000/2000; open 10am-5.30pm Tues-Sun Mar-Oct; 10am-4.30pm Tues-Sun Nov-Feb)* is full of screens showing action from the 1988 Seoul Olympics. You can also enjoy a simulated ride and test your skills on the do-it-yourself sports equipment downstairs (W500 coins needed).

The park also contains the **sports stadiums** that were used during the Seoul Olympics – the swimming pool, tennis courts and various gymnasiums. Professional cycling takes place in the velodrome on weekends during the summer months.

Next to the Wedding Hall, the **Children's Puppet Theatre** has fun puppet shows (W6000), although the puppets can only speak Korean. On summer evenings there are sometimes music or laser shows in the **outdoor concert arena** near the fountain.

On warm evenings and weekends hundreds of young people go to the park to rollerblade around the plaza, play rollerblade hockey and do skateboard tricks, while members of the older generation play badminton, jog, eat ice cream, picnic under the trees, or exercise tiny dogs.

To get here, take subway Line 8 to Mongchontoseong station.

World Cup Stadium & Parks 월드컵주경기장

Costing US$151 million, the 64,000-seat World Cup Stadium (Map 2) was built on what used to be a huge landfill site. The ultra-modern stadium, with Teflon-covered roof that is shaped like a traditional Korean kite, staged the opening ceremony of the 2002 World Cup soccer finals. Attractive parks and ponds have been created around the stadium, and a golf course is planned. Wind turbines, outdoor concert areas and a 202m fountain in Hangang are other features.

The best way to explore the stadium and the surrounding area is by bicycle – see the Cycling section later. However, it is also easily accessible by subway – take subway Line 6 to World Cup Stadium station.

Hongneung Arboretum 산림청수목원

Run by the Forestry Research Institute, this park-like arboretum *(Map 10; ☎ 961 2651; admission free; open 9am-7pm Sun)* covers 38 hectares and was established in 1922.

Restored after the Korean War, it has over 2000 plant species and 65 wildlife species (mostly birds) that include pheasants and weasels. Picnics are not allowed.

Nearby is the **Forestry Museum** *(☎ 961 2873; admission free; open 10am-5pm Sun)*, which is housed in an unusual wooden building. Its exhibits demonstrate the importance of Korea's mountains and forests. Also nearby are the **Hongneung Royal Tombs** *(admission W400; open 9am-5.30pm Tues-Sun)*, which the arboretum is named after. Many Joseon queens were buried here; as the burial location of royal bodies was a serious and contentious matter, they were sometimes dug up and moved. The **King Sejong Memorial Hall** *(☎ 969 8851; admission W1500; open 9am-6pm Tues-Sun)*, also in the area, has books, scientific and musical instruments and 14 portraits of Korea's most popular and admired scholar king.

To get to this area, take subway Line 1 to Cheongnyangni station and it's a 15-minute, 1km walk north.

WALKING TOURS

Inwangsan Shamanist Hillside Walk (Map 4)

On this short but uphill walk you can see Seoul's most famous shamanist shrine, visit small Buddhist temples and see part of the Seoul fortress wall. The walk only takes an hour if you just want a quick look but it's sensible to take longer and soak up the unique atmosphere.

Take subway Line 3 to Dongnimmun station, leave by Exit 2 and turn down the first winding alley on your left. Walk uphill past the golf driving range and grocery shops for 10 minutes, and you'll see a temple gateway on your left. Walk through it to the notice board.

Turn left to walk around the village where **Buddhist temples** and **traditional houses** cling to the rocky hillside. The temples have colourful murals on the outside that illustrate the Buddhist philosophy of life.

Back on the main path, a bronze bell marks the entrance to **Bongwonsa**, the largest of the temples. The paintings on the entrance gate doors depict the guardian kings of heaven who protect Buddhists from evil and harm. The shrine hall has five golden Buddha statues and a side shrine for the shamanist deities – Sanshin (the mountain god), Doksung (the river god) and Chilsung (the seven stars of the Big Dipper). Buddhism and shamanism have always coexisted peacefully in Korea.

Carry on up the steps to see Seoul's most famous shamanist shrine, **Guksadang**. It was originally built on Namsan by order of King Taejo, the founder of the Joseon dynasty, who established Seoul as the capital city. However, Guksadang was demolished by the Japanese in 1925 and Korean shamanists secretly rebuilt it on Inwangsan. The shrine is small but the altar inside is often loaded down with offerings of food for the spirits – rice cakes, fruit, meat and a pig's head – as shamanists believe that the dead still need food and drink. Ceremonies called *gut* usually take place inside or outside. These ceremonies involve contacting departed spirits who are attracted by the lavish offerings of food and drink. During some *gut* the drums beat and the *mudang* (female shamanist priest) dances herself into a frenzied state that allows her to communicate with the spirits and be possessed by them. Smartly dressed couples come here to ask for good fortune with a business project, to make contact with a deceased relative or to cure an illness. Another *gut* helps to guide the spirit of a recently departed person to find peace. Resentments felt by the dead can haunt and plague the living and cause them all sorts of misfortune. For shamanists death does not end relationships, they simply take another form.

Walk left and up some steps to the extraordinary **Zen rocks** that look like a Salvador Dali painting – two large rocks have been eroded into a semi-human shape. Women still come here to pray for a son.

The hillside above is full of eroded rocks that create an eerie atmosphere. In front of small crevices are candles, incense sticks and offerings of sweets. Climb up the hill for

10 minutes and you reach an altar where an **ancient Buddha** is carved on a rock.

People have been visiting this sacred area for thousands of years. One rock embodies the spirit of a famous general, while another is where children's spirits shelter. Shamanists perform their ceremonies under the shade of the trees – an old lady is bowing and waving five different coloured flags to attract the spirits, and a young girl is drumming and meditating. You can really feel the ancient atmosphere here, even though the traffic and the modern world is only a 20-minute walk away.

Natural springs in the area provide fresh water and you can easily walk to part of the **Seoul fortress wall**, which dates back to 1396 and is being renovated. From the wall you can walk down the hill using one of the many footpaths.

All visitors should treat the area and the people with respect, and remember that taking a photograph could interfere with an important ceremony. The walk can be combined with a visit to Seodaemun Prison and Dongnimmun Park, which are near the subway station on the other side of the road. See Historical Seoul at the start of the chapter for details.

Namsan & Seoul Tower Walk (Map 9)

This walk is popular with Seoulites, some of whom do it every morning as their daily exercise – the view from the top is definitely worth the climb. Walking time is about an hour, but allow a couple of hours so that you have time to look around.

Take Line 1 or 4 to Seoul Station subway and leave by Exit 10. Go up the steps and turn right towards the Hilton Hotel, then take the first left towards the multistorey car park and turn right up the steps and through the small garden. At the Hilton Hotel, go right and walk round to the front of the hotel. Cross the road, bear left, cross the second road, and go up the steps into the park.

Walk past the children's playground and the old men playing Korean chess, cross the road and go up more steps. Keep going straight and cross another road. Go up yet more steps and on the right is the **Ahn Choong-kun Museum** *(☎ 753 5033; admission W700; open 9am-6pm Mon-Fri)*, based around the Korean independence hero. Ahn Choong-kun went to Russia and in 1909 assassinated Ito Hirobumi, a top Japanese official who masterminded Japan's step-by-step takeover of Korea. Here you can learn all about his life and ideas.

From here walk to the indoor **botanic garden** *(admission W300)*. Over on the right is a **mini zoo**, but walk along the left side of the botanic garden for the shady 30-minute walk up the wide steps to the top of Namsan for some panoramic views of Seoul. If you don't like walking uphill, follow the signs to the **Namsan Cable Car Station** *(open Tues-Sun; adult one way/return W3000/4800, child one way/return W2200/2600; open 10am-11pm)* and take that to the top. See the High-rise Seoul section earlier in this chapter for details about Seoul Tower.

For a different route down, you can walk past Seoul Tower to the car park and follow the road right (there are signs). You share the road with cars, but a path is painted on

Seoul for Free

- Visit Olympic Park, the sculpture garden and Mongchontoseong Museum
- Look around one of the interesting markets
- Wander around the austere Namsangol Traditional Village
- Check out the Buddhist temples such as Jogyesa or Bongeunsa
- Go on a walking tour or a hiking trip
- Enjoy traditional music and dance on weekends at the open-air Seoul Norimadang
- View the art at the Insadong art galleries
- Watch the ice-skaters at Lotte World
- Relax in Marronnier Park in Daehangno on a warm weekend afternoon and enjoy the varied performers
- See the changing of the royal guard outside Deoksugung or look on at other royal re-enactments
- Log on to the Internet at KNTO or other free providers

the road. It takes 20 minutes to walk down to the indoor botanic gardens, where you can take a taxi or a bus or walk back to Seoul Station subway station.

Behind Deoksugung Walk (Maps 8 & 9)

This is a short 30-minute walk, but allow at least another two hours to look around the art gallery and the two museums and to have a cup of medicinal tea.

Take subway Line 1 or 2 to City Hall station (Map 9) and leave by Exit 1. Turn right and then go left along Deoksugung wall. It's a pleasant walk with shady trees and little traffic. After five minutes, **Seoul Museum of Art** on the left is worth a visit. The nearby **Cheongdong Methodist Church** was built in 1898 and is the oldest Protestant church in Korea.

Carry on straight ahead and on the right is **Cheongdong Theatre**, which puts on traditional music, song and dance shows. A **teashop** *(open 10am-10pm daily)* here sells *sibjeondaebotang*, a tea with 15 medicinal ingredients that's sweetened with honey quince syrup and served with Korean green tea, candied ginger and lightweight rice crackers. Some of the teas are alcoholic.

Continuing along the road, turn right at the sign for a short detour to **A&C Theatre**, which often puts on energetic musical shows designed to appeal to tourists, and a white tower, which is all that remains of the **Russian Legation Building** where King Gojong sought refuge for a year in 1896.

Back on the main road, you soon reach the **Star Six Cinema** and another **theatre** where the long-running 'kitchen-utensil drumming' musical *Nanta* has proved popular.

Turn left at the main road for a detour to the **Agriculture Museum**. It displays traditional wooden farming equipment and entry is free. Walk back to the cinema and cross over the main road to **Heunghwamun**, a traditional gate, in front of **Gyeonghuigung**, a palace that was completely destroyed by the Japanese during the colonial period. A few structures have been rebuilt but they are not open to the public.

Next door is the new **Seoul Museum of History**, which focuses on Joseon-dynasty Seoul. From here cross over the road using the footbridge to the moving giant **statue** of a Hammering Man. Walk down to Sejongno, turn right and go past Donghwa duty-free shop to the Seoul Metropolitan Council building. Turn right here to visit the **Anglican Church**, one of Seoul's few Renaissance-style buildings.

Between the Palaces Walk (Map 8)

This walk takes as little as one hour, but allow another hour or two to explore the park and the interesting shops, art galleries and teashops. The walk is shaded by trees most of the way and avoids crossing major roads.

Take subway Line 3 to Anguk station, leave by Exit 1 and turn right along the main road until you reach **Dongsipjagak**, an old watchtower. Turn right past **Seoul Selection Bookshop** and **Beomyeonsa**, an unusual Buddhist temple on the 3rd floor of a modern building, which are both worth a visit. Further on are lots of **art galleries** to look around.

Fork right and walk past a **hanbok shop** to a couple of **traditional restaurants** opposite the prime minister's residence, which has large white gates and guards outside. Past **Seomulseoduljae Teashop**, which specialises in medicinal teas, turn right and cross over the road to look around a fascinating little **antique shop**. Further on is the entrance to **Samcheong Park**, where a short loop walk takes you through attractive woodland. The spring water here is popular.

Cross back over the road and Seoul Tower appears in the distance. Walk down the hill to Bukchonhanok-gil on your right. Follow this alley through a quiet neighbourhood of traditional houses. At the end of the alley (building number 2 faces you) turn left and walk uphill. At the top is a splendid view of tiled rooftops that hasn't changed much in the past 100 years. The Joseon-dynasty aristocrats used to live here near the palaces while the poor lived in thatched houses further away.

At the next junction turn right, and then turn left at the red-brick public bath chimney. Turn left again at the end of this alley. On your right is the **Tibet Museum** *(admission including a cup of tea W5000; open 10am-7pm daily)*, which has a small but interesting collection of Tibetan items and Chinese teapots.

At the crossroads is **Art Sonje**, which houses an art gallery, a café, a cinema that shows international films, and Dal Restaurant, an excellent but expensive Indian restaurant. Further down the road on the right is the **Lotus Lantern International Buddhist Centre** where foreigners can study and practise Buddhism. At the main road, turn left for Anguk subway station or cross over the road to visit **Insadong** or **Jogyesa** temple.

COURSES

Language

International House *(Map 12; ☎/fax 762 5112; w www.ih.or.kr)* offers Korean lessons held in a friendly, informal atmosphere that cost a nominal W10,000 for three months. Six levels of classes are run on Tuesday and Thursday evenings and Saturday afternoons. Other language classes (Japanese, Chinese, Russian and Spanish) are organised as well as Latin dance and computer classes.

Yonsei University (Map 3) runs both part-time and full-time Korean-language classes for serious students. Ex-students of the classes recommend them. Don't forget that if you plan to study for four weeks or more, you must get a study visa.

Sisa Institute *(Map 8; w www.ybmedu.com)* is opposite Tapgol Park and offers month-long language courses for W180,000 (10 hours a week in the morning or afternoon), W120,000 (six hours a week in the evening) or W90,000 (three hours every Saturday).

Cheap Korean-language lessons are available at **World Village** *(Map 12; ☎ 018-239 9981)* in Daehangno.

Click on w www.metro.seoul.kr for a list of universities and institutes that offer Korean-language courses, or w www.korea.net for links to sites where you can learn *hangeul* on the Internet.

Traditional Culture

The **Son Family** *(☎ 562 6829; w www.sons-home.com)* in Gangnam-gu provide an introduction to Korean traditional culture. Three-hour programmes cost W70,000 and involve *dado* (a tea ceremony), making *gimchi,* dressing in *hanbok,* playing a traditional musical instrument, trying your hand at calligraphy and eating a typical Korean meal.

A similar programme is run by the four-generation **Yoo Family** *(☎ 3673 0323, fax 3673 0324; w www.korea-family.com)*, who live in a traditional *hanok* house north of Anguk subway station. The family's 3½-hour programmes cost W70,000 and are similar to those run by the Son family.

The **National Folk Museum** *(☎ 734 1341)* in the grounds of Gyeongbokgung runs practical courses that teach foreigners how to make fans, pottery, paper boxes and, of course, *gimchi*. The courses are free and numbers for each course are limited to 50 participants.

Cooking

The best way to learn Korean cooking is to do a homestay with someone willing to teach you. Otherwise there are a number of cooking classes conducted in English.

The **Yoo Family** *(☎ 3673 0323, fax 3673 0324; w www.korea-family.com)* will teach you how to make *gimchi* (W45,000 per hour).

The **Institute of Traditional Korean Food** *(☎ 741 5414, fax 741 5415)* operates Jilsiru Tteok Cafe (Map 8) and runs a three-hour, W70,000 course upstairs on making Korean rice cakes.

ACTIVITIES

Seoul offers a wide range of activities – hiking in the nearby mountains, cycling along the Hangang cycleway, bowling, billiards, saunas, and in winter skiing, snowboarding and ice-skating. Buddhist temple programmes and Korean-language and cooking classes are also available. For information on spectator sports (horse racing, baseball, soccer, basketball and *ssireum* wrestling), see the Entertainment chapter.

Cycling

Cycle paths line both banks of Hangang and bicycles can be rented in many of the parks along Hangang. In summer, swimming pools, paddle boats, windsurfing, water-skiing and jet-skiing can also all be enjoyed.

To cycle the routes described here, it's best to hire a bike on Yeouido from near the swimming pool in Hangang Park, or from another hut near the ferry boat terminal. Bicycles/tandems cost W2000/5000 per hour. There are more bicycle-rental huts in Yeouido Park but they cost a little more. Bicycle-rental huts are open every day from 9am to around 7pm but close in winter. Padlocks and bicycle helmets are not supplied and some form of ID is required.

To get to Yeouido Park, take subway Line 5 to Yeouinaru station and leave by Exit 2.

Yeouido Park (Map 5) A 2.5km cycle path runs around this park, which provides a splash of green in the middle of Yeouido.

Yeouido to the World Cup Stadium (Map 2) This tour is 7km return and takes 90 minutes, but will be longer if you spend time at the stadium and surrounding parks.

From Yeouido cycle past the National Assembly and after about 1km you reach the Yanghwa gardens. Five minutes beyond is Yanghwa Bridge, which you can use to cross Hangang. Walk up the steps of the bridge pushing your bike up the little bike path on the right of the steps. Have a look round Seonyudo (an island in the middle of Hangang), which is being transformed from a water treatment plant into an attractive park.

Wheel your bicycle down the narrow path on the right of the steps on the other side of the bridge and continue right along the cycle-way that runs along the northern side of the river. After 10 minutes, turn right at the orange bridge, ride over a small bridge and then turn right, following the green signs. After another 10 minutes you should arrive in the large attractive park that surrounds the World Cup Stadium.

Yeouido to Olympic Park (Map 2) This is a long route, 38km return, and takes four hours cycling, but nearly all of it is on a cycleway and there are no hills.

Along the way are parks, sports fields, and lots of bridges and fishermen. At Banpo and Jamsil windsurfers (W10,000), water-skis (W15,000) and jet-skis (W100,000) can be rented by the hour. Herons, geese and other birds live on and near the river.

Near the 18km distance marker, turn right (there is no sign), ride under a couple of bridges and follow the left side of a dry riverbed. At the road, turn left, cross over the minor road, and then cross the major road using the pedestrian crossing. Then turn right, go over the bridge and Olympic Park is on your left. It's worth spending at least an hour in Seoul's best park and looking around its museums, stadiums and outdoor sculptures.

Pool & Four Ball

There are pool halls all over Seoul. Look for the obvious signs outside. They often have pool tables (pool is called 'pocketball' in Korea) and tables for games of 'four ball' and 'three ball'.

Four ball is played in Belgium and the Netherlands but is most popular in South Korea. It's a kind of billiards or pool, but there are no pockets and players must hit cannons.

Two red balls and two white ones are used. The players (any number) hit the white balls in turn. The object of the game is to hit both of the red balls in one shot without hitting the other white ball. It sounds easy but it isn't.

You score minus one if you are successful and your white ball hits both the red balls and doesn't touch the other white ball, and you also get to take another turn. You score nothing if you hit just one red, and you score plus one if you hit the other white ball or miss everything. It's a handicap system, so beginners start with a score of three points. When you improve you start with five points, then eight, then 10 and so on. When your score reaches zero, to finish you must do a more difficult shot – hit one red and two side-cushions or two reds and one side-cushion without hitting the other white ball.

The loser buys everyone a meal, or pays the cost of the game – normally around W6000 per hour.

Tenpin Bowling

Tenpin bowling is available all over the city at a very reasonable price of around W3000 a game (plus W1000 shoe hire). **Doore Bowling Centre** (Map 12) in Daehangno and **Lotte World** (Map 7) are just two of the numerous alleys available. You can even have a game in the basement of Incheon International Airport. Log on to Ⓦ www.visitseoul.net for a complete list of alleys.

Skiing

The cold winters and mountainous terrain make Korea an ideal country for winter sports. There are a number of ski resorts just an hour away from Seoul by bus. Prices are reasonable and ski resorts offer a range of accommodation from youth hostels and basic *minbak* to condominiums and luxury hotels. The ski season runs from early December to mid-March.

It's easy to hire ski clothes and equipment, and there are usually ski instructors who speak English. The ski resorts have offices in Seoul and run all-inclusive package tours. Expect to pay around W38,000 for lift tickets (for a full day), W26,000 for equipment hire and W25,000 for a day of instruction. There are substantial discounts for children.

Contact **KNTO** (*☎ 757 0086; Ⓦ www.knto.or.kr*) or a travel agent for details on the ski resorts. The USO also organises weekend ski trips – see the Organised Tours section of the Getting Around chapter for details.

The following resorts are listed in order of distance from Seoul; phone numbers are given for both Seoul offices and resorts.

Seoul Ski Resort (*☎ 02-959 0864, 031 592 1220; season early Dec–late Feb*) has four slopes, a sledding hill, three lifts and hotel accommodation (66 rooms). The resort is 40 minutes east of Seoul.

Cheonmasan Ski Resort (*☎ 02-2233 5311, 346-594 1211; Ⓦ www.chonmaski.com; season early Dec–early Mar*) has five slopes and seven lifts. English-speaking instructors are available. The hotel has a pool. The resort is 50 minutes northeast of Seoul.

Bears Town Resort (*☎ 02-594 8188, 031-532 2534; Ⓦ www.bearstown.com; season late Nov–early Mar*) has 11 slopes, two sledding hills and nine lifts. Accommodation includes a youth hostel and a condominium, which has a pool, a sauna, a bowling alley and tennis courts. English-speaking instructors and night skiing are available. The resort has a golf course and is 40 minutes northeast of Seoul.

Yangji Pine Ski Resort (*☎ 02-542 8700, 0335-338 2001; Ⓦ www.pineresort.com; season early Dec–late Feb*) has seven slopes, one sledding hill and six lifts. Accommodation is in a hotel or condominium, and the latter has a pool and bowling alley. The resort is near Yong-in, 80km southeast of Seoul.

Jisan Forest Ski Resort (*☎ 02-3442 0322, 031-638 8460; Ⓦ www.jisanresort.co.kr; season early Dec–late Feb*) has nine slopes, snowboarding slopes and four lifts. English-speaking instructors are available. The resort is 50 minutes southeast of Seoul, near Ichon.

Blue Valley Ski Resort (*☎ 043-846 0750, fax 846 1789; season early Dec–early Mar*) has seven slopes, 13 lifts and night skiing. Accommodation includes a hostel, *yeogwan* and hotels. It is in Chungcheongbuk-do, a 2½-hour drive southeast of Seoul.

Yongpyeong Ski Resort (*☎ 033-335 5757, fax 335 5769; Ⓦ www.yongpyong.co.kr; season late Nov–early Apr*) is one of the best in Korea, with 18 slopes and cross-country trails. Accommodation includes a youth hostel, a hotel and a condominium. The resort is a 3½-hour drive east of Seoul.

Muju Ski Resort (*☎ 063-322 9000, fax 322 9993; Ⓦ www.mujuresort.com; season late Nov–late Mar*) is another excellent ski resort despite its southerly position. It has 23 slopes, 15 lifts and snowboarding is allowed. Accommodation is in a very expensive hotel, or in nearby *yeogwan* and *minbak*. The resort is a 4½-hour drive south of Seoul.

Swimming

The best places for swimming are on the sandy beaches of the unspoilt islands scattered off Incheon in the West Sea. See the Incheon section of the Excursions chapter for details.

In the hot and humid months of July and August, outdoor swimming pools in the parks along Hangang are open. One of the best, **Yeouido Pool** *(Map 5; admission W2500)*, is near Yeouinaru subway station on Line 5.

Large indoor pools are available at **Lotte World** (Map 7) and **Olympic Park** (Map 7) that cost W6500 and W4000 respectively. They are not always open to the public but are usually available in the afternoon.

Most top-end hotels have luxurious exercise facilities like 25m pools and saunas and some are available to non-guests. Prices start at W8000 but are reasonable considering the facilities provided. The **Dreamtel Youth Hostel** (Map 2) near Gimpo airport has a pool, sauna and exercise room that you can use for W7000 – you don't need to be a YHA member to enjoy the facilities. See the Places to Stay chapter for information on how to get here. The most expensive pools in Seoul must be the three outdoor ones at the **Sheraton Walker Hill Hotel** (Map 2), which cost W39,000 for adults and W27,000 for children in July and August.

Caribbean Bay is a wonderful aquatic centre at Everland, which is an hour south of Seoul by bus. See the Excursions chapter for details.

Gicheon Training

Nestled among the mountains of Gangwondo province, about 25km from Wonju City, is the Munmak Gicheon Centre, where I learnt the ancient martial art of Gicheon. Like taekwondo, Gicheon is an original Korean martial art, but most Koreans have never heard of it.

The Munmak Gicheon Centre opened in 1997 and has five small guesthouses and a large training studio. On the weekend I attended, my fellow students were from Korea, Indonesia, the Philippines, Australia and Canada.

Gicheon gets its name from Gi, the secret life force or energy paths that run through our bodies. Although it can be used for fighting, Gicheon concentrates on mind-body training, meditation and breathing to develop greater powers of concentration and to improve physical health and strength. The masters claim to have received enlightenment through Gicheon.

I was taught the six basic Gicheon postures, most of which stretched my joints considerably and were difficult to sustain for very long. The aim is to encourage the free flow of Gi throughout the body, which is essential for good health. In fact, the exercises relieved long-standing pain from carpal tunnel syndrome in my shoulders and wrists.

Training in the studio, planting lettuce in the fields, bathing in a mountain stream, and drinking *soju* under the stars with my teachers and fellow students was one of my most memorable experiences in Korea.

Lee Ki-tae, my Gicheon instructor, can be contacted on ☎ 016-420 0509 or e gicheon master@yahoo.com. You can learn more about Gicheon at his website: w www24.brinkster.com/thefringe or w www.gicheon.co.kr.

Melinda Sherwood

Taekwondo

This is the well-known traditional Korean martial art that developed out of *taekkyeon,* which can be traced back to ancient tomb murals in the Goryeo dynasty. Taekwondo is now an Olympic sport that is popular with martial arts fans all over the world. All Korean army personnel receive taekwondo training and five million people worldwide have reached certificate standard.

The headquarters of the **World Taekwondo Federation** *(Map 6; ☎ 566 2505)* is northeast of Gangnam subway station. It has a tournament hall, shops that sell taekwondo equipment and a small taekwondo museum. For information on tournament dates log on to w www.koreataekwondo.org or w www.wtf.org.

Hoki Taekwondo *(☎ 336 6014, fax 336 7925; w www.taekwontour.com)* runs a 1½-hour introductory programme at the War

Memorial Museum gymnasium that costs W30,000 and usually starts at 10am. The best thing about the programme is that you are given the opportunity to break a 2cm-thick wooden board. Contact Hoki first before turning up at the gymnasium.

Yonsei International Taekwondo Centre *(Map 3; ☎ 738 8397)* provides four training sessions in a week for W20,000.

See the Organised Tours section of the Getting Around chapter for details on martial arts tours.

Rollerblading

Popular areas for rollerblading are along the Hangang cycleways and in the Olympic Park entrance plaza. Rollerblades can be hired in **Jangchung Park** (Map 9) for W4000 and there is a small area to practise your skills.

Ice-Skating & Ice Hockey

Lotte World (Map 7) has a marvellous indoor skating rink that is open all year round. See the Amusement Parks & Zoos section earlier in this chapter for details.

There is an ice hockey team that's made up of Canadians, Americans, Koreans and Finns with a website at **w** www.glaciershockey.com.

Tennis

A few deluxe hotels have tennis courts, but public courts are available at **Olympic Park** (Map 7) for W6000 per hour Monday to Friday (W12,000 on Saturday and Sunday).

Jangchung Tennis Courts (Map 9) charges W8000 per hour Monday to Friday, W15,000 on Saturday and Sunday, and W25,000 at night.

Golf

There are golf courses near Seoul, but the private ones are usually reserved for members only. Some ski resorts have golf courses that cost W20,000 to W40,000 per round.

All in all, it is probably best to stick to the driving ranges, which you can find all over Seoul, as well as in some top-end hotels.

Adventure Sports

Rock climbing is growing in popularity, especially on the granite cliffs in Bukhansan National Park. For details on clubs and climbing walls log on to **w** www.visitseoul.net.

White-water rafting is available in Gangwon-do. See the Organised Tours section of the Getting Around chapter for more details.

Scuba diving lessons are available at Lotte World swimming pool (Map 7). Contact **Crystal Diving** *(☎ 415 5302, fax 3431 5554)* at the entrance to the pool.

Windsurfing, **water-skiing** and **jet-skiing** are available during the summer months at various places on Hangang, including Banpo (Map 6; Dongjak subway station, Line 4) and Jamsil (Map 7; Sincheon subway station, Line 2, Exit 7). Windsurfer hire is W10,000 per hour, water-skiing is W15,000 a ride and jet-ski hire is W100,000 per hour.

Squash

Log on to **w** www.visitseoul.net for a list of squash clubs and courts. The downtown Lotte Hotel and the Grand Hyatt Hotel in Itaewon have squash courts.

Traditional Korean Games

Baduk is known in the West by its Japanese name 'go', although it was originally introduced from China. It is a popular board game played between black and white counters. At each move you put a counter on the board and try to capture territory and encircle your opponent. The rules are very simple but the strategies are highly complex. The game has its own cable TV channel and you can often see groups of old men playing it in summer under the trees in Seoul's many parks.

Another game that the old men play in the parks is **changgi**. This game also derives from China and is a form of chess. The board and pieces are the same as with Chinese chess, but the moves that the pieces can make are quite different. Both versions are played on the line intersections rather than on the empty squares as with Western chess. Some pieces move in similar ways to Western chess pieces and all three games share the same objective – to checkmate your opponent. Korean chess is a fascinating game and well worth learning if you have the time.

Go-Stop is a popular gambling game that can keep groups of men up all night. It is a card game using small cards with flowers on them. The rules and strategy are not easy to pick up, so if you take part in a game expect to lose money.

Yut is an entertaining board game usually played by children and is similar to the Western game of ludo. Each player has four counters and you chase your opponent around the board and try to get all your counters home first. Four wooden sticks (each with one flat side) are used instead of dice to decide how many spaces on the board your counters can move forward.

Bathhouses & Saunas

Don't leave Seoul without experiencing a public bath. Unfortunately you have to go to Ichon, 50km southeast of Seoul, to soak in an *oncheon* hot bath fed from mineral-laden hot spring water, or to Incheon for a seawater hot bath, but there are plenty of ordinary hot baths known as *tang* in Seoul. *Tang* have the same symbols as *yeogwan,* which causes confusion.

The rather sparse traditional *tang* bathhouses only cost around W4000, which is less than half the price of the more palatial facilities offered by luxury hotels.

Undress in the locker room and then take a shower, as you must clean yourself thoroughly before getting into the bath. Soap and shampoo is supplied, as well as toothpaste and toothbrushes. A thorough clean is part of the bath experience; the ladies section has hairdryers, foot massagers and all sorts of lotions and perfumes. You can often have your hair cut as well.

The water in the big public baths varies from hot to extremely hot, but there may also be a cold bath (including a 'waterfall' shower). Relaxing and turning pink in a hot bath is good therapy, especially on a cold winter's day. The heat soaks into weary bodies, soothing tired muscles and minds.

Most *tang* have saunas – some made of wood, some of stone – but all are as hot as a pizza oven. If you want to suffer more, you can be pummelled by a masseur. But check the price first as massages are usually expensive. Most people also take a nap lying on a wooden floor with a block of wood for a pillow.

If you make an excursion outside Seoul, try to find an *oncheon* with an outdoor section, which is a real Garden of Eden experience, although the Adams and Eves are separated. At night you can look up at the stars and it's the perfect way to relax after a hike in the mountains.

Seoul has some unusual **saunas**, such as steam or mugwort herbal saunas. Many are open 24 hours a day, but they are segregated and some only have facilities for men. Male-only saunas are available downtown at the New Seoul Hotel (W10,000) and the Koreana Hotel (W13,000).

Health and beauty tours in Seoul are popular with Japanese tourists, but these upmarket facilities are expensive. **Seoul Mud** *(Map 11; ☎ 747 8012, fax 749 8097; open 9am-midnight)* in Itaewon is one such place. A two-hour stay, bathing in its special soft mud, then in a ginseng pool and an orange pool, and finished off by a sauna, costs W78,000. It's a cheap price to pay for beauty if it works.

A less-expensive option is offered at **Dreamtel Youth Hostel** (Map 2). A 45-minute subway ride west of the city centre, it has a sauna, an exercise room and an indoor swimming pool that you can use for W7000 a day. See the Places to Stay chapter for information on how to get here.

A swelter in **Yu Young Sauna** (Map 11) costs W3500, while **Niksantang** (Map 12) is a public bathhouse with a sauna and massage facilities.

Korean Buddhist Temple Programmes

Some Korean temples, including Jogyesa (Map 8), offer visitors the chance to participate in a number of activities with the monks. See **W** www.templestaykorea.net for details and the Places to Stay chapter for more details on temple stays.

Buddhist Prayer Before Eating

Now we take our meal that caused no harm to any sentient beings.

Let us consider whether our behaviour deserves this meal.

Let us cultivate our minds away from greed, anger and foolishness.

We eat this meal to become enlightened.

Bongeunsa (Map 7) offers a **four-hour programme** for W20,000. It starts with a typical temple four-bowl lunch of rice, soup, vegetables and water. No talk is allowed and not even a scrap of food should be wasted – Buddhists are strict.

A guided tour of the beautiful temple buildings is followed by Seon meditation. Everyone sits cross-legged and a monk tells participants to concentrate and use their minds to focus on their breathing only. After this a monk prepares organic green tea, which must be served at exactly the right temperature and should be drunk in three sips. Tea calms the mind and the body, and if Korean monks have a dis-agreement they settle it over a cup of organic green tea.

Lotus Lantern International Buddhist Centre *(Map 8; ☎ 735 5347, fax 720 7849; W www.lotuslantern.net)* has a shrine hall and a library of Buddhist books in English. The centre runs classes and meditation practice, and holds a service on Sunday at 6pm. Meditation retreats are organised on Ganghwado, a large and unspoilt island northwest of Seoul.

Mountain Hikes Around Seoul

Seoul is fortunate to have plenty of forested mountains nearby and hiking is a very popular activity with all age groups. Nearly everyone likes to get away from the concrete and cars in the city and escape to natural surroundings where they can breathe fresh air. You're best to avoid heading for the mountains at weekends or public holidays, otherwise you'll find yourself standing in a long queue to reach the summit.

Koreans are serious about the great outdoors: any excursion away from the concrete of Seoul is prepared for with a thoroughness worthy of an expedition primed to assault Everest. Koreans must also be the best-dressed hikers in the world – check out the red waistcoats, yellow caps and multi-coloured, knee-high socks.

If your energy begins to flag, consider taking a shot of the Korean hiker's friend – pine-needle *soju*. One mouthful should be enough to help you make it to the top.

BUKHANSAN NATIONAL PARK

Just north of Seoul is Bukhansan (Map 10), a national park with impressive granite peaks, forests, temples and tremendous views. Many peaks are over 500m and rock climbers particularly enjoy Insubong (810m). Insubong is a free-climber's dream, with some of the best multi-pitch climbing in Asia and routes of all grades. Guides can be found through Seoul climbing shops or through mountaineering clubs, though solo climbers new to the mountain should find the local climbers eager to help. More information on Insubong can be obtained though the **KNTO** *(☎ 757 0086; Ⓦ www.knto.or.kr)*.

Bukhansan's park entry fee is W1300 for adults and W300 for children, and the ticket booths sell a hiking map (mostly in Korean) for W1000.

Camping is possible, alternatively you can stay in basic hiking huts. Contact the **park authorities** *(☎ 909 0497, fax 918 9063; Ⓦ www.npa.or.kr)*. Huts are not usually open in winter, and in peak periods (10 July to 20 August and 1 October to 14 November), on public holidays and weekends some huts and campgrounds have an online reservation system.

Bukhansan receives four million visitors a year and to reduce environmental damage, footpaths are closed in rotation, so don't ignore 'track closed' signs.

The following two hikes are recommended, the first in the south of the park and the second in the northern section. Both are all-day hikes.

Title Page: One of the white granite peaks at Bukhansan National Park, just north of Seoul (Photograph by Bill Wassman)

Baekundae Hike

This is a moderate to strenuous hike that takes six hours, including short breaks.

Take subway Line 5 to Gwanghwamun station, leave by Exit 1 and walk round to the front of the Sejong Cultural Centre. Get on bus No 156 (W600) and tell the driver 'Bukhansan'. The journey takes 35 minutes in normal traffic conditions and will take you to a bus stop at the western edge of the park.

Follow the other hikers as they walk to the end of the small village, turn right and walk to the ticket booth. The park's highest peak, Baekundae (836m), is 4km or two hours away. A five-minute walk brings you to the fortress wall and Daeseomun gate. The wall is 9.5km long and was made of earth in the Baekje dynasty. It was rebuilt with 13 gates and stone blocks in 1711 during the reign of King Sukchong and encircled 12 temples and numerous wells.

Fifteen minutes after leaving the gate the road crosses a bridge. Fork left following the sign to Baekundae – keep a look out for little striped squirrels. Spring water is available at Yaksu-am, a hermitage which you reach 45 minutes after leaving the road. Past Yaksu-am there are stairs up to another fortress gate and then you use metal cables to haul yourself up to the Baekundae peak. Surrounded by granite cliffs and with a 360-degree view, it's a top-of-the-world feeling.

The easiest option is to return the same way, but it's more interesting to turn left on the stairs and walk along a scenic, rocky route to Yongammun, another fortress gate 35 minutes away. Then walk along the remains of the wall to Dongjang-dae, a command post, and on to Daedongmun, which is 40 minutes from Yongammun.

At Daedongmun, walk down to the toilets and take the path that follows the river bed. There is no sign but the track is clear. The path goes through an attractive valley and passes the small temples Taegosa, Yonghaksa and Beopyongsa to the beginning of the road, which you reach after 45 minutes. From here it's another 40 minutes back to the bus stop.

Dobongsan Hike

Dobongsan is a mountain with three rocky peaks. This cool shady hike (Map 10) takes about five hours to cover 10km, but add time for a picnic lunch. Moderate fitness is required but if Korean grandmothers can do it, you can too.

Take subway Line 1 north to Dobongsan station; the journey costs W800 and takes 45 minutes from City Hall if your train goes all the way (not all do). Exit the station and cross the road, walk through the market and food stalls and past the bus terminal to the ticket booth.

Keep on the main path, following the sign to Jaunbong, one of Dobongsan's peaks, 2.7km away. Five minutes past the spring, turn right, following the sign to Manjangbong (another Dobongsan peak). Keep a look out for woodpeckers and squirrels.

About an hour from the subway station, you arrive at Dobong Hut. Bear right following the sign to Manwol-am. Then follow signs to Jaunbong, go past the police rescue post and up the final steep and rocky stretch to the top, which is between two rocky peaks. Here the adventure begins as you scramble down a ravine helped by metal cables, then up and along a rocky ridge and through narrow crevices.

Follow the signs to Mangwolsa, but don't miss the turning to the right marked 'Wondobong Ticket Box'. Follow this less-used short cut down the hillside past a small spring. Half an hour from the right turn you join the main track down to the car park. Follow the road, bearing left as you enter the town to Mangwolsa subway station (Line 1).

WESTERN NAMHANSANSEONG HIKE

This easy hike in Namhansanseong Provincial Park, 20km southeast of the city centre, takes less than two hours and follows part of the ancient fortress wall, which is 3m to 7.5m high and stretches 9.6km (although the inner circle is only 6.5km). Completed in 1626, Namhansanseong guarded the southern entrance to Seoul, while Bukhansanseong guarded the northern approaches. It was garrisoned by tough Buddhist monks who were soldiers rather than pacifists in those days.

In 1636 King Injo fled to this fortress when the Manchus invaded from China. After a siege of 45 days the king surrendered and his son was kept hostage in China for eight years.

To get to Namhansanseong, take subway Line 8 to Namhansanseong station and leave by Exit 1. Then take any bus the short way up the road to the park entrance. From here, walk for 30 minutes along the concrete road past fresh water springs and small temples up to Nammun, the southern gate of the fortress. Pay the W1000 entry fee at the ticket booth and ask for the free map. Near the gate is Nammungadeun restaurant where one of the items on the menu is *gamjajeon* (potato pancake), which is as big as a pizza and costs W6000. Nearby a stall sells *makgeolli* bread, another cheap but filling food that's popular with hikers.

Turn left and walk along the wall that has extensive views of Seoul and Hangang – look out for big butterflies

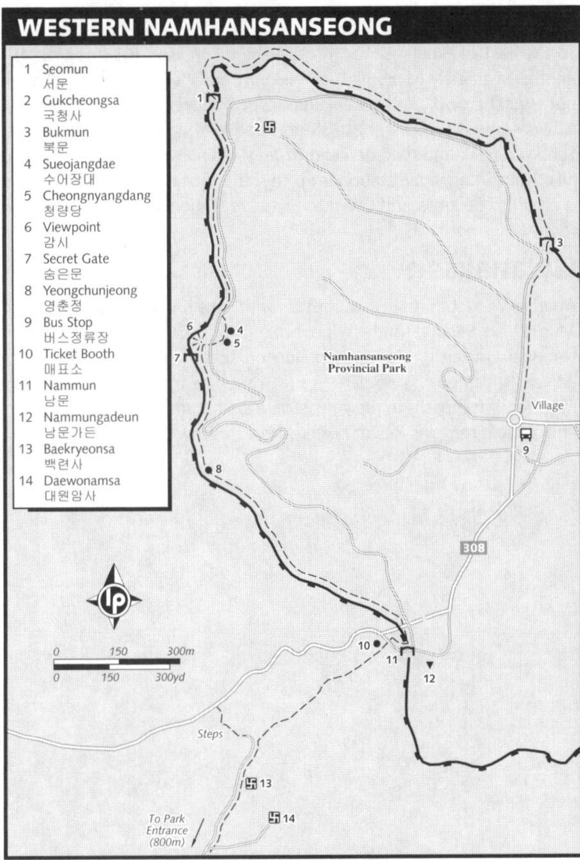

and golden dragonflies. Pass Yeongchunjeong pavilion and a secret gate before reaching Sueojangdae command post and Cheongnyangdae, Yi Hoe's shrine. Yi Hoe was killed after false accusations were made that he had embezzled funds meant for the fortress's construction. His wife and concubine both committed suicide when they heard of his execution.

Ten minutes further on, go through Seomun (West Gate) and walk along the outside of the wall for 30 minutes to Bukmun (North Gate); Bukmun is usually locked but most people can squeeze through.

From here you can carry on round the wall for another 4km or else it's just a five-minute stroll down to the village of traditional houses that are mainly restaurants. The bus stop is near the roundabout and bus No 9 provides a frequent service for the 20-minute journey to Namhansanseong subway station (W1000).

Suraksan

To the east of Bukhansan National Park is Suraksan (638m; Map 10), another attractive climbing and hiking area. It's not a national park, but expect crowds at the weekends. One relatively easy hike is to take subway Line 4 to Danggogae station and hike up past Heungguksa to Suraksan peak and then descend to Jang-am subway station. A shorter hike from Danggogae station is up to the top of Bulamsan (508m) and then on to Bulamsa and down to Sanggye station.

Gwanaksan

Another mountain that is a popular with hikers is Gwanaksan (632m; Map 2) on Seoul's southern boundary. Take subway Line 2 to Seoul National University station and hop on to the bus that goes to the university campus. From here you can see the mountain, which has a network of footpaths to the peak. There are natural springs, two temples and a cable car, plus lots of hikers who can show you the way.

Places to Stay

Seoul has a wide range of accommodation, including backpacker guesthouses, budget hotels, homestays, and plenty of mid-range and top-end hotels. However, single travellers are at a disadvantage in Seoul because accommodation is usually charged per room, with little or no discount for people who are on their own. Hotel rooms with Western-style beds are most common, but for the same price you can often opt for a Korean-style room where you sleep on a *yo* (padded quilt) on the *ondol* (heated) floor.

Guesthouses & Youth Hostels

Seoul has a handful of guesthouses that cater specifically for budget-conscious foreigners. They are usually small, offer dormitory accommodation (W15,000 a night), single rooms (W25,000) and double rooms (W35,000), and the staff speak English. They usually provide a TV and video lounge, a kitchen, a free washing machine, a free breakfast and free Internet access. Toilets and showers are usually shared.

There are also two luxurious youth hostels, Dreamtel and Olympic Parktel, that are worth considering, although they lack the friendly atmosphere of the guesthouses and are not centrally located. YHA membership costs W20,000.

Yeogwan & Motels

More than 3000 *yeogwan* (budget family-run hotels) are scattered around Seoul. Most are almost identical and follow the same pattern, so it is difficult to make recommendations, although the cheaper ones are usually shabbier; all generally accept credit cards. Don't be put off by the dimly lit corridors and the proprietor napping in a cubicle at the entrance. The rooms are small but full of facilities – en suite toilet and shower, TV, video, telephone, fridge, drinking water, air-conditioning and heating, even toothbrushes and hairdryers. Nearly all the rooms have beds, but some also offer Korean-style rooms with a padded quilt on the floor. The staff rarely speak any English, there are no kitchen facilities and prices may be W5000 higher on Saturday nights. Room prices start at W25,000 and those in the upper range (W40,000 a room) merge into the love-motel category.

Some *yeogwan* call themselves a motel or a *jang* but they are all similar and have a symbol as follows:

Unfortunately the same symbol is used by public bathhouses and saunas, which can cause confusion.

Sometimes looking like fairyland castles, love motels cater for daytime, pay-by-the-hour couples, but they also accept conventional guests. Facilities are good considering the cost, although you might get a round bed, satin sheets and a boudoir decor with stars painted on the ceiling.

To make a reservation at a budget hotel, log on to **w** www.worldinn.com.

Homestays

Some Korean families in Seoul offer rooms in their apartments to foreigners. The cost for bed and breakfast is around W30,000 a night for a single person and W60,000 for a couple. It's a particularly good deal for singles, who normally have to pay almost the same as a couple for a hotel room; however, not all families are keen on hosting single males. Rates are greatly reduced if you stay long-term. Homestays offer visitors the chance to experience Korean food, customs and family life at close quarters; guests are often treated like royalty in Korea and you might become life-long friends with your host family. You can sometimes find families offering free homestays – they usually do this because they want to meet foreigners and improve their English.

A well-established homestay organisation is **Labostay** (*☎ 817 4625, fax 813 7047;* **W** *www.labostay.or.kr*), which has organised over 18,000 homestays. A single person pays US$30 a night for bed and breakfast, while a couple pay US$50. Children from four to 10 pay $15 and children under four are free. Dinner is $5 extra per person, which is a bargain. A big reduction on the daily rate is possible if you stay for a month – singles pay around US$500. Pick-ups from Incheon airport cost US$70, while pick-ups from downtown Seoul cost US$20. Booking online at least two weeks before your arrival date is the best method of making a reservation.

Seoul Homestay (*☎ 723 8656, fax 723 8353;* **W** *www.seoulhomestay.co.kr*) has 1000 families in Korea, including 200 families in Seoul who are willing to host foreign visitors in a spare room; log on to the website and you can find brief details about the families. Guests have access to a kitchen, TV, telephone, computer and washing machine. Some families offer guests private bathroom facilities but some are shared. Breakfast is included and so is dinner if you stay more than three nights.

If you stay a week or less, singles pay US$30 a day and couples sharing a room pay US$44. If you stay for more than a week but less than a month, singles pay US$20 a day and couples US$30. If you stay for more than a month, the daily cost goes down to US$15 for a single and US$24 for a couple. The placement fee is US$30 and you pay the rest on arrival. An optional pick-up from Incheon airport costs US$50.

Korea Homestay (**W** *www.komestay.com*) charges US$30 to register and the homestay cost is W30,000 per night for a single person (W500,000 per month) or W50,000 per night for a couple (W700,000 per month).

Homestay websites include **W** www.koreahomestay.com, **W** www.visitkorea.net, **W** www.home-stay.co.kr, **W** www.hotel-homestay.co.kr and **W** www.billboard.pe.kr.

Temple Stays

Overnight stays in temples throughout Korea usually run from 4pm to 10am the next day and cost around W50,000. Participants wear Buddhist robes and stay in single-sex dormitory-style accommodation, sleeping on padded quilts on the floor. Don't go to bed late, you have to get up for the Buddhist service, which begins at 3am.

Sweeping paths, making stone rubbings and hiking in the mountains could also be on the programme, as well as meditation, temple meals and the tea ceremony. Temple stays are an enlightening experience revealing genuine insights into the lifestyle and beliefs of Korean monks. These programmes were started to provide an unusual experience for visitors who came for the 2002 World Cup soccer finals but are being continued. See **W** www.templestaykorea.net for details.

Minbak & Yeoinsuk

Both these types of establishment have disappeared in Seoul, but you will come across them on the West Sea islands and in other rural and seaside areas. *Minbak* are rooms that you can rent in people's homes, which are usually inexpensive but have only basic facilities. Expect to pay W20,000 a room, though the price usually goes up in summer. A group of people can share one room if everyone sleeps on *yo* padded quilts on the floor. A *yeoinsuk* is a budget *yeogwan* usually with shared toilet and shower facilities.

Hotels

There is no shortage of mid-range and luxury hotels in Seoul. Hotels with history and character are hard to find these days; however, standards are high and prices reasonable for the level of services and facilities that are provided – the best hotels in Seoul rate with the best hotels anywhere. It is often worthwhile bargaining down the price of your stay, as both mid-range and top-end hotels tend to copy each other and provide almost identical rooms and facilities.

Often Mid-range hotels that cost around W100,000 have a restaurant, coffee shop, bar and sauna.

Top-end hotels cost over W300,000, but provide half a dozen restaurants, a coffee shop, bars and nightclubs, as well as a fitness centre, an indoor swimming pool, a sauna and other facilities. There are American-style top-end hotels (such as the Grand Hyatt, the

Sheraton Walker Hill and the Hilton), deluxe local *jaebol*-run hotels like Shilla and Lotte, and ultramodern business hotels south of the river, such as the Inter-Continental Hotels at the COEX Conference Centre, JW Marriot and the Seoul Renaissance Hotel.

Several websites offer discounted prices if you use their booking services. Log on to **w** www.koreahotels.net, **w** enhotel.infocus.co.kr and **w** www.khrc.com for reduced prices at a number of mid-range and top-end hotels in Seoul. Some luxury hotels offer 50% discounts to regular customers and at less busy times of the year, so it is always worth bargaining.

Don't forget that 21% (10% service charge plus 10% VAT) is invariably added to all bills charged by these hotels.

Where to Stay?

Insadong (Map 8) has some budget accommodation and is a pleasant area to stay, full of interesting restaurants, teashops, art galleries and antique shops, with a Buddhist temple and palaces nearby. Other downtown locations are popular, with numerous budget *yeogwan* in the Tapgol Park (Map 8) area and more expensive hotels grouped around Central Hall in Gwanghwamun (Map 8). But if you want to be near the nightlife, stay in Itaewon (Map 11; the main expatriate entertainment district) or the Hongik/Sinchon/Ewha area (Map 3; the main local student entertainment district with live-music venues and dance clubs). Daehangno (Map 12), the other student area, has a few *yeogwan* but no other accommodation. The Myeong-dong (Map 9) shopping area has a handful of *yeogwan* and more upmarket hotels. Namsan (Map 9) is home to some of the luxury hotels. South of Hangang, Gangnam (Map 6) is home to numerous mid-range and top end hotels.

Generally, it doesn't matter too much where you stay as long as you are near a subway station, although taxis are also plentiful and cheap.

Budget accommodation is defined as dorm beds or rooms that cost W35,000 or less. Mid-range hotels cost from W35,000 to W180,000 a room. Top-end hotels cost over W180,000 a room.

PLACES TO STAY – BUDGET

Gwanghwamun (Map 8)

Inn Daewon *(☎ 738 4308; dorm beds/singles/doubles W15,000/20,000/25,000)* is a guesthouse in a rundown traditional-style building with a courtyard where you can sit and chat. It's popular and cheap but needs some cleaning and renovation work. Although conveniently located near City Hall and the subway, the living conditions are very cramped and some rooms have no windows. The kitchen is tiny and everyone shares two toilets and a shower. There is a TV lounge and free tea and coffee, but the washing machine costs W1000. The owners are friendly and helpful, speak some English and have been running this guesthouse for many years.

Deoksu Motel *(☎ 737 3119; rooms W35,000)* has typical facility-filled en suite Western and *ondol* rooms, some of which are bigger than others, although they all cost the same.

Gwanghwajang *(☎ 738 0751; rooms W38,000)* is slightly over the budget hotel limit, but is fancily decorated in a homey, frilly style and worth the extra cost.

Tapgol Park (Map 8)

Wongap Inn *(☎ 734 1232; rooms Sun-Fri W25,000, Sat W35,000)* is used to looking after foreigners and is good value. It's behind the YMCA in Pimatgol, an alley full of cheap restaurants that runs parallel to Jongno, a broad highway that used to be frequented by Joseon aristocrats who were carried along in sedan chairs. Since ordinary citizens had to prostrate themselves when a sedan chair approached on Jongno, they preferred to use Pimatgol.

Paradise Motel *(☎ 730 6244; rooms Sun-Fri W35,000, Sat W40,000)*, another option near Jongno, has the usual small but facility-filled en suite rooms.

Seoul Backpackers *(☎ 3672 1972, fax 743 4878; **w** www.seoulbackpackers.com; dorm beds/singles/doubles W15,000/25,000/35,000)* has modern and smart facilities. The dorms have two or three double bunks, and every room has its own toilet and shower facilities. The guesthouse has *ondol* underfloor heating, a TV lounge, kitchen, outside area, free washing machine, free breakfast, free Internet and free weekly films shown on a big screen. The helpful staff speak English, and the Incheon airport bus fare (W6000) is refunded if you stay three nights. It's brand new, clean and tidy, centrally located and one of the best budget options, so book ahead.

Motel Jongnowon (☎ *763 4249;* **w** *www.jongnowon.com; rooms Mon-Fri W25,000, Sat & Sun W30,000)* is just behind Seoul Backpackers. The owner speaks English, is helpful and offers free Internet access for 30 minutes a day. Lots of foreign guests have enjoyed their stay here over the years.

Seahwajang (☎ *765 2881; rooms W23,000)* has cheap but shabby rooms that vary a lot – ask to see more than one. Small rooms cost W450,000 per month (which works out at W15,000 per day) or larger rooms are W550,000 (W18,000 per day), making Seahwajang popular with long-term residents.

Guesthouse Korea (☎ *3675 2205;* **w** *www.guesthouseinkorea.com; dorm beds/singles/doubles W15,000/25,000/35,000)* is located behind Hyundai Oilbank petrol station. One dormitory has two double bunks and the other has four double bunks. The building is old and rundown, and some rooms have no windows. However, there are four showers and toilets, and it has a small kitchen, TV lounge, outdoor area, free Internet, free breakfast, and the staff are helpful and friendly. The Incheon airport bus stop is nearby at Anguk and the fare of W6000 is refunded if you stay three nights.

Emerald Hotel (☎ *743 2001; rooms Sun-Fri W25,000, Sat W40,000)* is a big pink building in a quiet alley just north of Nakwon Arcade. It boasts cable TV and the comfortable rooms have a table and chairs – items usually lacking in *yeogwan* rooms in Seoul. The staff speak some English and it has received favourable reviews from travellers. Just outside the door are small shops selling homemade *tteok* rice cakes.

Next door is **Yongjin Yeogwan** (☎ *765 4481, fax 765 9521; small/large rooms W30,000/35,000)*, which has been recently renovated. The staff speak some English.

Opposite is **Hwaseong Yeogwan** (☎ *762 2111, fax 725 0834; rooms W25,000)*, which provides another option. The lady in charge is a classic Korean *ajumma* (married or older woman).

Ritz Hotel (☎ *764 0353; rooms W40,000, Sat, Sun & public holidays W50,000)* has a space-age exterior so you know it's a love motel. The rooms have big TVs, circular beds and starry skies painted on the ceilings. It offers Internet access, a lift, a sauna and you can check out at noon. Although it's a bit above the budget range, it's a good deal for the price and you shouldn't leave Seoul without spending one night in a love motel.

Cala Motel (☎ *741 4455; small/large rooms W32,000/35,000)* is less exotic than the Ritz and is cheaper too, but is often booked up on Saturday nights.

Paradise Motel (☎ *763 3000; small/large rooms W35,000/40,000, Sat & Sun W40,000/45,000)* is another smart, large motel in the Tapgol Park area and has a receptionist who speaks some English.

Yuhwajang *(rooms W35,0000)* is a large *yeogwan* with a medieval castle turret but the facilities inside are modern.

Gyeongbukjang *(rooms Sun-Fri W30,000, Sat W40,000)* is another option in this area, which could be useful if the others are full, as can happen on Saturday.

Gukjejang (☎ *732 0801; small/large rooms W30,000/35,000)* is a large *yeogwan* in a bunch of cheap hotels northwest of Jonggak subway station (Line 1). It has 30 Western-style and *ondol* rooms, and the owner speaks some English.

Also in the area are **Sejongjang** (☎ *732 7856, fax 732 7176; rooms W35,000)*, which has recently been renovated; **Cheongjin Motel** (☎ *733 3863, fax 739 8543; rooms Sun-Fri W35,000, Sat W40,000)*, with an owner that speaks some English; **Dongwonjang** (☎ *735 8011; rooms W25,000)*; **Useong Motel** (☎ *734 4866, fax 736 1554; rooms W25,000)*; and **Sinjinjang** (☎ *732 4997; rooms W25,000)*.

Out near Jongmyo Shrine are more *yeogwan*. **New World Hotel** *(Yuhwa;* ☎ *766 2121, fax 764 9833; rooms W35,000)* is large, smart and even has a lift; also try **Daerimjang** *(rooms Sun-Fri W30,000, Sat W35,000)*.

PLACES TO STAY

Dongdaemun (Maps 4 & 8)

Travelers A Motel *(☎ 2285 5511; W www.travelersa.com; dorm beds/doubles W12,000/30,000)* is near Dongdaemun Market and is bigger than the other guesthouses. It has lots of well-equipped double rooms and the cheapest dorm beds in Seoul (two or three double bunks in a room). Prices are reduced by 10% for a week's stay. The double rooms have their own toilet, shower, air-con, heater, TV, fridge and telephone, and are similar to *yeogwan* rooms. There's also a lounge with satellite TV and free Internet access, but the kitchen facilities are poor. The owner is helpful, speaks good English and has done some redecorating recently. The guesthouse is centrally located but is not in a residential area and is hidden away down a small alley of sewing machine shops; to get here, take subway Line 2 or 5 to Euljiro 4-ga station, leave by Exit 4, turn right down the second alley and then take the first left.

Yuseongjang *(☎ 2273 3438; rooms W25,000)* has 20 rooms and is probably the best of the bunch of *yeogwan* you'll find down an alley on the fringe of Dongdaemun Market opposite the National Medical Centre. It's the place to stay if you want to be close to the all-night shopping, as well as the cinema facilities.

Insadong (Map 8)

Seoul Guesthouse *(☎ 745 0057, 011-9134 7741; W www.seoul110.com; dorm beds/singles/doubles/family room W15,000/30,000/40,000/100,000)*, north of Anguk subway station (Line 3), offers a rare chance to stay in a traditional *hanok* house; it's wonderful that some of these houses are being restored and put to use. You sleep on a *yo* on an *ondol* floor in a small room of the beautiful Joseon-era house built around a garden courtyard. There are no en suite facilities except in the family room. Guests can use the TV lounge, kitchen, free Internet and washing machine – the facilities are ultra modern even though the house is a century old. The owner, Mrs Lee, speaks English and is very helpful. Book in advance; if it's full enquire about Hanok Sarang, a similar guesthouse nearby, which may be available. Mrs Lee and her house are equally delightful and Japanese tourists love staying here.

Yeongbinjang *(☎ 732 4731; rooms W25,000)* is near the famous Sanchon restaurant in an interesting area to stay, with lots of traditional Korean restaurants, unusual teashops and craft shops.

Gwanhunjang *(☎ 732 1682; rooms W35,000)* is just off Insadong 4-gil on the left. It has been recently renovated and the owners are helpful.

Singungjang *(☎ 733 1355; rooms Sun-Fri W30,000, Sat W35,000)* is another option in the heart of Insadong. One foreigner stayed here a year, which must mean something.

Myeong-dong (Map 9)

Gyeongdojang *(☎ 755 5437; rooms W30,000)* has a good location next to the Prince Hotel in this popular shopping and entertainment district.

Gyerimjang *(☎ 998 4294; rooms W30,000)* is a *yeogwan* located next to the Pacific Hotel, but it has no beds, only *yo* mattresses on the floor. The owner speaks a little English.

Palace Yeogwan *(☎ 227 4878; rooms W30,000)* and **New Mountain Villa** *(☎ 2267 3632; rooms W30,000)* both have a good location behind the Astoria Hotel, but are typical *yeogwan* and don't live up to their fanciful names.

Itaewon (Map 11)

Seoul Motel *(☎ 795 2266, fax 797 0300; rooms Mon-Fri W30,000, Sat & Sun W40,000)* has been recently renovated and is probably the best budget option in Itaewon. It's above McDonald's and the manager speaks English. If you want to party all night in Itaewon and not worry about getting a taxi home, this is the place to stay.

Hilltop Motel *(☎ 793 4972; rooms Sun-Thur W25,000, Fri & Sat W30,000)* is in the middle of the hostess bar area. Rooms are small but have cable TV, and the en suite toilets and showers are tiled. The decor is a bit tatty as is usual at this price. The owner speaks some English and has seen just about everything over the years, so nothing is likely to shock him.

Tae Pyeong Motel *(☎ 792 8514; rooms W25,000)* is also in the heart of the Itaewon action behind the Grand Ole Oprey.

At the eastern end of the main street is **Namsan Motel** *(☎ 795 0860; rooms W30,000)*, a rabbit warren spread over three floors.

Ihwajang *(☎ 795 9575; rooms W30,000)*, at the other end of the street, attracts some foreign guests.

Donginjang *(☎ 795 6409; rooms W25,000)* is down a back alley, but is reasonably priced.

Daehangno (Map 12)

Gungjeonjang *(☎ 745 3578; rooms W25,000)* is a good cheap place to stay in an area that has little accommodation of any kind. You could drink in a different bar every night for a year and they'd all be within walking distance of this *yeogwan*.

Daeseong Yeogwan *(☎ 3673 2028; rooms W30,000)* is better than it looks from the outside.

Lone budget travellers could consider the *hanok*-style **Friends House** *(☎ 3673 1515, fax 3673 1513; ⓦ www.friends-house.com; beds per person W40,000)* as it's one of the few places in Seoul to charge on a per person basis.

Hongik, Sinchon & Ewha (Map 3)

Guesthouse Korea *(☎/fax 3142 0683; ⓦ www.guesthousekorea.com; dorm beds/singles/doubles W15,000/25,000/35,000)* is a brand new comfortable guesthouse in a quiet residential location. It has a TV room, kitchen, free Internet, free breakfast, free washing machine and a free pick-up service. One dormitory has two double bunks and the other has three double bunks. It's a 15-minute walk to Hongik University subway station (Line 2) and the nearby nightclub and entertainment area. The nearest Incheon airport bus stop is at Seogyo Hotel (bus No 601 or 602). Telephone from there and someone will pick you up, as it is difficult to find.

Yeongbinjang *(☎ 392 2038; rooms W35,000)* is behind the Mirabeau Hotel near Ewha Women's University.

Northeast of Sinchon subway station (Line 2) is a cluster of *yeogwan* and **Onyangjang** *(☎ 393 0468; rooms W24,000)* is one of the cheapest. **Geurin Motel** *(☎ 392 4574; rooms W30,000)* is more modern, but is up on the 5th and 6th floors. **Prince Hotel** *(☎ 363 4700; rooms W38,000)* is better still, has 48 rooms and the staff speak some English. There are also lots more *yeogwan* in this area.

Southwest of Sinchon subway station (Line 2), **Dongbojang** *(☎ 717 5649; rooms W30,000)* and **Geumsil Motel** *(☎ 717 8426; rooms W30,000)* are cheaper but not as good as the recently renovated **Cheongsujang** *(☎ 715 3292; rooms W35,000)*.

Kims' Guesthouse *(☎ 337 9894, fax 3141 7203; ⓦ www.kimsguesthouse.com; dorm beds/singles/doubles W15,000/25,000/35,000)* is outside the main entertainment area and is more of a homestay than the other guesthouses. Everything is new and modern, and it has satellite TV in the lounge, a kitchen, a large balcony, free breakfast, free tea and coffee, a free washing machine and Internet access is W1000 per hour. The dorm has two double bunks, and guests share two toilets and showers. The owners speak English and are very helpful. It's located in a quiet area near Hangang, a 12-minute walk from Hapjeong subway station (Line 2 or 6).

Incheon International Airport

Budget *yeogwan* and motel accommodation are available a few kilometres away near the airport island's attractive west-coast beaches. Take bus No 301 (W1200) or a taxi to Eulwangni Beach. See the Incheon section of the Excursions chapter for a map and information on the airport area. The Getting Around chapter also has airport information.

Gimpo Domestic Airport (Map 2)

You may want to stay near this airport if you have an early domestic flight or a late arrival from elsewhere in Korea. It can also be useful if you arrive at Incheon airport very late at night or are leaving very early in the morning because there is a special congestion-free highway between the two airports that only takes 30 minutes by bus or taxi.

Gimpojang *(☎ 663 1311; Western & ondol rooms W35,000)* is located south of Songjeong subway station (Line 5). The staff speak some English.

Another option (if you are a youth hostel member) is the luxury **Dreamtel Youth Hostel** *(☎ 2667 0535, fax 2667 0744; W www.hostelbooking.com; dorm beds/4-person rooms W22,000/72,600)*, west of Gimpo airport. Although far from downtown, the facilities are modern and more like a resort hotel than a youth hostel. Most rooms have three double bunks, but the four-person family rooms have a double bunk and two single beds. All the rooms have their own toilet, shower, TV and fridge. The hostel has a shop, café, restaurant, sauna, exercise room (W3500), indoor swimming pool (W3500) and a woodland park behind. Its location is west of Gimpo airport. Take subway Line 5 to Banghwa station (the end of the line and 45 minutes from downtown) and leave by Exit 4. Go straight, turn left at the end of the road and then turn left again at the end of the next road; altogether it's a five-minute walk from the subway station.

Other Areas North of the River (Map 10)

Exciting Korea Guesthouse *(☎ 3217 8231, fax 725 1238; W www.excitingkorea.com; dorm beds W14,000)* has accommodation in rooms with two or three double bunks. Guests share two showers and toilets inside, but there are more outside. Popular with long-termers, it offers a kitchen, TV lounge, small garden, free Internet, free washing machine, free breakfast and a free T-shirt if you stay long enough. The only downside is that the location is inconvenient – take subway Line 3 to Gyeongbokgung station, leave by Exit 3 and walk to the bus stop. Take any bus to the Boam Art Hall stop (5 minutes). Walk up Baeksasil-gil, go left and it's on your right. It's easier to telephone if you've just arrived from Incheon airport and someone will pick you up from the nearest airport bus stop. The guesthouse owners also run inexpensive tours – see the Organised Tours section of the Getting Around chapter.

South of the River (Map 7)

Olympic Parktel Youth Hostel *(☎ 421 2111, fax 410 2100; W www.hostelbooking.com; dorm beds W22,000)* is an unusual hostel and is part of a luxury hotel that overlooks Olympic Park. The rooms have two double bunks and two futon beds on the floor, which can be rolled up when not in use. Each room has its own small toilet, shower, air-con, heater, fridge, cable TV (55 channels), telephone and a good view – all the rooms are on the 7th, 8th or 9th floors. You can use the hotel swimming pool, exercise room and sauna for W6500 a day, and eat a hotel breakfast for half-price. Don't forget your YHA card, as the cost of a hotel room is W170,000. The 2nd floor has a **YHA office** *(☎ 410 2144; open 9.30am-6.30pm daily)* where you can become a YHA member for W20,000. The Incheon airport bus stop is outside and the hostel is a 10-minute walk from Mongchontoseong subway station (Line 8). The location is not ideal and other dorm beds are cheaper, but it's worth considering.

PLACES TO STAY – MID-RANGE

Gwanghwamun (Map 8)

New Seoul Hotel *(☎ 735 9071, fax 735 6212; W www.bestwesternnewseoul.com; doubles, twins & ondol rooms from W160,000)* is the Best Western hotel with the best location. It offers a restaurant, coffee shop, *noraebang* (karaoke rooms) and a sauna, and attracts plenty of Japanese guests.

New Kukje Hotel *(☎ 732 0161, fax 732 1774; doubles & twins from W150,000)* has restaurants, *noraebang,* saunas for men and women, and location, location, location.

Tapgol Park (Map 8)

Seoul Hotel *(☎ 735 9001, fax 733 0101; doubles/twins including tax & service W80,000/85,000)* is a modest place with plenty of facilities at a fair price. Western and Korean meals – breakfast (W9900), lunch (W15,500) and dinner (W27,500) – are available.

YMCA *(☎ 734 6884, fax 734 8003; W www.ymca.or.kr/hotel; singles/doubles/twins/triples W40,000/55,000/60,000/80,000)* is reasonably priced and centrally located on Jongno near a subway station, but the rooms, which have a TV and fridge, are somewhat shabby and old-fashioned. Western-style breakfasts cost W4000 to W10,000, while lunch and dinner cost from W6000 to W25,000. The reception desk is on the 6th floor – take the lift.

Central Hotel *(☎ 265 4121, fax 265 6139; singles/doubles W82,000/94,000)* is one block south of Jongno 3-ga subway station (Line 1 or 3). Facilities include a restaurant, coffee shop, nightclub and sauna.

Dongdaemun (Map 4)

Dongdaemun Hotel *(☎ 741 7811, fax 744 1274; doubles W110,000, twins & ondol rooms W130,000)* is part of the Best Western chain. Perfectly located for dedicated shoppers on the edge of Dongdaemun Market, it overlooks Dongdaemun gate, which looks beautiful when lit up at night. The restaurant offers a good-value multicourse steak meal for W25,000. On the 8th floor is an 'Adult Business Club'.

Insadong (Map 8)

Saerim Hotel *(☎ 739 3377, fax 735 3355; rooms Sun-Fri W45,000, Sat W50,000)* has 31 small but comfortable Western and *ondol* rooms at a reasonable price in this attractive area that is quiet late at night. The electronically controlled toilets are impressive but confusing.

Myeong-dong (Map 9)

Metro Hotel *(☎ 752 1112, fax 757 4411; singles/doubles/twins W55,000/72,000/83,000)* is a short walk from Euljiro 1-ga subway station (Line 2), and has a restaurant, bar and coffee shop. The price is reasonable given its central location.

Prince Hotel *(☎ 752 7111, fax 752 7119; singles/doubles/twins/suites W80,000/90,000/90,000/145,000)* is a business hotel with small rooms, but a good location in Myeong-dong. The coffee shop provides an American-style breakfast.

Astoria Hotel *(☎ 268 7111, fax 274 3187; doubles/twins including tax & service W72,470/90,818)* has a restaurant, *noraebang*, and good views of Namsan and Seoul Tower.

Savoy Hotel *(☎ 776 2641, fax 755 7669; singles/doubles/triples W100,000/120,000/180,000)* is near the heart of the very busy Myeong-dong shopping area, has Japanese and Western restaurants, shops and the bar has live jazz music.

New Oriental Hotel *(☎ 753 0701, fax 755 9346; singles/doubles W69,000/83,500)* has a bar and coffee shop.

Itaewon (Maps 4 & 11)

Kaya Hotel *(☎ 798 5101, fax 798 5900; deluxe doubles/twins/ondol suites W48,000/53,000/58,000/80,000)* has 50 rooms and lacks facilities but is good value and is popular with visiting GIs. The hotel is not in the Itaewon entertainment area but is near the American military base and is one subway station south of Seoul Station. The restaurant serves American and Korean food, and you can relax in the sauna after a hard day of sightseeing. To get here, take subway Line 1 to Namyeong station, turn right at the exit and right again at the main road.

Hamilton Hotel *(☎ 794 0171, fax 797 8087; W www.hamilton.co.kr; singles/doubles/twins W100,000/135,000/135,000)* is an Itaewon landmark with a large shopping mall on four levels that contains 100 stores. Every room has Internet and satellite TV, and there is an outdoor swimming pool. It's in the heart of the Itaewon action and *the* place to stay if you want somewhere in this price range.

Crown Hotel *(☎ 797 4111, fax 796 1010; rooms including tax & service W100,000)* is some distance away from the main Itaewon area. Facilities include three restaurants, a nightclub and a golf range on the roof. The sauna (open from 8.30am to midnight daily) offers steam baths, green tea and ginseng baths, and face and body massages.

Itaewon Hotel *(☎ 792 3111, fax 795 3126; rooms W140,000)* is on the main street and offers comfort at a reasonable price. It has three restaurants and a disco. Discounts are possible.

Daehangno (Map 12)

Friends House *(☎ 3673 1515, fax 3673 1513; W www.friends-house.com; beds per person W40,000)* is a traditional *hanok* house but everything inside is brand new. With a pricing system that is unusual in Seoul, this accommodation is a better deal for singles than for couples. You sleep on a *yo* on the floor in a small room, and there is a 20% discount for more than two people in a room. Facilities include a TV lounge, kitchen, free Internet access and free use of the washing machine. To get here, take subway Line 4 to Hyehwa station and leave by Exit 4. Walk north up the main road to the roundabout and turn left at the post office. Then turn left again at Yun Hyun Pharmacy and it's down the second turning on the right, altogether a 10-minute walk from the station.

Hongik, Sinchon & Ewha (Map 3)

Gallery Hotel (*☎ 711 7794; rooms W60,000*) is one of the many options in this area southwest of Sinchon subway station (Line 2), which is full of budget and mid-range accommodation.

Mirabeau Hotel (*☎ 392 9511, fax 392 3829; doubles/suites including tax & service W92,570/137,940*), near Ewha Women's University, has a grill restaurant, bar and coffee shop.

Incheon International Airport

A cluster of new hotels has been built in Airport Town Square, which is less than 10 minutes' drive east of the airport. Remember to dial ☎ 032 if ringing from Seoul, and that 21% extra will be added to your bill for service and tax. However, you can always try for a discount.

Hotel Sky (*☎ 752 1101, fax 752 1109; w www.hotelsky.co.kr; twins/doubles/suites W70,000/70,000/100,000*) has themed rooms, restaurants and a bar.

Hotel Hub Herb (*☎ 752 1991, fax 752 1990; w www.hotelhh.com; twins & doubles from W80,000*) also has a bar and Korean and Western restaurants.

Hotel Sevilla (*☎ 752 1170, fax 752 1175; w www.hotelsevilla.co.kr; twins/doubles/suites W105,000/100,000/160,000*) has a business club.

Hotel New Airport (*☎ 752 2066, fax 746 2067; e hotelnewairport@yahoo.com; semi-deluxe/deluxe doubles W100,000/120,000*) is the most luxurious. Deluxe rooms have free Internet access and free fax, digital 34-inch TV, spa bath, DVD player and bidet, and facilities include a free golf driving range.

Gimpo Domestic Airport (Map 2)

Airport Hotel (*☎ 662 1113, fax 663 355; w www.hotelairport.com; doubles & suites W91,000-173,000*) is located just outside Songjeong subway station (Line 5) or a five-minute taxi ride from the airport. Facilities include two restaurants, a coffee shop and a *noraebang* lounge.

Bukhansan (Map 10)

Green Park Hotel (*☎ 900 8181; doubles/twins W67,000/73,000*) is in northern Seoul and is a good base for hiking in Bukhansan National Park.

Bugak Park Hotel (*☎ 395 7100, fax 391 5559; doubles & twins W133,000*) is located on the southern slopes of Bukhansan National Park. Facilities include a restaurant, coffee shop, bar and nightclub, and weekday discounts are offered.

South of the River (Maps 5, 6 & 7)

Yeouido Hotel (*☎ 782 0121, fax 785 2510; rooms W124,000*) is one of the few accommodation options on Yeouido. Facilities include a business centre, two restaurants, including a Western-style grill, *noraebang* and a nightclub.

Princess Hotel (*☎ 544 0366, fax 544 0322; rooms/suites W80,000/120,000*) is a metal-clad, ultra-modern love hotel with 10 styles of room decor and photos to help you choose. Located in the middle of the upmarket Apgujeong shopping area, the hotel is a 10-minute walk from Apgujeong subway station (Line 3). Rooms and suites are discounted about 20% if you book in after 11pm.

Sunshine Hotel (*☎ 541 1818, fax 547 0777; singles/doubles/twins W96,000/139,000/153,000*) is a 10-minute walk south of Apgujeong subway station (Line 3). Facilities include a bar and a sauna.

Hotel Popgreen (*☎ 544 6623, fax 514 1810; doubles/twins including tax & service W157,300/164,400*) has small functional rooms, but is very near Apgujeong subway station (Line 3). It has its own restaurant, coffee shop and men's sauna.

Yujinjang (*☎ 548 2298; rooms W40,000*) is next to Dynasty Hotel and a 10-minute walk north of Gangnam subway station (Line 2).

The cost is a little higher than similar *yeogwan* in other areas. Ask to see a large room. The owner speaks some English.

Dynasty Hotel (☎ *540 3041, fax 540 3374; doubles & twins including tax & service W145,200)* is opposite the Ritz Carlton Hotel. Facilities include two restaurants, a nightclub and a *noraebang* bar.

Youngdong Hotel (☎ *542 0112, fax 546 8409; doubles/twins W109,000/133,000)* is a five-minute walk northeast of Sinsa subway station (Line 3), and has three restaurants, a nightclub and a men's sauna.

Samhwa Hotel (☎ *541 1011; rooms/suites W68,000/98,000)* is north of Sinsa subway station (Line 3) and is more Korean-style than most of the modern but rather sterile hotels you find south of the river.

New Hilltop Hotel (☎ *540 1121, fax 542 9491; rooms W140,000)* is a five-minute walk southwest of Hak-dong subway station (Line 7). Facilities include a restaurant, bar, coffee shop and nightclub.

Samjeong Hotel (☎ *557 1221, fax 562 6628; doubles/twins W166,000/188,000)* is a five-minute walk north of Yeoksam subway station (Line 2). Facilities include restaurants, a coffee shop, a sauna and a nightclub.

Green Grass Hotel (☎ *555 7575, fax 554 0643; doubles/twins W157,000/186,000)* is a five-minute walk from Seolleung subway station (Line 2) and a 10-minute walk from the COEX Mall. Facilities include a Western restaurant, coffee shop, sauna and games room. The nearby royal tombs in a wooded area make for a pleasant afternoon stroll.

Olympic Parktel Hotel (☎ *421 2111, fax 410 2100;* **w** *www.parktel.co.kr; doubles & twins including tax & service W170,000)* is out of the central area but is near Mongchontoseong subway station (Line 8) and overlooks Olympic Park. It has a pool, sauna and exercise room (W6500), and a W32,000 buffet with nightly live music on the top floor. Part of the hotel is a youth hostel.

There is a cluster of a dozen mid-range hotels and love motels along the Olympic Expressway near Olympic Park. A cheap one is **Aida Motel** at W40,000, while the others are around W65,000.

PLACES TO STAY – TOP END

Gwanghwamun (Maps 8 & 9)

Radisson Plaza Hotel (☎ *771 2200, fax 755 8897;* **w** *www.seoulplaza.co.kr; singles/doubles W310,000/330,000)* is opposite City Hall and has all the usual luxury hotel facilities, including a well-designed fitness club and pool. Prices are negotiable.

Westin Chosun Hotel (☎ *317 0404, fax 777 4444;* **w** *www.westin.com; singles/doubles from W372,000/392,000)* has some Art-Deco style and was the first Western-style hotel in Seoul. It's also popular because it has kept up-to-date with all the facilities offered by top hotels in Seoul. It runs the popular O'Kim's Bar, as well as the Sheobul Buffet and Ninth Gate restaurants. In the garden is a renovated pavilion that was originally built at the time when King Gojong proclaimed himself an emperor and had an altar built to give thanks to heaven.

Lotte Hotel (☎ *771 1000, fax 752 3758;* **w** *www.hotel.lotte.co.kr; singles/doubles from W340,000/370,000)* has 1500 rooms decorated in 13 different styles and a classical decor. It is well located, and the nearby duty-free shop has 50 boutiques that sell goods produced by 400 international brand-name companies. The Vine Restaurant does a Sunday brunch buffet for around W30,000. Stay here if you want to be near posh shops and the ever-reliable Lotte *jaebol* will accommodate you in grand style.

Koreana Hotel (☎ *730 9911, fax 734 0665;* **w** *www.koreanahotel.com; doubles/twins from W195,000/205,000)* has elegant rooms, five restaurants, a bakery and a great location.

Insadong (Map 8)

Fraser Apartments (☎ *6262 8888, fax 6262 8889; 1-/2-/3-/4-bedroom apartments W8.2m/9.1m/10.4m/11.7m; penthouse W16.9m)* are ultra-modern luxury apartments that can be rented on a monthly basis. The 200 apartments share a baby-sitting service, restaurant, bar, coffee shop, sauna, gym and indoor pool. Worth considering if someone else is paying, as even luxury hotels in Seoul tend to have smallish rooms, and these apartments give more space as well as more privacy if you are staying with your family.

Myeong-dong (Map 9)

Pacific Hotel (*☎ 777 7811, fax 755 5582; singles/doubles/twins/ondol rooms/suites W150,000/175,000/185,000/195,000/90,000*) is well located and offers discounts at weekends. The sauna is popular, and an evening dance show and meal costs W100,000 for four people.

Sejong Hotel (*☎ 773 6000, fax 755 4906; W www.sejong.co.kr; singles/doubles/twins/triples/suites W160,000/220,000/230,000/320,000/400,000*) has a good location between Namsan and Myeong-dong. It has the usual facilities, including a 24-hour sauna, fitness club and a supersonic wave tub. The dinner buffet, which costs W32,000 including tax and service, is deservedly popular. The hotel has a more Korean style than the foreign-owned luxury hotels.

Royal Hotel (*☎ 756 1112, fax 756 1119; W www.seoulroyal.co.kr; doubles/twins including tax & service W240,000/275,000*), opposite Myeong-dong Catholic Cathedral, is double-glazed, and has three restaurants, a business centre, free wireless Internet and a sauna.

Hilton Hotel (*☎ 753 7788, fax 754 2510; W www.hilton.com; singles/doubles/suites W340,000/360,000/400,000*) has a 1982 Henry Moore bronze sculpture in the lobby, a new and classy nightclub, and with its top location you can eat in a different restaurant every day for a week. To stop all that food making you put on weight you can join local Seoulites walking or jogging up Namsan for an early-morning panoramic view over Seoul.

Namsan (Map 9)

Sofitel Ambassador Hotel (*☎ 2275 1101, fax 2272 0773; singles/doubles W260,00/330,000*) is a few minutes' walk northwest of Dongguk University subway station (Line 3). Facilities include three restaurants, a deli, a sauna, hydrotherapy, an indoor pool, a golf driving range and free shuttle buses.

Hotel Shilla (*☎ 2233 3131, fax 2236 3349; W www.shilla.samsung.co.kr; rooms W350,000, suites W500,000-7m*) is a large hotel with spacious rooms that is situated at the foot of Namsan and run by Samsung, one of Korea's mighty *jaebol*. No expense is spared on their flagship hotel. It has a duty-free shop, five restaurants, swimming pools, a fitness centre, tennis courts, a golf driving range, sculpture garden, sauna and 24-hour massage service.

Tower Hotel (*☎ 236 2121; singles/doubles/twins W230,000/278,000/290,000*) is up on Namsan near the National Theatre. Sports facilities here include an outdoor pool, tennis courts and a golf driving range.

Itaewon (Maps 6 & 11)

Grand Hyatt Hotel (*☎ 797 1234, fax 798 6953; W seoul.grand.hyatt.com; singles/doubles & twins from W255,000/355,000*) is on a hill overlooking Itaewon and is popular with American visitors. The decor is functional but stylish, and the facilities include five restaurants, a popular bar, outdoor swimming pool, sundeck, tennis courts and squash courts. The presidential suite (where American presidents have actually stayed) costs a cool W6.5 million.

Capital Hotel (*☎ 792 1122; rooms W278,000*) is south of the main Itaewon tourist area. Facilities include four restaurants, a coffee shop, a nightclub, a health club, an indoor pool, a golf driving range and a sauna with a ginseng bath. Discounts are possible.

Hongik, Sinchon & Ewha (Map 3)

The only luxury accommodation in Hongik is **Seogyo Hotel** (*☎ 333 7771; W www.hotelseokyo.co.kr; doubles & twins/suites including tax & service W242,000/302,500*). A buffet lunch is W20,000 in one of the four restaurants. Other facilities include *noraebang*, a business centre, and a fitness centre with a men's sauna, aerobics and a pool.

Bukhansan (Map 10)

Olympia Hotel (*☎ 396 6000; rooms from W230,000*) is located near the southern slopes of Bukhansan National Park. The bar, nightclub and four restaurants may not get you fit, but the indoor and outdoor pools, sauna, health club, golf driving range and mountain hikes should help to keep you in shape. Prices are negotiable.

Other Areas North of the River (Map 2)

Sheraton Walker Hill Hotel *(☎ 453 0121, fax 452 6864; W www.walkerhill.co.kr; rooms W320,000-3.2m)* is way out east but provides free shuttle buses to Itaewon and Dongdaemun Market. Rooms overlook Hangang and facilities include tennis courts, a golf driving range, a health club, a spa pool, a sauna and, in summer, outdoor swimming pools. The hotel is well known for its 24-hour casino, cabaret dance show and duty-free shop.

South of the River (Maps 5, 6 & 7)

New Manhattan Hotel *(☎ 6670 7000, fax 6670 7578; rooms W250,000)* is the best hotel on Yeouido. Facilities include four restaurants, a coffee shop, a nightclub, a health club and a sauna. Discounts are possible.

JW Marriott Hotel *(☎ 6282 6262, fax 6282 6263; W www.marriott.com; rooms from W360,000)* opened in 2000 and has large rooms, four restaurants and excellent health-club facilities. It's next to Central City Mall and Seoul Express Bus Terminal. Discounts of 25% to 35% are available for advance bookings.

Ritz Carlton Hotel *(☎ 3451 8000, fax 3451 8188; W www.ritz.co.kr; singles/doubles/suites W350,000/380,000/W5.5m)* in Gangnam has European-style furniture, a golf driving range, live piano music in the lobby and louder live music in the nightclub, where a beer costs W10,000. Afternoon tea is even more expensive at W28,000. Seasonal discounts are available.

Novotel Ambassador *(☎ 567 1101, fax 564 4573; W www.ambassadors.co.kr; singles & doubles from W297,000)* is next to the Ritz Carlton Hotel. It has every facility, including a golf driving range and a rocky waterfall view from the lobby.

Elle Lui Hotel *(☎ 514 3535, fax 548 2500; W www.ellelui.co.kr; doubles & suites W160,000-400,000)* overlooks Hangang and is near the designer boutiques in Apgujeong. Facilities include a 24-hour sauna and a nightclub.

Hotel Riviera *(☎ 541 3111, fax 541 6111; W www.hotelriviera.co.kr; rooms W200,000-800,000)* is also near Apgujeong. Facilities include a deli shop, four restaurants, a sky lounge, a bar, an indoor golf range, a health club and a pool.

Hotel Amiga *(☎ 3440 8000, fax 3440 8200; W www.amiga.co.kr; rooms & suites W230,000-800,000)* is a five-minute walk southeast of Hak-dong subway station (Line 7). It gives a big discount for Internet reservations. Facilities include four restaurants, a bakery and a music bar.

Seoul Renaissance Hotel *(☎ 555 0501, fax 553 8118; W www.renaissance-seoul.com; rooms W320,000-550,000)* offers 15 restaurants and lounges, a health club, a swimming pool, tennis courts, a nightclub, a golf driving range and a sauna. Discounts are available in summer. This was where the Korean soccer team stayed during the World Cup finals in 2002.

New World Hotel *(☎ 557 0111, fax 557 0141; doubles & twins W210,000)* has restaurants, a bar, a nightclub, a health club, a sauna, a swimming pool and a golf driving range. The COEX Mall is a 10-minute walk away.

Grand Inter-Continental Hotel *(☎ 555 5656, fax 559 7990; W seoul.intercontinental.com; singles/doubles & twins from W300,000/320,000)* is one of two Inter-Continental hotels at the COEX Mall. Facilities include seven restaurants, a disco, a beauty salon, a 50m-lap pool and a business floor.

COEX Inter-Continental *(☎ 3452 2500; W seoul-coex.intercontinental.com; singles/doubles & twins from W310,000/330,000)* is the other Inter-Continental luxury business hotel in this area.

Lotte World Hotel *(☎ 419 7000, fax 417 3655; W www.hotel.lotte.co.kr; standard/executive rooms from W216,000/300,000)* is the place to stay if you have youngsters with you and can afford the rates. Next door is Lotte World and the COEX Mall is three subway stations away. Facilities include four restaurants, a sauna, a pool and a duty-free shop.

LONG-TERM RENTALS

Most foreign workers in Seoul live in accommodation that is supplied by their employers, but a few live in a guesthouse or *yeogwan* on a monthly basis and negotiate a reduced daily cost. Apartment sharing is another option, although spare rooms may be difficult to find – try the notice boards on the Seoul government or newspaper websites, or in magazine classifieds.

Renting an apartment is difficult because of the traditional payment system. *Chunsee* is when you loan W30 million to W500 million (70% of the value of the property) to the landlord and get it all back at the end of the rental period. *Wolse* is when you pay a smaller returnable deposit of W3 million to W10 million (a year's rent) plus a monthly rental fee. However, some accommodation in Seoul is available to foreigners on the Western system with a small returnable deposit and a monthly rent.

If you are looking to rent, take note that real estate is measured in *pyeong* (1 *pyeong* is 3.3 sq m). A medium-sized apartment in Seoul is about 30 *pyeong,* though smaller budget ones of 15 *pyeong* to 20 *pyeong* are common. There are even some super-tiny studios of seven to 10 *pyeong,* which are only suitable for a single person. At the opposite end of the scale are enormous apartments of 50 *pyeong* to 60 *pyeong*.

Places to Eat

FOOD

The cuisines that are widely available in Seoul are Korean, Japanese, Western and Chinese. Korean restaurants are everywhere, and generally provide a reasonably priced and well-cooked meal. Japanese restaurants are popular with budget-minded students. Western restaurants include well-known chains so you know what you're going to get. Chinese restaurants offer either very budget Koreanised food or an expensive authentic menu, with not many in the middle price range.

Usually in Korea the host pays for everything and if you're ever invited out for a drinking session or a meal with Korean friends, you'll find it difficult to pay the bill or even contribute towards it. As a foreigner, the same applies even if it is you that's doing the inviting. All manner of tricks will be used to beat you to the cashier and, even if you get there first, the cashier will be ordered not to accept your money.

Note: for a convenient glossary of Korean dishes, see the Food section in the Language chapter at the back of the book.

Korean

Sampling the very wide range of Korean cuisine is one of the delights of visiting Seoul. Korean food is healthy and simple, with plenty of pickled or fresh vegetables. Spicy soups, vegetable side dishes and white rice or noodles combined with meat, fish or seafood form the basis of many dishes. Most meals come with cold vegetable side dishes – often including *gimchi* (김치; cabbage, white radish, cucumber or other vegetables that have been pickled and fermented in a red pepper and garlic sauce), radish, spinach, cucumber or bean sprouts. Soups are a Korean specialty and are eaten with the rest of the meal, not at the beginning. Meals you cook yourself on a small portable gas cooker are also common. Koreans use a spoon to consume soup and rice and chopsticks for the side dishes.

Korean food has a reputation for being packed with fiery red peppers, but there are plenty of dishes for those who prefer something more mild.

The Wonderful World of Korean Food, published by KNTO, is a free booklet that provides an excellent introduction to Korean food and drinks.

A do-it-yourself barbecue at your table can involve thin slices of marinated beef (불고기; *bulgogi*), beef ribs (갈비; *galbi*) or bacon-type pork (삼겹갈; *samgyeopsal*). Expect to pay around W15,000 per person for the beef meals and W10,000 to W12,000 for the pork, but they will cost more in smart restaurants. Dip the meat in a sesame oil or red-pepper sauce and wrap it in a lettuce and sesame leaf together with garlic and thin strips of onion *and* eat it with side dish vegetables. All three are delicious meals usually eaten in a group, but the cheaper pork is like bacon and can be fatty.

Chicken is another popular dish. *Samgyetang* (삼계탕) costs around W8000 to W10,000 and is a small whole chicken stuffed with glutinous rice, red dates, garlic and ginseng and boiled in a soup. It's commonly eaten in summer with ginseng wine. *Dakgalbi* (닭갈비) costs W6000 to W8000 and is pieces of boneless chicken, cabbage, other vegetables and finger-sized pressed rice cakes, which are all grilled at your table in a tasty sauce. Somewhat similar but more expensive (around W10,000) is fashionable *jjimdak* (찜닭), which is a spicy mixture of chicken pieces, transparent noodles, potatoes and other vegetables. It is not usually available for one person. Seoul also has numerous 'chicken and beer' places where a plate of barbecued chicken and a small salad costs around W10,000.

Bibimbap (비빔밥) is a tasty mixture of meat, vegetables and an egg on top of a bed of rice, and usually costs around W5000 to W7000. Take out some of the *gochujang* (고추장; red pepper sauce) before you mix it all up if you don't want it too hot. It is usually served with a soup, but don't mix that in too! Another version, *dolsotbibimbap*

Samgakgimbap

Samgakgimbap (삼각김밥; triangular sushi) is only sold in convenience stores and it's a challenge to unwrap the plastic cover without unwrapping the dried seaweed. The rice has a variety of fillings – marinated beef, tuna and *gimchi*, chicken, octopus or spicy vegetables. Someone with a sense of humour gives these small snacks big names – *maeunmatjeyuk-bokkeum samgakgimbap* (매운맛제유보끔 삼각김밥) is *samgakgimbap* with spicy fried pork, while *sutbulgochujangchikin samgakgimbap* (숫불고추방치킨 삼각김밥) is *samgakgimbap* with chicken marinated in chilli sauce.

A healthy and tasty snack that only costs W700, it's hard to understand why triangular sushi has failed to achieve the global fame and popularity of its close relative, circular sushi.

(돌솟비빔밥) is served sizzling hot in a stone pot. Both can be ordered without the meat (and egg) as a vegetarian meal.

A meal that is popular in summer is *naengmyeon* (냉면; cold noodles), a simple and cheap (around W6000) meal of buckwheat noodles in a broth that is garnished with chopped-up vegetables and half an egg. It tastes better than it sounds and is often eaten after a meat dish as a kind of dessert.

Mandu (만두) is another budget-priced favourite (W4000 or less) – small dumplings that are filled with meat, vegetables and herbs. Fried, boiled or steamed, they make a tasty snack. However, they can be turned into a cheap W6000 meal called *tteokmanduguk* (떡만두국) if eaten with pressed rice cakes, meat and seaweed in a soup.

Gimbap (김밥; sushi) is another cheap meal (W4000) – strips of vegetables, egg or meat are rolled in rice and covered in dried seaweed. Without the dried seaweed cover it is known as 'nude' *gimbap*. Another unusual *gimbap* has purple-coloured rice.

Dubujjigae (두부찌개; spicy tofu stew) and *doenjang jjigae* (되장찌개; soya-bean paste stew) often appear as part of *hanjeongsik* (한정식), a group banquet meal, which includes fish, meat, soup, rice, noodles, steamed egg, shellfish and lots of cold vegetable side dishes. It's a good way to sample a wide range of Korean food at one sitting and prices range from W12,000 to W50,000 or more.

Korean soups vary from spicy seafood and crab blends to bland broths such as *galbitang* (갈비탕; beef short-ribs and vegetable soup with rice) or *seolleongtang* (설렁탕; slices of beef with spring onions and rice in a milky broth). Both cost around W6000. Culinary adventurers can try more expensive *doganitang* (도가니탕; a soup made with jellified cow's knee cartilage) or the infamous *bosintang* (보신탕; dog soup) for around W9000.

Japchae (잡채) is a dry noodle dish with Chinese origins made using sweet-potato noodles that are fried in sesame oil and mixed with strips of egg, meat, mushrooms, carrots and other vegetables. It costs around W7000. A mild-tasting meal for special occasions such as birthdays, it is a pity that not many restaurants serve it.

More expensive at W15,000, *sinseollo* (신선로) is another mild dish that is eaten on special occasions. Consisting of sliced meat, vegetables and seafood in a beef broth, it is cooked at your table in a special metal pan.

Desserts Although desserts are not usually provided in Korean restaurants, a Baskin Robbins ice-cream shop can be found on almost every street.

Convenience-Store Snacks Small convenience stores, such as Mini Stop, 7-Eleven, Buy The Way, LG25 and Family Mart, can be found all over Seoul. They're open long hours, sometimes all day and night. Pop into one whenever you want a quick, cheap meal.

A bowl of instant *ramyeon* (라면) noodles costs from W700 – just add hot water and eat it at the stand-up counter. Other options are *gimbap* (W1700), *samgakgimbap* (삼각김; W700), egg salad (W1600) or a sandwich (W1500). For dessert, buy a W500 ice cream (try Enjo for a chocolate blast) or a chocolate bar for W700. Various types of coffee cost around W500. Fruit is more expensive – W1000 for a kiwi fruit, orange or small apple. Soft drinks start at W500, a can of local beer is W1500 and a small bottle of *soju* (소주; local vodka) is W1000.

Street-Stall Food Thousands of food stalls sell cheap food for around W2500. *Tteokbokki* (떡보끼), finger-sized pressed rice cakes and other items in a sweet and spicy orange sauce, is the most popular. *Pajeon* (파전) – big pancakes with spring onions or seafood – are another tasty snack. *Dakkoyakki* (다꼬야끼) are balls of octopus with a tasty garnish, but they are not easy to find – try at Seoul Grand Park (Map 2).

Other street-stall food includes chicken kebabs, which have a delicious sweet and tangy sauce brushed over them, plain roasted potatoes, roasted honey-coated sweet potatoes and 20 types of hot dogs, including fishy ones. *Ppeondaegi* (뻔대기), silkworm larvae, smell bad and taste like earth, but even children seem to enjoy munching this weird snack.

Hotteok (호떡) is a kind of sweet pita bread that costs around W500 and comes in various forms – it can be crispy or soft and some stalls sell it as a small thick pancake, while others make it into a big thin crispy pita bread and the Chinese version (*gonggalpang;* 공갈팡) is a round, hollow ball. But all types of *hotteok* contain a cinnamon and honey paste and are delicious when freshly made.

Delimanjoo (데리만주) are freshly baked, custard-filled minicakes that are sold in subway stations. Waffles, *churros* and red-bean paste snacks are also common. In Insadong (Map 8), try *kkultarae* (꿀타래), fine threads of honey and cornflour wrapped around a nut sauce, and *daepaesaenggangyeot* (대패생강엿), a huge slab of toffee, which is shaved off in strips and served on a stick.

Tteok This is the word (떡; pronounced 'dock') for the vast array of rice cakes available in Seoul – pressed ones are chewy and smooth and are often eaten in a spicy soup, while lightweight ones are fluffy and eaten with tea; others are steamed, boiled or fried and flavoured with fruit, nuts, spices, flower petals and even *makgeolli* (막걸리; milky white fermented rice wine). Besides traditional *tteok* that are flavoured with mugwort, pine-pollen powder or azalea flowers, you can sample modern fusion *tteok* flavoured with coffee or chocolate.

Specialist *tteok* shops that cluster around Nakwon Arcade (Map 8) and department stores sell packets of rice cakes for around W3000. Traditionally a food for special occasions, they are a popular gift, but the splendid-looking giant gift sets can cost W100,000.

Japanese

Seoul has many Japanese restaurants and most provide cheap W6000 meal sets based on fried, breadcrumbed cutlets – pork (*donkkaseu;* 도까스), fish (*saengseonkkaseu;* 생선까스) and chicken (*chikinkkaseu;* 치킨까스) – with a shredded cabbage and mayonnaise salad, and *miso* (미소; soya-bean paste) soup. Other options are *udon* (우돈; noodles) or *tempura* (*twigim* in Korean; 튀김), which is vegetables and seafood that has been deep-fried in batter. Other Japanese restaurants offer a more expensive raw fish and seafood menu.

Western

The usual Western-style food outlets are everywhere in Seoul. Lotteria is the local version and offers *bulgogi, bulgalbi* and *gimchi* burgers. Its rice burgers use rice cakes instead of a bun. More upmarket restaurant chains are also plentiful.

Italian food is very popular in Seoul – not just pizza chains but numerous small pasta and spaghetti restaurants, which serve reasonably authentic meals.

A recent trend is fusion restaurants, some of which provide a Mexican/American/Italian menu. Others offer Asian/European combinations such as spaghetti sauce with fiery red peppers – the possibilities are endless. Anyone for *ppeondaegi* pizza or a *gimchi* Caesar salad?

Chinese

Budget Chinese restaurants concentrate on *bokkeumbap* (볶음밥; fried rice that often includes chopped-up ham), *jjajangmyeon* (짜장면; a bland concoction of noodles and a thick black-bean sauce) and *tangsuyuk* (탕수육; thin strips of sweet and sour pork that are 90% batter) – Koreanised Chinese dishes that have probably never been seen outside Korea. Some restaurants offer authentic Chinese meals, but they tend to be expensive.

Vegetarian

Although Koreans love meat, fish and seafood, vegetables also play a large part in their diet. Restaurants such as Pulhyanggi (Map 6), Sanchon (Map 8), Dimibang (Map 8), Dagyeong (Map 8) and idame (Map 3) provide special vegetarian meals. Indian restaurants usually offer some vegetarian meals as well.

Vegetarians can try *bibimbap* or *dolsotbibimbap* without the meat (or egg), *beoseotjeongol* (버섯전골; hotpot with different kinds of mushrooms), *doenjang jjigae* (된장찌개; spicy soya-bean paste stew), *dubujjigae*, *jjajangmyeon,* vegetable *pajeon* or *dotorimuk* (도토리묵; acorn jelly) but check before you order that these meals don't have any meat, seafood or fish. Some *gimbap* is vegetarian, or you can always eat a meal of rice and vegetable side dishes. *Gimchi* sometimes has seafood in it but is usually made of just vegetables, so *gimchi mandu* or *gimchi* fried rice *(gimchibokkeumbap)* are other possibilities.

Not all restaurants understand the needs of vegetarians, so occasionally you will find small clams or anchovies in a 'vegetarian' dish. There isn't much you can do about it except pick them out.

Ethnic

Itaewon (Map 11) is home to Thai, Indian, Turkish, Egyptian, Indonesian, Vietnamese, Swiss, German and French restaurants. The food is usually produced by expat chefs and is authentic. The highly competitive restaurant scene in Seoul ensures that prices are generally reasonable and W10,000 to W30,000 would cover most meals. The number of ethnic restaurants outside Itaewon is growing but is still very few.

DRINKS

Nonalcoholic

All the usual soft drinks are available in cans or bottles plus some unusual ones that are worth trying – *sikhye* (식혜; rice punch), aloe, grape juice with real grapes, vitamin-packed Bacchus and Condition F, which is supposed to reduce hangovers.

A wide range of unusual teas can be sampled in traditional teashops – see the boxed text 'Unusual Teashops that Serve Unusual Teas' in the Entertainment chapter. Traditional teas are regarded as a kind of medicine, with beneficial physical and psychological effects. Green tea and the tea ceremony play a role in Buddhist temple life as the monks believe tea can help them achieve serenity and enlightenment.

Boricha (보리차; barley tea) is popular and is sometimes served free in restaurants instead of water. *Ssukcha* (쑥차; mugwort tea) and *ssanghwacha* (쌍화차; herb tonic tea) are regarded as cure-alls. Add hot water to the burnt rice you scrape from the rice cooker bowl and you have *sungnyung* (숭룽; burnt-rice tea). It tastes better than it sounds.

Even more numerous than teashops are the coffee shops – it would take years to visit all of the outlets in Seoul.

Alcoholic

Many Koreans enjoy drinking alcohol and socialising with their friends or work colleagues. *Maekju* (맥주; beer), such as the locally produced lagers Hite, OB and Cass, are popular, but stout, Guinness and an increasing range of imported bottled beer is also available.

Soju (소주), vodka-like and usually made from rice or sweet potatoes, is the local firewater. Although it comes in all sorts of flavours – lemon, peach, pear, apple, apricot and guava – most people prefer it unflavoured.

Makgeolli (막걸리) is a fermented rice wine that looks and tastes a bit like yoghurt. It used to be popular with the peasant farmers and is traditionally served in a kettle and drunk from a small bowl. *Dongdongju* (동동주) is similar and is often drunk with a meal. Neither are as strong as *soju*.

There are hundreds of traditional rice wines and fruit liquors with ancient secret recipes that are brewed or distilled in different regions of Korea. Like traditional Korean teas, these drinks are regarded as a kind of medicine with numerous health benefits. Sansachun (산사춘) is a plain rice wine, while Baekseju (백세주) is rice wine flavoured with ginseng and herbs. Igangju (이강주) contains ginger, turmeric and cinnamon, which makes it sound more like a curry than an alcoholic beverage. Wolfberry wine

Free Food Samples

Department stores offer their customers numerous products to taste in the supermarket section, which is usually in the basement. In just one store you may be able to sample such items as sesame soup, cold noodle soup, potato and buckwheat pancakes, rice wrapped in bean curd, grilled eel, ham with mustard, hamburgers, chicken wings, dumplings, baked potato, and various types of nut jelly and *gimchi*. For dessert, kiwi fruit, yellow melon, gingko nuts, cheese slices, yogurt and an aloe drink may all be on offer for you to try.

uses not just the fruit but also the leaves and roots of the plant. One to avoid is *baemsul* (뱀술), which has a dead snake in it.

Korean custom dictates that you should keep filling the glasses of your fellow drinkers (being especially attentive to anyone older than you) and wait for them to fill your glass. This makes it difficult to keep track of how much you have drunk.

WHERE TO EAT

With many thousands of restaurants scattered throughout every neighbourhood of the city, there is no problem finding somewhere to eat. Small unpretentious Korean restaurants serve up local food at reasonable prices, and Italian, Japanese and fast-food restaurants are everywhere.

Restaurants in top-end hotels generally add 21% to the bill (10% service charge and 10% VAT) but otherwise tipping is not necessary or expected.

Not all Korean restaurants offer a table and chairs option; in some traditional restaurants customers sit on floor cushions. Only a small minority of restaurant staff speak any English, but fortunately most restaurants have pictures or plastic replicas of the meals they offer and this makes it easy to order what you want.

In Seoul, eating out (like everything else) is a group activity and you don't see many people dining alone. Some Korean meals are not usually available to one person, so invite someone out with you if you want to try *bulgogi*, *jjimdak* or *hanjeongsik*.

Like the shops, most restaurants open every day, usually from late morning until 10pm. In general the main problem is deciding which of the many restaurants to eat in. Probably the best method is to decide what you want to eat rather than choosing a particular restaurant; competitive pressures ensure that most restaurants provide a good deal.

Department stores are good places to go for a meal since they have a range of expensive and inexpensive restaurants as well as reasonably priced food courts that are usually in the basement. But keep in mind that most department-store food courts close around 7.30pm.

Budget restaurants in the following listings are defined as those where most meals are W7000 or less, mid-range restaurants offer meals mainly in the W8000 to W18,000 range and the top-end restaurants provide meals that generally cost more than W18,000. Of course, the definitions are not exact, as many restaurants offer meals at a wide variety of prices and some expensive restaurants offer a range of cheap lunches.

GWANGHWAMUN (MAPS 8 & 9)

Budget

Hwanggeumjeong (*☎ 739 4343; meals W5000; open 24hrs*), near the Sejong Centre for the Performing Arts, has a sign written in Chinese characters and blue tiles on the porch. You sit on cushions on the floor and tuck into *bulgogi*, *jjigae*, *galbi* or *tteokmanduguk* for W5000.

In the street that runs alongside the Sejong Centre for the Performing Arts are a number of cheap **Japanese restaurants**, although conveyor-belt sushi costs W2200 per small plate.

Goryeo Supermarket Food Court has only three restaurants, but they cook up a wide range of food for W4000 or less. Try the *gamjatang* (potato and pork-rib soup). The supermarket is also useful for self-caterers or anyone looking for something for a picnic lunch.

Witch's Table (*☎ 732 2727; drinks & snacks W3000-6000*), near Goryeo Supermarket, offers large filled bagels or bacon, lettuce and tomato on wholemeal bread for

W5500, while banana toast or half a bagel with toasted cheese are W3500. Tea or coffee is W3000.

Gwasai Restaurant *(meals W4000)* near Deoksugung is a no-frills eatery that offers a wide range of Korean food at budget prices.

Top End

Yongsusan *(☎ 771 5553; B1 Seoul Finance Centre; meals W20,000-100,000)* serves royal-cuisine meals. Set lunches are W20,000 to W40,000, while set dinners start at W30,000. The food is special – for instance five-grain rice cooked in bamboo, ginseng porridge, noodle and vegetable sausage *(sundae)* and pink *omija* tea. Another branch is north of Insadong.

Buck Mulligan's *(☎ 3783 0004; Seoul Finance Centre; meals W16,000-35,000)* offers lunch specials, such as stew, roast beef or fish pie for W16,500, and other Irish food, such as salmon, mussels, potato cakes and Jameson chicken. Mains are W25,000. Desserts, such as brown-bread ice cream or apple crumble, are W8000. A Guinness will add W13,000 to your bill. Live music starts around 8pm.

TAPGOL PARK (MAP 8)

Budget

Midarae *(meals W2500-5000)* on Jongno is one branch of a popular chain that serves all sorts of budget meals and offers a variety of unusual *gimbap*.

Gamjatangjip *(meals W4000-6000)* can be found behind Pizza Hut and serves typical Pimatgol peasant fare. The W4000 *gamjatang* has big meaty bones and a big lump of potato in a spicy soup, while the W5000 *samchi* is a tasty barbecued fish served whole. Wash it down with *sansachun* rice wine, although it costs more than the food at W7000 a bottle.

Tomoko *(☎ 722 2970; meals W3500-6000)* is south of Jongno and offers the usual Japanese fare of noodles and a choice of pork, tuna or cheese cutlets.

Jilsiru Tteok Café *(☎ 741 5414; lunch set W5000)* is the place to go for unusual and colourful *tteok* rice cakes; try tropical fruit, coffee, *gimchi* or pumpkin rice cakes, which cost W1000 each. It also serves traditional teas for W5000. Upstairs is a *tteok* museum and *tteok*-making classes are available (W70,000). Take Exit 6 of Jongno 3-ga subway station (Lines 1, 3 & 5) to get here.

Mid-Range

Outback Steakhouse *(W www.outback.co.kr; meals W10,000-28,000)* has outlets across Seoul and offers steaks with an Aussie theme.

Top End

Top Cloud Restaurant *(☎ 2230 3000; W www.topcloud.co.kr; set lunches W40,000-47,000, set dinners W70,000-130,000)* is on the 33rd floor at the top of Jongno Tower, Seoul's most striking skyscraper building. It's a place to go for special occasions as long as you don't suffer from vertigo. The seven-course dinners feature items such as foie gras, lobster, rack of lamb or king prawns, and the food has French and Asian influences. If you go à la carte, soups are W11,000, mains W30,000, desserts W9000 and a glass of wine is W10,000.

Next door is **Top Cloud Cafe** *(☎ 2230 3002; drinks W6500-10,000)* where the views are less expensive – soft drink is W6500, beer is W8000, wine and cocktails are W9000, and juices and coffee are W10,000.

DONGDAEMUN (MAP 4)

Budget

PYCCKUU *(meals W10,000-15,000)* is a Russian-style restaurant near Dongdaemun market with unusual decor – large plastic pot plants and flashing Christmas tree lights. No English is spoken and there is no English menu. Order the small version of the first item on the menu, which consists of a pile of mixed vegetables and pieces of pork surrounded by slices of tomato. It costs W10,000 and is enough for two or three people. Bread, hazelnut coffee and sweet wine are included in the price. Vodka is W3000 extra.

Freya Town, Migliore and Doota malls in Dongdaemun market have popular **restaurants** and **food courts**. Hundreds of **food stalls** in the market offer cheap meals.

Top End

Dongdaemun Hotel Restaurant *(☎ 741 7811; meals W15,000-30,000)* is conveniently situated for shoppers on the edge of Dongdaemun market. Its six-course steak or prawn meals for W25,000 make for a good deal.

INSADONG (MAP 8)

Insadong is home to a host of traditional-style Korean restaurants selling old-fashioned, hometown Korean food. *Hanjeongsik* restaurants offer a banquet of items so you can try many Korean dishes (especially side dishes) at one sitting. There are also a number of vegetarian restaurants, including ones that serve Buddhist temple food.

Budget

Shinpouri Mandu *(meals W2000-5000)* on the main road in Insadong is one branch of a restaurant chain that serves up good basic meals in a bright clean environment. The meals include home-made shrimp, pork or *gimchi mandu* for around W3000. Equally good is its *dolsotbibimbap. Mandukalguksu* is dumplings, flat noodles, an egg, vegetables and shellfish in a spicy soup.

Hayangim Pureunnae *(☎ 737 5805; meals W6000-12,000)* is a typical Insadong restaurant with a relaxing atmosphere and cushions on the floor. The mushroom hotpot is a good deal at W14,000 for two and comes with unusual side dishes, such as mashed potato and egg. Also recommended is the meat, vegetable and mushroom soup that is cooked at your table.

Insa Art Plaza Food Court *(meals W5000)* is hidden away in the basement and offers traditional Korean food at bargain prices; however, it's open only for lunches.

Father's Restaurant *(meals W5000-12,000)* is worth visiting more for its rustic, junkshop decor than its food. However, octopus and other fried rice meals are only W5000. Railway lines lead to the garden shed front door and the interior transports you back in time.

Kuay Yin Lo *(☎ 723 7601; meals W3000-8000)* is north of Insadong in building No 40 near Art Sonje and is run by an ethnic Chinese family. Noodles, *mandu* and rice meals cost W3000, while seafood-based dishes are W8000.

Hyangnamusegeuru *(☎ 720 9524; meals W5000-12,000)* is further north and has three trees outside. No English is spoken but just ask for *moksalsogeumgui*! This is pork barbecued at your table, which you eat like *bulgogi* wrapped in lettuce with sauces and spicy vegetables. You can cut some of the fat off the pork with the scissors provided. It's a good deal for W6000. Also try the *doenjang jjigae*.

Mid-Range

Dimibang *(☎ 720 2417; meals W6000-30,000)* is a vegetarian restaurant well known for its use of *hamcho* root and other medicinal herbs and roots. It also serves herbal alcohol and teas. You can order *doenjang jjigae* or *bibimbap* for W6000, or set meals cost W10,000, W20,000 or W30,000. You sit on bamboo mats on the floor and eat with wooden spoons and chopsticks.

Yeongbin Garden *(☎ 732 3863; meals W5000-15,000)* in Insadong-gil has *galbitang* for W5000 and barbecued *galbi* for W15,000.

Anjip *(☎ 3672 7070; meals W6000-15,000)* offers a great *hanjeongsik* meal at a great price – W8000 per person (minimum two people). Sit on embroidered cushions in your own private room and 20 dishes are laid out in front of you. The *bulgogi,* spicy cockles and steamed egg are particularly delicious, and there is fruit and cinnamon tea to finish off the meal.

Hanmoechon *(☎ 766 5535; meals W6000-25,000)* is a traditional-style mainly vegetarian restaurant that serves a set vegetarian meal for W15,000. Otherwise you can have *gujeolpan* for W20,000 or *sinseollo* for W25,000. Lunches are cheaper and start at W6000.

Seoul Moemaeul *(☎ 720 0995; meals W10,000-20,000)* further north of Insadong offers excellent food in a rustic decor. You sit on cushions on the floor with classical music in the background. Order the *moejeongsik* (W16,000 per person) for a sumptuous banquet. The pork is excellent, the broths and sauces are tasty, the salad is fiery, the *gujeolpan* is interesting (eight types

PLACES TO EAT

of shredded vegetables, which you wrap in a thin slice of white radish) and the jujube tea finishes the meal off perfectly.

Top End

Sanchon *(☎ 735 0312; W www.sanchon.com; set lunch W19,000, set dinner W32,000)* serves up Buddhist temple vegetarian food but the prices are not very Buddhist. You sit on cushions on the floor in a soothing atmosphere with candles on the tables. The set meal has 16 courses served in wooden bowls and includes sesame and rice gruel, wild roots, mini vegetable pancakes, tofu and medicinal tea. The marinades, glazes and sauces are excellent. An à la carte menu is also available. A traditional dancer performs at 8.15pm and you can join in at the end.

Dagyeong *(☎ 725 5754; set meals W30,000-50,000)* serves Buddhist temple vegetarian sets but they are expensive. A cheaper deal is a regional set meal for W7900.

Min's Club *(lunch W15,000-18,000, dinner sets W50,000)* is a restaurant housed in a restored traditional house filled with antiques. It serves dishes like crab roulade, steaks, pumpkin chowder, or pork with ginseng, chestnuts and seared sesame leaves.

Dal Restaurant *(☎ 736 4627; meals W14,000-35,000)* is a luxurious Indian restaurant in the Art Sonje centre and small private rooms are available. The sumptuous decor makes you feel that you are in a maharajah's palace. Vegetarian curries and dahl cost around W16,000, while tandoori meals cost W18,000 to W28,000. Mango lassi is W6000. Lunch specials cost W25,000 to W35,000.

Yongsusan *(☎ 739 5599; meals W22,000-100,000)*, further north, is a classy restaurant with staff dressed in traditional *hanbok* and expensive art on the walls. It serves royal cuisine of the highest quality.

MYEONG-DONG (MAP 9)

Budget

Seochogol *(☎ 777 6911; meals W5000-12,000)* is located behind Popeye's and specialises in *galbi* that is charcoal-grilled at your table, giving the whole place a smoky atmosphere. It comes with side dishes and costs W7000.

Nakwon Restaurant *(meals W5000-10,000)* is popular and has a salad bar that costs W1000 for 100g, making a plateful around W5000.

Mid-Range

Baekje Samgyetang *(☎ 776 3267; meals around W10,000)* is on the 2nd floor and the restaurant sign is in Chinese characters. It specialises in *samgyetang*, a whole steamed chicken stuffed with rice in a ginseng, chestnut and jujube broth. The W10,000 price includes side dishes and a small glass of ginseng wine. Other meals include fried and roast chicken, and a ginseng and abalone rice porridge with egg, both of which are W9000.

Nutrition Centre *(meals W5500-8500)* has outlets in Myeong-dong, Jongno and other locations. It's a 'no-frills' restaurant that offers a simple menu of *samgyetang* or roast chicken for W8500. A chicken lunch costs W5500.

Top End

Eunhasoo Dinner Buffet *(☎ 3705 9141; lunch/dinner W31,000/36,000)* in Sejong Hotel offers more than 70 different types of food. It's generally Western-style but there are plenty of Korean dishes to sample, such as *galbi*, pork hocks, spicy crab soup, pumpkin porridge, rice cakes, rice punch, raw seafood, deliciously sweet raw meat, sea ginseng and cow cartilage soup.

ITAEWON (MAPS 4 & 11)

Budget

Sigol Bobsang *(☎ 794 5072; meals W7000-10,000; open 24hrs)* has a rustic decor and traditional music playing in the background. 'Countryside food' is the name of the restaurant and you can order *sigol bobsang* – 20 mainly vegetarian small side dishes, including some unusual ones, with spicy tofu soup and rice for W7000 per person (two people minimum). If you want meat order the W10,000 *bulgogi*.

Chunchon is in a street full of cheap restaurants and offers *dakgalbi* – boneless chicken pieces cooked on a metal barbecue plate at your table with cabbage and other vegetables and covered with a spicy sauce. It costs W6000 per person (two people minimum).

Bali (☎ *749 5271; meals W5000-12,000*) is next to 3 Alleys Pub and offers genuine Indonesian food at a reasonable price. Nasi goreng, *gado gado* and chicken satay are W6000, while fried prawns are W10,000.

Ali Baba (☎ *790 7754; meals W10,000*) on the main street is an authentic Egyptian restaurant with a relaxing atmosphere enhanced by Arabic music, a tiled floor and attractive seat cushions. Salads, hummus, *babaganesh* and falafel are W5000, while beef and lamb dishes are W10,000.

Salaam (☎ *793 4323; meals W10,000*) is behind the mosque and offers basic Turkish food. The obvious choice is the eight-course try-everything set for W15,000. Otherwise various kebabs in pita bread cost W5000. No alcohol is served but a smoke on the *shisha* pipe is a pricey W10,000.

Shakranthi (☎ *792 7585; meals W10,000*) is a new Indian restaurant that is rather hidden away, but offers delicious and relatively inexpensive food. Portions are small but you can order three between two people, as the curries cost W6000 to W8000.

The **United Service Organizations' Canteen** (☎ *795 3028; breakfast/lunch US$2/5; open 7am-2.15pm Mon-Fri*) is out of the main Itaewon area, but offers some genuine Americana. The diner boasts red and blue plastic seats, a juke box, real breakfasts and you can pay in US dollar bills. Big burgers and salads are US$2, coffee or tea is US$0.50 and lunch platters are US$5.

PLACES TO EAT

Mid-Range

Itaewon Galbi (☎ *795 9716;* **W** *www.kalbi.co.kr; meals W6000-15,000*) specialises in *galbi,* which costs W15,000 – the secret of its success is the quality beef and the sweet marinade. Otherwise W10,000 buys a tasty mushroom and meat *bulgogi* soup, which is cooked at your table in an earthenware bowl. For vegetarians there's a meatless *bibimbap* for W6000.

Top End

Gecko's Garden (☎ *790 0540; meals W10,000-30,000; open noon-2am*) offers eating and drinking indoors, on the veranda or outdoors in the garden. The Mediterranean feel is accentuated by the Spanish tapas, which cost W9350 for five plates of snacks. Otherwise the mains are W18,000 to W38,000, or you can splash out on the W70,000 set dinner.

Ashoka (☎ *792 0117;* **W** *www.ashoka.co.kr; daily lunch buffet W25,000; Sat & Sun dinner buffet W31,000*) is an Indian restaurant in the Hamilton Hotel. It offers vegetarian meals and tandoori mains from W20,000.

Chalet Swiss (☎ *797 9664*) has soups, appetizers and salads for around W8000, *roesti* and other mains are around W15,000, fondues and grills are around W24,000, and desserts are W5500.

Memories (☎ *795 3544; lunch/dinner W10,000/25,000*) is a little oasis of authentic Deutschland in Itaewon. German beers are W7000, and bratwurst, schnitzel and steaks range from W12,000 to W16,000. Substantial set dinners are W25,000. This is real German food served by a real German chef.

Thai Orchid (☎ *792 8836;* **W** *www.thaiorchid.co.kr; set lunch/set dinner W17,000/30,000*) has a large menu with all the usual favourites. With over 100 items not everything can be excellent, but it maintains its popularity. Vegetarian meals are W7000 and mains range from W10,000 to W20,000. It's on the 3rd floor – not the 2nd floor, which has a different Thai restaurant.

Moghul (☎ *796 5501; meals W20,000*) is an Indian restaurant with a garden section that is popular on summer evenings. Mains are W13,000 to W20,000, while buffets on Saturday and Sunday are W20,000 (lunch) and W22,000 (dinner).

DAEHANGNO (MAP 12)

There are hundreds of restaurants in Daehangno and they are spreading out from around Hyehwa subway station (Line 4) up to the roundabout and branching off west down a street of cheap eateries. If you want Western food this is the place to come; it's a competitive free-for-all that keeps prices lower than in Itaewon.

Budget

Bongchu (☎ *3676 6981; meals W9000*) is a popular *jjimdak* restaurant, with another branch in Hongik. This fashionable dish consists of a big platter piled high with chicken pieces, potatoes and carrots on a bed of noodles, and a sweet and spicy soy sauce covering everything. There are no side dishes and you need a minimum of two people for this party food.

Beer Oak *(☎ 745 0087; meals W8000-12,000)* has irresistible barbecued chicken that is cooked on a spit over a wood fire for W9000.

Mid-Range

Obseoye *(☎ 742 4848; meals W6000-15,000)* is one of those rural-retreat restaurants where you go to forget about bustling, stressful city life. The restaurant serves good side dishes, the W9000 beef and noodle soup is tasty, and the dark *chikcha* (arrowroot tea) is special too.

Sale e Pepe *(meals around W10,000; open 11am-2am)* has various zones but outdoors under the smart tent roof is the best option. Despite the Spanish-style broken-mosaic designs, the food is Italian pasta. Set lunches start at W8000, while in the evening most pasta dishes are around W10,000. This is a stylish place with good food that is hard to beat.

World Village *(w www.ih.or.kr; meals W11,000)* is the place to go if you want to eat your way around the world – meals from nine different countries cost W10,000 to W12,000 each. The owner, Mr Moon *(☎ 018 2399981; e mbh45@hanmail.net)*, also runs almost-free Korean-language lessons upstairs.

El Paso *(☎ 3675 0111; meals W7500-15,000)* is a Mexican restaurant in Korea run by a man who used to run a Korean restaurant in Mexico. It offers genuine Mexican food surrounded by Mexican artworks and souvenirs. Kidney-bean soup is W3500, lunch specials and salads are W7500, while mains are W11,000 to W13,000.

Kijoam *(☎ 766 6100; meals W7000)* is a Japanese restaurant with the usual reasonable meals at a reasonable price.

HONGIK, SINCHON & EWHA (MAP 3)

Hongik has a number of Chinese restaurants in a mini-Chinatown that is a short walk from Hongik University subway station (Line 2). Take Exit 4 and walk straight ahead for five minutes and you should come to Hsiang Yuan on your left. Backtrack and turn right for Mei Hwa and Hongbok. Continue along this road and turn right at the traffic lights for Jen Beijing and Sandong Shui Jao Daewang (the latter is a 15-minute walk).

Budget

Opposite the front of Ewha Women's University is **Andrew's**, a small shop that sells delicious Chinese-style custard tarts for W1200. Next door you can buy **bubble tea**, which originated in Taiwan and involves putting little balls of something into a range of drinks from tea and coffee to juice (W4000). There are plenty of **Western restaurants** in the street between the main entrance to Ewha Women's University and the subway station.

Nolboo *(☎ 3141 7766; meals W4000-8000)* in Hongik is one outlet of a chain that serves up cheap student grub. Try the ham, sausages, vegetables, beans, tofu, noodles and anything-else-hanging-around that is all thrown into a big wok and cooked at your table. It's served with rice and good side dishes for W5000. This meal, which some people call Johnson-*tang,* is said to have originated after the Korean War when just about the only meat available in Seoul was 'black market' tins of ham and sausages that were smuggled out of the US army base at Yongsan.

Naniwa *(☎ 333 5337; meals W3000-6000)* is a cheap Japanese restaurant selling the usual cutlet-and-salad meal sets. One outlet is near Hongik, the other near Sinchon.

Coco's provides American-style food and desserts, with salads for W9000 and steaks for W25,000. There are other branches around town too.

Haejeodon *(☎ 322 0205; meals W6000-10,000)* has a pleasant outdoor area and specialises in pork *bulgogi,* which costs W6800 if marinated in wine, or W7500 if marinated in ginseng. *Bibimguksu* is also on the menu – cold noodles and a few vegetables in a hot sauce, which you mix up as you do with its more famous brother, *bibimbap*.

Zen Zen *(☎ 335 3420; meals W6000-10,000)* has a beer-hall atmosphere and serves up *bulgogi* pork that's been marinated inside a bamboo container; it's barbecued at your table and served with *doenjang jjigae* for W7200. You can take as much salad wrapping as you want from the salad bar. Try the pungent sesame leaf – it's the bright green leaf with serrated edges.

Huedeura Ramyeon *(meals W3000-5000)* is a tiny, dark place that is said to serve the hottest *ramyeon* in Seoul. You can take up the challenge for only W3000.

Gio *(meals W4500)* is only a shack but it often has a queue outside because the food is unique and cheap. There is no need to order, as it only provides two dishes that are both cooked at your table. First is a bowl of mushrooms and home-made noodles, the widest in Seoul. Take out some of the red pepper paste and cook it for 15 minutes. Next is a rice, seaweed and herb mixture cooked in the same pot. Gio has another branch in nearby Sinchon but the second branch's decor is smart and it doesn't have the atmosphere of the original, which features a 'bawling *ajumma*', one of those wonderful, hard-working, middle-aged waitresses who really shouts your order out to the cook in the kitchen.

Dangang Andong Jjimdak *(meals W5000)* is worth a mention as its tasty *jjimdak* is only W5000.

Chicken Rice *(meals W4000-8000)* has unusual chicken fusion dishes, including an interesting chicken salad served in an edible pastry basket for W3500. However, the tables are tiny and squashed together.

Hongbok *(☎ 323 1698; meals W4000)* is in Hongik's mini-Chinatown and sells *pow* (steamed filled buns) for W1000 or *mandu* soup for W4000.

Mid-Range

Sandong Shui Jao Daewang *(☎ 333 6355; meals W5000-12,000)* is in Hongik's mini-Chinatown and offers large portions at reasonable prices. The usual strips of battered pork in sweet and sour sauce cost W9000, an unusual noodle, rice and vegetables dish with a fried egg on top is W5000, and fried dumplings are W4000.

idame *(☎ 392 5051; W www.idame.co.kr; meals W6000-15,000)* is a genuine vegetarian restaurant that serves an excellent vegetarian *bulgogi* for W15,000. It offers 10 original mains that are clearly described in English on the menu. Fried rice, noodle and salad dishes cost W6000. The white sofas and decor are relaxing as is the background music. This special restaurant can be found on the 2nd floor in an alley near the front entrance of Ewha Women's University.

Top End

Hsiang Yuan *(☎ 336 3421; most meals W25,000)* has a lengthy but expensive menu with seven fried egg rolls for W25,000. Cheaper items include shrimp fried rice for W6000 and 'eight treasures' sweet rice for W5000.

Mei Hwa *(meals W15,000-40,000)* offers set menus for W20,000 to W40,000 with a minimum of three people. Noodles are W5000 or small dishes around W15,000.

Jen Beijing is another expensive Chinese restaurant where you can have Beijing duck for W50,000.

OTHER AREAS NORTH OF THE RIVER (MAPS 7 & 9)

Budget

Techno Mart Food Court *(meals W3000-8000)* has 40 stalls offering everything from raw fish to pizza from *samgyetang* to *tteokbokki*. Many offer huge platters of food that you share – a W10,000 platter feeds three hungry people. Giant fruit and ice-cream desserts are also available, as is yogurt ice cream. All the stalls display plastic replicas of the food they offer, so it's choosing rather than ordering that is the problem.

Hankook *(☎ 2273 7507; meals W5000)*, right near Korea House, is a good place for a quick budget lunch. Two tasty meat and vegetable broth soups *galbitang* and *seolleongtang* are both W4500.

Top End

Korea House *(☎ 2266 9101; set menus W30,000-80,000)* is near Namsangol Traditional Village. Enjoy a buffet of traditional Korean royal-court food and drink for W30,000 (lunch) or W33,000 (dinner) in a Joseon era *yangban* house. Every evening top-class performers put on one-hour folk music and dance shows, which cost W29,000. The performances start at 7pm and 8.50pm, except on Sunday when there is only one show at 8pm.

SOUTH OF THE RIVER (MAPS 5 & 6)

Budget

Myeongdong Restaurant *(☎ 761 1414; meals W4000-8000)* is 50m from the 63 Building on Yeouido. You sit on cushions on the floor and delicious *naengmyeon* cold noodles with meat, egg and vegetables in a salad-type spicy sauce; *bibimbap* and *samgyetang* are both reasonably priced.

Mandoo World *(☎ 555 8133; meals W4000)* in Gangnam offers tasty cheap Korean meals for under W5000.

Mid-Range

Pavilion *(☎ 555 6284; meals W8000-15,000)* is a huge and popular Californian/European/Asian fusion restaurant near Gangnam subway station (Line 2). The Cajun chicken pasta is good, but our shrimp gratin was lacking shrimps and flavour. Also on the large menu are such items as snails (W9500) and tiramisu (W3500).

Priveé *(☎ 564 4314; meals W8000-15,000)* is further up the street, similar to Pavilion and serves pleasant but smallish fusion meals. The Szechwan shrimp spaghetti sounds interesting but ours had more meat than shrimp and no detectable Szechwan flavour.

Yeotnal *(☎ 3481 1252; food W8,000-15,000)* is in the basement of the red-brick Uncle 29 Building in Gangnam. Little wooden thatched huts give this basement an unusual Pacific Island feel. Beer is only W2000 but the food is relatively expensive.

Pulhyanggi *(lunch sets W7000, dinner sets W18,000-50,000)* is a well-known restaurant in Apgujeong that offers mainly vegetarian food. Lunches cost W6000 to W8000 and various dinner set menus offer a banquet for W18,000 to W50,000. It also has a branch in the basement of Seoul Tower on Namsan.

Hard Rock Cafe *(☎ 547 5671; meals W8000-24,000; open 5pm-2am Mon-Fri, 12pm-2am Sat & Sun;)* in Apgujeong offers steaks for W24,000, while burgers and salads are W8000. Different specials are available every night. After eating you can drink at the bar and dance to live rock music among the usual rock-star memorabilia.

Marché *(meals around W14,000)*, in the COEX Mall (Map 7), offers continental European food served from counters in an informal market-like atmosphere. The food looks fresh, and organic salads, muffins and other culinary delights are available.

A bunch of **Western-style restaurants** can be found outside Exit 5 of Gangnam subway station (Line 2).

Top End

Lapalooza *(☎ 591 4258; 9-course set meal W27,000)* is a smart Chinese restaurant in Gangnam.

Plaza Fountain Buffet is a famous restaurant in the basement of Yeouido's 63 Building. It offers a cosmopolitan buffet (W35,000 to W40,000) on tables grouped around a 'dancing' fountain.

Noryangjin Fish Market Restaurants *(meals W25,000-90,000)* are up on the 1st floor of the fish market south of Yeouido. All five restaurants are similar and you sit on cushions on the floor. It specialises in raw fish that is guaranteed to have been swimming around not long before you eat it. Raw fish and seafood costs a minimum of W50,000, but it comes with side dishes and can be shared. If you don't want raw seafood, the restaurant at the end does cooked fish, sea cucumber and octopus dishes for W25,000. There are no menus in English and it's difficult to find anyone who can speak it either.

Entertainment

NIGHTLIFE

Pubs, Clubs & Bars

Hof is the Korean word for a pub or bar and there are hundreds in every entertainment district. Many serve food, such as barbecue chicken and salad, or expect you to buy *anju* – snacks such as dried squid, peanuts or rice crackers and seaweed – which can be pricey, especially in nightclubs.

All the top hotels in Seoul provide bars that are popular with foreigners and locals who don't mind spending W10,000 or more on a beer. The hotel bars offer a luxury atmosphere with good service and a wide range of drinks and food; many provide live music or have nightclubs. Try O'Kim's (Map 9), JJ Mahoney's (Map 11) or Bobby London (Map 9).

Live music venues and dance clubs often have a cover charge of around W5000 but this includes a free drink.

See the Nightlife Zones section later for listings.

Noraebang

Noraebang is the Korean version of Japanese karaoke and consists of singing along to the backing track of a well-known song while reading the words on a screen. It's popular with people of all ages in Seoul and every Korean seems to be able to sing at least one song well.

The best way for any foreign businessman to really impress his Korean hosts is to go to a *noraebang* bar or room with them and perform a heartfelt version of Frank Sinatra's *My Way*.

The expensive option is to go to a *noraebang* bar, especially one with hostesses hovering around who applaud loudly to make you feel like a rock star. A cheaper option is for a group of friends to go to a private *noraebang* room to enjoy a sing-along on their own. There are lots of English-language songs to choose from and the cost is a modest W12,000 to W15,000 an hour. Most are open from 5pm to 2am, and you can buy beers and soft drinks. A few also have hostesses to help patrons have a good time – for a fee.

Cafés

Seoul has an astonishing variety of cafés, each with its own unique decor, music and atmosphere. Some are all-white, while others are all-black; some play classical music and have valuable old paintings on the wall, while others have walls decorated by their customers' scribbles and messages; some are tiny with room for only a handful of guests, while others are multistorey complexes with a dozen themed areas and room for hundreds of people; you can sit on modernistic plastic and metal chairs, on sofas, or on cushions on the floor.

Some cafés dream up all sorts of original fusion food and drink concoctions – cold fruit teas, alcoholic coffees, herbal infusions, red-bean drinks, rice punches, drinks flavoured with flowers and even tea mixed with coffee.

There are cafés full of dogs (see the boxed text 'Dog Mania in Apgujeong' later), cafés where the waiters entertain you with magic tricks, cafés where you can breathe pure oxygen, cafés where you can watch films, women-only cafés, live music cafés – the list is endless. You could write an entire book about the cafés in just one small area of Seoul.

Café drinks can cost as much as a cheap meal (W5000), but you can usually stay as long as you want. Meeting friends and chatting in unusual or luxurious cafés is part of the Seoul way of life.

See Nightlife Zones following for listings.

NIGHTLIFE ZONES

Unless indicated, admission to all venues is free.

Downtown (Maps 6, 8 & 9)

The downtown area is not noted for its nightlife but there are some hotel bars, such as O'Kim's and Bobby London.

O'Kim's *(☎ 317 0388; open 11.30am-2am daily)*, in the Westin Chosun Hotel, is popular with both Koreans and foreigners. It has darts, pool and bar football, as well an Irish band that plays at 8.30pm every night except Sunday. Irish stew is W18,000, lamb chops are W33,000 and the set dinner is W45,000. OB draught is W9000 but a Guinness is a record-breaking W22,000.

Bobby London *(☎ 317 7091; open 5pm-2am daily)* is a 'British-style' pub in the basement of Hotel Lotte, with draught beer, live music and themed rooms – you can choose Charles Dickens' study, a nautical cabin or a sports room. Happy hour is from 5pm to 8pm, with 50% discounts on draught beer.

Two hotel nightclubs are **Nix & Nox** *(☎ 3451 8444; open 6pm-3am daily)* in the Ritz Carlton Hotel, which has a bar, a pizza oven, live music, a disco and *noraebang* rooms, and **Areno's** *(☎ 317 3244; open 6pm-2am Sun-Thur, 6pm-3am Fri & Sat)* in the Hilton Hotel. This new Egyptian-themed entertainment zone has four DJs, different events every night, pub games and *noraebang*.

Buck Mulligan's *(☎ 3783 0004; Seoul Finance Centre)* is a very smart Irish bar that offers live rock music every evening between 8pm and 11.30pm, followed by a classical fusion band. Drinks are W10,000 for wine or W13,000 for Guinness.

Myeong-dong is mainly a shopping area but there are cinemas and plenty of restaurants and bars. It does have one unique live venue called **Feel** *(☎ 778 2401; admission W5000)*, an informal upstairs and downstairs den run by Shin Kyung-so and packed with the mementoes of a lifetime. It has live rock and folk music provided by Shin and his friends from 8pm to midnight daily. Admission includes a drink, and more drinks are also W5000. To get here, take subway Line 4 to Myeong-dong station, leave by Exit 10, walk to the elevated expressway, turn left and it's on the left past the school.

Itaewon (Map 11)

Most of Seoul's expat bars and clubs can be found in Itaewon, a shopping and entertainment street that caters to the US troops stationed nearby. It's the only area where you see lots of foreigners and it has a different atmosphere from the rest of Seoul.

The clubs open early but don't start getting busy until 10pm or later. Friday and Saturday nights have a real party atmosphere.

Bars Popular bars to start off the evening include the following:

Seoul Pub *(☎ 793 6666; open 3pm-2am daily)* is a friendly place and has a jukebox, pool, darts and meals, such as German sausages, Korean snacks and English shepherd's pie. Draught beer is W4000 and draught Guinness is W8000 a pint.

Gecko's *(☎ 749 9425; W www.geckosterrace.com; open 10am-2am daily)* is a popular, smart bar and eatery with a party atmosphere and loud music. Draught beer is W2500 (1.7L pitchers are W8000) while Newcastle Brown is W7000 and a Guinness is W10,000. More than 50 cocktails are available at W5000 to W7000. Pub meals and salads are W6000 to W10,000 and Mexican or Italian mains are W16,000 to W23,000. Lunch specials at W8000 to W12,000 include dessert and coffee.

3 Alley Pub *(☎ 790 0540; open 4pm-midnight daily)* has quickly become a popular watering hole. An English-style pub, it offers eight draught beers from W2500 (pitchers cost W9000) as well as pub grub that includes home-made sausages.

JJ Mahoney's *(☎ 797 1234; open 6pm-2am Sun-Thurs, 6pm-3am Fri & Sat)* is in the Grand Hyatt Hotel, which is on a hill overlooking Itaewon. You can play pool or darts here, as well as dance in the disco later on.

Nashville *(☎ 798 1592; W www.nashvilleclub.com; open 5pm-2am daily)* is an Itaewon institution. Its **Sports Pub** *(open noon-2am daily)* offers darts, pool, bar football and a jukebox (W500 for three songs). Draught beer is W2500 but W1700 during happy hours between 6pm and 8pm. Upstairs is **Club Caliente**, which gets hectic on Friday and Saturday nights as customers dance to the Latin beat. On the roof is an outdoor **rooftop beer garden**, a rare phenomenon in Seoul and the perfect place to cool off on a humid summer evening. The basement has a popular but scruffy diner with American action movies on the TV screen and paintings of cowboys on the walls. Burgers are W6000, vegie meals are W8000, barbecued chicken is W12,000 and steaks start at W18,000. Breakfasts are also served.

Hollywood Bar & Grill *(☎ 749 1659; open 4pm-2am daily)* is similar to Nashville but smarter; beer is W6000. The bar has a giant TV screen, pool and a dartboard, and the restaurant offers steak meals, imported wines and lunch specials.

Clubs The popular country-and-western **Grand Ole Oprey** has a large dance floor, scribbles on the walls, a huge library of LPs, beers at W2300 and salutes the American flag at midnight.

Nearby is **Chi-Chi**, which plays American '50s and '60s music, while **East'n'West** is more of a disco.

King Club *(☎ 790 8303; admission free; open 7pm-4am daily)* has been around for a fair time. A large dance place, it can get very crowded. Dancing girls put on various shows, and it stays open until 5am or later on weekends. The music ranges from rhythm and blues to hip-hop, and beers start at a reasonable W3000.

OB Stadium *(☎ 797 4663; open 11.30am-10pm daily)* has all-you-can-drink beer and soft drinks and all-you-can-eat beef and chicken dishes for W17,000. Alternatively, you can just drink all you want for W12,000. A two-hour limit applies on Friday and Saturday nights and it closes relatively early at 10pm. Facilities to help you enjoy yourself include *noraebang* and a dance floor with disco lights and a big screen.

Live Music Itaewon is not noted for cultural activities, but it does have some venerable live-music venues.

All That Jazz *(☎ 795 5701; admission free Mon-Wed, W3000 Thur-Sun; open 5pm-midnight daily)* has been operating since 1976 and is an intimate venue providing live jazz nightly. Piano music can be enjoyed from 7pm and then bands play from 9pm. Beers cost W6000 and meals such as seafood spaghetti cost W8000, while steaks are W15,000.

Just Blues *(☎ 749 0960; admission free Sun-Thur, W3000 Fri & Sat; open 7pm-2am daily)* is another Itaewon live-music institution. Beers cost W5000, the sofas are comfortable and live music (usually rhythm and blues) starts at 9pm. Sunday features live jam sessions.

JR Blue *(admission free)* is up the alley that goes past KFC and is another live-music venue that generally offers jazz, but sometimes blues. It's a funky dark cellar with candles on the tables and is more informal than the other two options. It also has a dance floor. Live music starts at 9.30pm and drinks cost W5000. When live music isn't being played, the bar staff have a choice of 6000 LPs as well as numerous CDs.

Woodstock *(☎ 334 1310; admission free; open 4pm-7am daily)* puts on some kind of live rock band every night at around 9pm and, although it's next to a church, that doesn't mean that the music volume is turned down. Darts and a pool table are also available and it's relaxing sitting on the sofas in spite of the psychedelic designs on the walls.

Hostess Bars These can be found all over Itaewon, but many are concentrated on the hill across the main road from the Hamilton Hotel, known locally as Hooker's Hill. Males walking around this area on their own or in groups will frequently be called 'honey' and offered a good time by scantily clad girls plastered in make-up. If you step inside one of these bars, a drink for yourself may cost only W5000, but a drink for one of the young ladies could set you back W20,000.

It's usually fairly obvious which bars are the hostess variety, as the staff are more scantily clad than elsewhere. Some have signs outside that read 'Sweetheart Club – Drink Food Woman', 'Woman & Cocktails' or the more subtle 'For Gentlemen', which is a strong hint about what you will find inside.

Gay & Lesbian Venues Itaewon has the only gay and lesbian bar and club scene in Seoul that attracts foreigners and English-speaking Koreans. Most venues huddle together in an alley near Hooker's Hill.

Why Not *(☎ 795 8193)*, a 'Male Meet Market' according to a sign there, is the leader of the pack, with a dance area, stools around the bar and a small stage for drag shows, which start at 11pm. Not much happens until 10pm, even on Friday and Saturday.

Always Homme *(☎ 798 0578)* is a large bar decorated with bric-a-brac that has a wide selection of drinks and English-speaking staff. Also in the area is the bar **Queen**.

Soho *(☎ 797 2280)* is a smart bar modelled on a London gay bar, while **Trance** *(☎ 797 3410)*, which has drag shows that are popular with foreigners, and **G**, are dance clubs.

California *(☎ 749 7738; open 6pm-late daily)* is down some steps off the main road. Quiet and comfortable, it was Itaewon's first gay bar. Beers are W5000, and there are tables and chairs or you can sit at the bar. There's a gay disco in a basement next door that is open and buzzing on Friday and Saturday nights.

Daehangno (Map 12)

Although Daehangno is best known for its small theatres (see the Theatre section later), it also has plenty of large restaurants and bars with outdoor sections. They are particularly popular on summer evenings, but even in cooler months the management supply outdoor heaters to encourage customers to sit outside under the stars. Different types of do-it-yourself entertainment are available in the **billiard halls**, the **Doore Bowling Centre**, as well as in a number of **noraebang** where you can enjoy a sing-along for W15,000 an hour.

Motzart Café *(☎ 744 7651)* near Marronnier Park has European-style decor and furniture, smart-looking staff and plays relaxing classical music. Tea, coffee and juices are W3500.

At **Mindeulreyeongto Café** *(Minto; ☎ 745 5234)* you pay W4000 for a drink with endless refills, enjoy free *ramyeon* noodles and watch free movies downstairs. There is a choice of seven themed rooms, all of which have different furniture, colours and style. One seems to be a school homework room. Special drinks are W5000 to W7000 and fusion meals cost W10,000.

The **Seoul Jazz Academy** is nearby and the stylish **Live Jazz Club** *(☎ 743 5555; admission W15,000; open 6.30pm-2am daily)* puts on three live bands every night. Everything in the club is black – the floor, the walls, the ceilings, the tables, the waiters' outfits and even the resident dog. The cover charge is steep but it includes a free drink, so you could sip it very, very slowly and enjoy two or three different jazz bands for the price. Further drinks are W7000 and meals are W25,000 for steak or salmon.

At **Bier Hall** *(☎ 744 9996)* the main attraction is 2.7L pitchers of draught OB lager for W10,500. Meals such as smoked pork or chicken are W11,000. The brick archways and murals give it a Mediterranean feel, although it is meant to be German style.

The **Red Lion Irish Pub** *(☎ 743 6331; open until 4am daily)* is not very Irish, like most of Seoul's Irish pubs, but does sell Guinness (W8500) and sometimes plays an Irish CD on the sound system.

Hudson's *(☎ 744 2255)* has a large outdoor patio and sells beers from around the world for W5000 to W9000. It also provides a wide range of food, including barbecue meals, German sausages, pig's feet and Caesar salad.

Other bars include **Chicago Sports Bar**; **Wild Bill's**, a restaurant bar with a cowboy theme; **Boogie Boogie Bar**, '50s American decor and music with a '56 Chevrolet Bel Air over the front door; and **Santana's** dark beer and Mexican food.

Hongik (Map 3)

Bars & Cafés There are hundreds of bars in the Hongik area, but **Gold** *(☎ 333 9905; open 5pm-6am daily)* is hard to beat. It has an English-speaking owner, wood cabin decor, bar food and, best of all, a draught beer or a shot of tequila costs only W1500.

Queen's Head *(☎ 3143 0757)* looks like an English pub, with rustic decor, leather armchairs, bar stools and even a Victorian fireplace, but the food is Italian and no English beers are available.

Y'sorno Cafe is a women-only feminist café with black decor.

Labris *(☎ 333 5276; open 3pm-2am Sun-Mon, 3pm-4am Sat)* is a low-key women-only lesbian bar. It has comfortable sofas and a big screen, and beers cost W4500.

Live Indie Music Clubs This area is famous for street murals and live indie music played in tiny underground music venues by bands with names like Psychy 69, Jacob's Ladder, X-sample, No Brain and Vaseline. The venues usually open around 6pm and stay open a couple of hours after the live music has ended. Live concerts usually run from 7pm to 10.30pm, but as with live music all over the world, musicians don't always start or finish on time. Entry is usually W5000 and this includes a drink, but it can go up to W15,000 for popular bands or special events.

Drug *(☎ 326 3085; admission W5000; open from 7.30pm Fri-Sun)* is the most famous live club and has been open since 1994. Its band Crying Nut is the only indie band that has made it in the mainstream music world and has so far put out three successful CDs. Their style is mainly punk rock: 'Shut up and listen to me!/We have to run/We can't become idiots/We have to gallop/We have to fight against lies/Let's gallop our horses'. Unfortunately the entire group were called up to do their military service in 2003 so they are going to be out of the music scene for two years. However, Lazy Bone is another act you can catch in the Drug cellar and their music style is described as 'ska punk rock'.

SLUG.er *(☎ 3142 0643; admission W5000 Tues-Thur, W6000 Fri-Sun; open Tues-Sun)* has a cover charge that includes a beer. Live indie bands (mainly rock and hip-hop) perform from 8pm to 10.30pm, but it doesn't close until 2am. Beers cost W4000.

Rolling Stones *(☎ 325 607; admission W7000-10,000; open Tues-Sun)* features live heavy-metal rock from 8pm to 11pm in a tiny cellar with no chairs. Admission includes a drink, otherwise beers are W5000, although the bar is hard to find – look for a cardboard box on the floor.

Free Bird *(☎ 333 2701; open 7.30-midnight daily; admission free)* is a rough-looking venue that puts on live music most nights from 7.30pm to 11pm. The live music varies from jazz and rock to death metal. Beers are W6000.

Dance Clubs Hongik is also Seoul's hot dance spot and offers a couple of excellent Latin American dance clubs, as well as a flock of techno, trance, house, rock, rap, funk, jungle and drum 'n' bass dance venues. Entry usually costs W5000 and includes a free drink, but some clubs charge more on Friday and Saturday nights.

Hongik Club Day happens once a month, usually on the last Friday of the month. Clubbers pay W15,000 and gain free entry to 10 dance clubs in the Hongik area. The clubs start to get busy after 10pm and you can roam around from club to club until you run out of energy or the sun rises. The music and atmosphere is different in each club, but what they all have in common is their small size, so expect some jostling on the dance floors. The clubs that currently participate in this scheme are nb, dd, Saab, Sk@, Hooper, Joker Red, Hodge Podge, MI, Myungwolgwam and matamata but this could change. Most of them are close to each other, so you shouldn't have trouble finding them even without the map that comes with the Club Day ticket.

Sk@ *(☎ 323 8750; admission W5000; open 7pm-5am daily)* is a typically tiny, cellar-like dance club, which has had three different owners in its 11-year life and plays rock and funk dance music. The admission price includes a beer, otherwise beers cost W3000.

Hodge Podge *(☎ 6259 2302; admission Sun & Tue-Thur W5000, Fri & Sat W10,000; open 7pm-4am Tue-Sun)* is another funky dance club. It plays rock, hip-hop, hardcore and every kind of dance music.

Macondo *(☎ 011-449 1660; admission Sun-Thur free, Fri & Sat W5000; open 7pm-midnight daily)* is near Hongik University subway station (Line 2) and is a Latin American dance club playing great music that makes everyone jump up and dance. It has a homely decor with candles on the tables and beers cost W3000. Entry on Friday and Saturday includes a drink.

PATRICK HORTON

The botanic garden glasshouse at Changgyeonggung

MARTIN VINCENT ROBINSON

Gardens along the Hangang River are a glorious carpet of colour in early summer

MARTIN VINCENT ROBINSON

Silkworm larvae *(ppeondaegi)* is a popular street stall snack

MARTIN MOOS

It is possible for vegetarians to feast in Seoul.

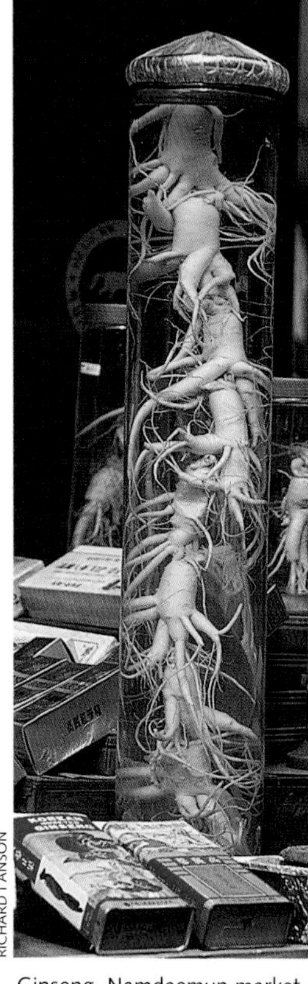

RICHARD I'ANSON

Ginseng, Namdaemun market.

SIMON CHARLES ROWE

Fast food near Changdeokgung

Bahia *(☎ 335 1512; admission W8000; open 6pm-midnight Tue-Thur, 6pm-2am Fri & Sat)* is another great Latin American dance club, but larger than Macondo. Admission includes a drink and beers sell for W3000.

Jazz Clubs Hongik has a number of live jazz venues and bars and cafés with jazz-type names also play jazz CDs for their customers.

Hot House Live Jazz *(☎ 332 2174; admission W6000; open 6pm-late daily)* puts on live jazz every night from 8.30pm to 11pm, with a jam session on Saturday. The cover charge includes a soft drink.

Be Bop Jazz Club *(☎ 338 4932)* has live jazz most nights and always on Friday, Saturday and Sunday. Drinks start at W5000. It's on the 5th floor (take the lift) and below it is a smart sports bar, a café and an Internet room.

Sinchon & Ewha (Map 3)

Sinchon becomes a neon wonderland in the evening, when it is packed with young people out for a good time. It merges with the shopping and eating area near Ewha Women's University.

Bars Many of the bars take their music very seriously and have a wall of CDs to choose from. Their names often have a musical theme like 'The Who', 'Lennon', 'Sting', 'Velvet Underground', 'Abba', 'Rolling Stone' and 'The Cure'. Some play requests from their customers.

Woodstock *(☎ 334 1310)* is a dark den with scribbles on the walls, rough-hewn tables and chairs, and is the place to go for loud rock music. Beer is W2000 a glass or W7000 a pitcher.

Doors *(☎ 334 54630; open 3pm-5am daily)* is similar to Woodstock but the music is not so loud. A 2L pitcher of beer costs W7500.

Beatles *(☎ 323 5463; open 8pm-5am daily)* is a basement bar opposite Doors with over 10,000 LPs. It describes itself as an 'old music bar'. The place looks like a log cabin, has an English-speaking owner and a beer costs W3000.

Birdland *(☎ 312 7021, open 11am-midnight daily)*, which is outside the back entrance of Ewha Women's University, has live jazz music from 7.30pm.

Free Crocodiles *(☎ 3141 4403)* has dark beer on draught (brewed in its own microbrewery) at W2000 for 500ml, sausages for W6500 and smoked chicken for W10,000, and free Internet access.

Voodoo *(☎ 336 5021; open 7pm-midnight Mon-Fri, 7pm-2am Sat & Sun)* plays interesting music and the staff speak some English. Cocktails cost W5000, while beers are W3500.

Wallflowers *(☎ 3142 5234; open 6pm-3am daily)* has a stylish black-and-chrome interior and plays quiet jazz music. Beers are W4000 and Guinness is W10,000.

Clubs Nearby Hongik has nearly all the clubs but there are a few in Sinchon.

Blue Monkeys *(☎ 322 0097; admission Sun-Thur W5000, Fri & Sat W7000; open 6pm-4am daily)* is a disco with balcony seats that plays 90% hip-hop music. The cover charge includes a drink and beers cost W5000.

Haeyuljae *(☎ 332 8955; admission W3000; open 6pm-late daily)* is an unusual club where patrons put on a wig, make-up and fancy dress – anything from army uniform to a monkey outfit or Dracula to a rabbit is available – be someone completely different. The cave-like club room has benches and sofas, disco lights and a screen, and is a good place to hold a party. It has a DJ on Friday and drinks cost W5000.

Cafés At **Bagdad Magic Cafe** *(☎ 336 2773; open 1pm-1am daily)* customers are regaled with magic tricks involving coins, cards, straws and rubber bands. The magic tricks are free, coffee is W4000 and food costs W5000 to W10,000. On Friday and Saturday evenings at 7pm and 9pm and on Sunday at 7pm, you can enjoy a 20-minute magic stage show. Oh Eun-young is an excellent performer and doesn't say a word. The stage shows are also free, but the prices rise to W4000 for a beer and W7000 for refillable coffee.

Bubble Tea Shop *(drinks W4000; open 8.30am-10pm Mon-Sat, 2pm-10pm Sun)* at the front entrance to Ewha Women's University sells a range of juices and teas. The bubble tea comes from Taiwan and has chewy black balls in it. The drink might sound strange but its popularity is spreading all over Asia.

South of the River (Map 6)

The alleys north of Gangnam subway station (Line 2) are crammed with cinemas, DVD rooms, Internet rooms, CD shops, bars and restaurants.

Woodstock *(☎ 556 9774; open 6pm-1am daily)* plays the usual '60s and '70s rock music, but the decor is smarter than its Sinchon namesake. Woodstocks seem to be multiplying. Beers cost W3000.

Dog Mania in Apgujeong

At present Koreans are more famous for eating dogs than loving them but this is changing. Dogs, the smaller the better, are fast becoming a must-have fashion accessory in the streets of Apgujeong (Map 6).

At **Igloo Fusion Dog Mania Café** in Apgujeong, customers are greeted by over 30 dogs of all shapes and sizes. They run freely around the café causing noisy chaos. Some customers go there with their own dogs, which adds to the bedlam. The menu has snacks for dog customers (chicken and doggy corned beef) as well as drinks and snacks for human customers, which start at W7000.

Patrasche is another dog café in Apgujeong, but less dogs are resident here so it's more peaceful. The chicken hamburger and tuna salad on the menu at W5000 is for dogs not humans.

Pet shops in Apgujeong add a new dimension to the phrase 'pampered pets'. They sell dog toothbrushes and poultry-flavoured toothpaste. Dog shoes cost W15,000 but you do get four of them, while pet jewellery cost W20,000. Other items on sale are dog backpacks – their owners keep tissues inside them. You can also buy dog hair dyes – dye your pet's ears purple or give him (or her) a fashionable green tail.

At **New Orleans Jazz** *(☎ 566 6676; open 3pm-1am daily)* you can listen to swing and jazz CDs as you relax in your armchair. Beer, coffee and tea cost W4500.

Rock Star 2000 *(☎ 558 7922)*, above Joyplanet, is decorated with car parts and customers sit on jazzily covered airline seats with plenty of legroom. The bar plays hip-hop music and beers start at W2000.

Joyplanet *(admission W7000)* has smart DVD rooms and offers free coffee, popcorn and Internet access.

XXXX Club *(☎ 019-669 1659; admission free)* is a techno dance club that attracts foreigners; beers are W5000.

On the same side of the road is **Gensia Oxygen Cafe**, which offers free oxygen when you buy drinks that range from W4500 to W7000.

The Apgujeong area is known more for its upmarket department stores and brand-name boutiques, but it does have some rather expensive nightlife.

Once In a Blue Moon *(☎ 549 5490; admission free; open 5pm-2am Mon-Sat, 5pm-1am Sun)* is a classy jazz club. Beer costs W10,000 and snacks start at W22,000. Live jazz bands play from 7pm to 8pm and from 8.30pm to 12.30am (until 11pm on Sunday).

Rock'n'Roll Bar *(open 8pm-5am daily)* attracts some foreigners but beers are W8000.

On the other side of Apgujeong subway station is **Rico's** *(admission W7000 Tues-Thur, W8000 Fri & Sat)*, a Latin American dance bar that's admission price includes a drink. To get here, take subway Line 3 to Apgujeong station, leave by Exit 4, turn right, then turn left at Mr Pizza, turn right at Hyundai golf driving range and it's on your left.

O'Kim's *(☎ 511 0778)* is on the 9th floor of the Gaonix Building opposite Hyundai department store. It has live music at 9pm and draught Guinness costs W10,000. A buffet lunch is W22,000, but bangers and mash or fish and chips are W19,000.

Tea Museum Cafe *(☎ 515 2350, open 10.30am-9pm daily)* is a shop, café and exhibition room. It stocks 80 teas from more than a dozen different countries around the world. Some teas have unusual names like gunpowder, snow and golden Buddha.

Unusual Teashops that Serve Unusual Teas

Insadong (Map 8) has many small teashops that serve traditional hot and cold teas made from roots, leaves, herbs and fruit. The teas are usually delicious and the teashop owners put a lot of effort into creating an unusual decor. Some are so full of old junk and works of art that there is hardly room for the customers. A cup of tea costs from W4000 to W6000 (as much as a cheap meal), but it's a quality product and is served with rice-cake snacks.

Dawon is opposite Kyongin Gallery and you can sit in the pleasant courtyard under the trees or on floor cushions in small rooms in a 19th-century building. The *omijacha* is a cold, delicious pink tea made from dried *omija* fruit the size of small currants – it's supposed to have five flavours. The *nokcha* (green tea) is unusual, as it's served with milk and syrup.

Yetchatjip (Old Teashop) is an old established teashop up some stairs that has an artistic bric-a-brac decor and half a dozen little songbirds flying around freely. It offers nine hot teas and seven cold ones – the hot *mogwacha* (quince tea) has a subtle fruity flavour, and the cold nashi-pear tea used to be enjoyed by Joseon kings and queens.

Dalsaeneun Dalman Saeng Gakhanda (Moon Bird Thinks Only of the Moon) is a romantically named teashop packed with plants and rustic artefacts. Bird song, soothing music and flowing water add to the atmosphere. Among the 14 teas on offer are some unusual ones – *gamipcha* is persimmon-leaf tea while *yeongjicha* is mushroom tea. The *saenggangcha* (ginger tea) has a peppery but sweet taste and is recommended.

Hakgyo Jongi Ttaeng Ttaeng Ttaeng (School Bell Goes Ding, Ding, Ding!) is owned by a famous Korean comedian and is furnished like an old school classroom with a blackboard and small wooden tables and chairs. The menu is written on a wooden school ruler. The *mogwacha* is excellent and has lots of real fruit.

Sinyetchatjip (New Old Teashop) has a junk-shop decor and a peacock and a monkey to entertain its customers who sit on cushions on the floor. The *maesilcha* (plum tea) is deliciously sweet and sour.

South African rooibos tea is popular and iced hibiscus tea is very pleasant. A cup of tea costs from W6000 to W10,000, and the classical music is free. Teapots and teacups are for sale too.

TEASHOPS

Teashops *(tabang)* offer a taste of old-style social life and are mainly found in Insadong (Map 8) – see the boxed text 'Unusual Teashops that Serve Unusual Teas'. While the drinks may be pricey at around W5000 per cup, you are paying for a special product that usually includes a rice-cake snack.

DVD BANG

A DVD *bang* (room) is the place to go to see Korean movies, as they can be shown with English subtitles. You watch the film in your own private room sitting on a comfortable sofa. The usual cost is W7000 per person (the same as a cinema ticket) and they are popular with dating couples. A DVD *bang* is a lot smarter than a *bideobang* (video room).

Cinecastle *(Map 3; ☎ 334 0627)* in Hongik charges W7500 for one person, W14,000 for two, W20,000 for three, W25,000 for four and W30,000 for five.

CINEMAS

Luxurious new multiplex cinemas with large screens and the latest sound equipment are opening all over Seoul. Films usually run from 11am to 11pm, but the **Freya Town Multiplex** (Map 4) in Dongdaemun shows films 24 hours a day and the **COEX Mall Multiplex** (Map 7) has some midnight films. The good news is that English-language films are shown in cinemas in their original language with Korean subtitles and are not dubbed. However, Korean-language movies don't have English subtitles, so it's better to see them in DVD *bang*, where they do have

English subtitles. Cinema tickets cost W7000 and seating is allocated so look at your ticket for the row and number of your seat.

The *Korea Herald* and the *Korea Times* print film listings on Friday, and you can also find listings and reviews on their websites at W www.koreaherald.co.kr and W www.koreatimes.co.kr. However, with the new multiplex cinemas having so many screens, many people just turn up and then wait in a nearby coffee shop until it is time for a particular film to begin.

The **Korea Film Archives** at Seoul Arts Centre (Map 2) screens classic Korean films with English subtitles during programmes that it runs every spring and autumn. This is a good opportunity to see Korean films that are not normally available.

Korean Films

DVD rooms are a great way to see Korean films subtitled in English in a private mini cinema – singles pay W7000 and couples W13,000. Korean films have improved markedly in recent years and the ones outlined below are some that are worth seeing.

Peppermint Candy (2000) is written and directed by Lee Chang-dong. Although bleak and sometimes brutal, this thought-provoking film begins with a man's suicide and then goes back in time, step by step, to reveal his tragic life. Ultimately it's the portrait of a romantic young man corrupted by his years in the army and police force. A complex and ambiguous film, it has real drama and substance.

JSA (2001) is a taut thriller directed by Park Chan-wook about a friendship that develops between soldiers on opposite sides of the Demilitarized Zone that separates North and South Korea. The theme of ordinary people from both Koreas caught up in the politics of a divided nation made this a memorable film about present-day realities and hopes of eventual reunification.

Crazy Marriage (2002) is an amusing film with a message that is directed by Yu Ha, a well-known poet. Gam Woo-sung plays an unemotional university lecturer who meets up with sexy Uhm Jung-hwa. The film focuses on their ups and downs in and out of bed. She marries a doctor, but their relationship continues. In one scene Gam refuses to eat a fancy birthday cake that Uhm gives him and eats a small tomato instead. That sums up his character and their relationship, which is a kind of 'crazy marriage'.

A Bungee Jump of Their Own (2001) is directed by Kim Dae-sung. A shy student, In-woo, falls in love with a girl called Tae-hee, but she is killed in an accident and he becomes a high-school teacher and marries someone else. The film becomes an emotionally charged drama when In-woo falls in love with one of his male students whom he believes is the reincarnation of Tae-hee. Any director who tackles the topic of homosexuality in Korea deserves a medal for bravery and somehow Kim Dae-sung makes this unlikely tale convincing.

Eunuch (1968) is a classic film directed by Shin Sang-ok, who was kidnapped together with his actress wife by North Korean secret agents in 1978 and forced to make films in the North until he escaped in 1986. Based on true events, this historical drama focuses on the eunuchs, who were employed in the Joseon palaces as sexless slaves, but sometimes rose to high positions in the government. The film also tells the tragic story of a woman forced to become the king's concubine by her father, although she loves someone else. An artistic film, it reveals what went on in those now-empty palaces in Seoul.

The Way Home (2002), written and directed by Lee Jeong-hyang, is an unsentimental but poetic study of an ancient rural grandma and her selfish, rude young grandson from Seoul who comes to stay with her. This unusual and engaging film was a surprise hit with local audiences.

Chihwasun (2002) won Im Kwon-taek the director's prize at the 2002 Cannes Film Festival. The film is based on the true story of a talented but wayward painter who lived at the end of the Joseon dynasty. A non-conformist, his life was a series of personal misfortunes that nevertheless inspired his best art.

My Sassy Girl (2001), directed by Kwak Jae-young, is a role reversal comedy about a girlish guy and his aggressive, bossy girlfriend. Based on a true story that was posted on the Internet, hilarious scenes and film parodies give this film a wider appeal than just the youth market.

KNTO *(Map 8; ☎ 757 0086; w www.knto.or.kr)* screens Korean films with English subtitles for free at 4pm on Tuesday and **Seoul Selection Bookshop** *(Map 8; ☎ 734 9565; w www.seoulselection.com)* shows Korean DVDs with English subtitles three times a week – Wednesday at 7.30pm, Saturday at 2.30pm and Sunday at 11.30am – and entry costs less than a cup of coffee. The **Seoul Art Cinema** at Art Sonje (Map 8) screens artistic films from around the world.

The gold-tinted 63 Building (Map 5) on Yeouido has a large screen **Imax Cinema**. Adult tickets cost W6000 and English is available on headphones.

THEATRE

Seoul has a very lively small-theatre scene mainly based around the area northwest of Hyehwa subway station (Line 4) in Daehangno (Map 12), but also in Hongik (Map 3). Admission prices are generally W8000 to W25,000.

Although Seoul's theatre performances are usually in Korean, **Munye Theatre** (Map 12) and **Hakjeon Green Theatre** *(Map 12; w www.hakchon.co.kr)* sometimes have a screen by the stage that shows English subtitles. Munye Theatre is also the centre of the annual Dance Festival, which includes local and foreign dance groups.

Large theatres often put on musicals like *Taekwon* and *Nanta* that can be enjoyed by foreigners since there are few or no words. Check w event.kf.or.kr to find out what's on.

Marronnier Park (Map 12) is a busy and free performance area in Daehangno. On a typical summer Saturday or Sunday afternoon, high-school rock bands play on the glass-roofed stage, while a traditional *samulnori* troupe bang their drums and cymbals and dance under the chestnut trees. A white-faced clown entertains children, and nearby 'Mr Guitar', a musician and comedian, performs in front of a large and appreciative audience. Later, traditional masked dancers in white, long-sleeved gowns go through their slow-motion routines. In contrast, teenagers are practising their hip-hop moves – there's a **hip-hop school** behind the park. At the entrance to the park, a group of Christians sing songs and smile at everybody who stops to listen. In one corner a group of young artists draws portraits for a fee.

Seoul Norimadang (Map 7)

This outdoor circular arena for traditional performances *(☎ 414 1985)* puts on excellent and entertaining two-hour free shows that usually start at 3pm on Saturday and Sunday in April, May, September and October. Shows start at 5pm in the heat of summer from June to August. Local pensioners in the audience get up and dance in a stately manner.

To get here take subway Line 2 or 8 to Jamsil station, take Exit 3, go straight, cross the road and turn left – it's only a few minutes' walk. If you are in Lotte World, walk through Baby World and take the stairs on your right.

Seoul Arts Centre (Map 2)

This huge cultural complex *(☎ 580 1300; w www.sac.or.kr)* has a circular **opera house** with a roof shaped like a Korean nobleman's horse-hair hat and seats over 2000 people. Other theatres here are the 700-seat **Towal Theatre**, the smaller **Chayu Theatre** and a large **concert hall**.

To get here, take subway Line 3 to Nambu Bus Terminal station and leave by Exit 5. You can take a frequent shuttle bus (W400), or walk to the end of the bus station building, turn left and Seoul Arts Centre is at the end of the road – a 15-minute walk.

National Centre for Korean Traditional Performing Arts (Map 2)

The Centre for Korean Traditional Performing Arts *(☎ 580 3300; w www.ncktpa.go.kr)*, next door to the Seoul Arts Centre, includes two theatres and a **museum** *(☎ 580 3333; admission free; open 9am-6pm Tues-Sun)* that houses unusual musical instruments from Korea and around the world. The *eo* is a wooden tiger, which is played by scraping a bamboo stick over the 27 teeth on its back.

Every Saturday from March to December eight different styles of traditional music, singing and dancing are performed starting at 5pm; tickets cost W10,000 and W8000 (students half-price). Numerous other traditional performances are held here.

National Theatre (Map 9)

The splendid National Theatre *(☎ 2274 3507; W www.ntok.go.kr)* building houses two theatres and a restaurant, but is inconveniently located near Namsan.

To get here, take subway Line 3 to Dongguk University station, leave by Exit 6 and walk for 20 minutes up the hill past Hotel Shilla. Alternatively, you can take a taxi (W2000) or hop onto bus No 17 at the subway station.

Cheongdong Theatre (Map 9)

The Cheongdong Theatre *(☎ 751 1500; W www.chongdong.com; open Tues-Sun)* puts on 1½-hour performances of traditional music, singing and dancing at 8pm (from April to September) and at 4pm (from October to March). An excellent feature is that English subtitles appear on a screen and explain the meaning of the songs. After the show you can also take photographs of the performers in their traditional clothes. Tickets cost W30,000 to W40,000 but there are discounts for students.

To get here, take Line 1 or 2 to City Hall subway station, leave by Exit 1 and it's a five-minute walk along Deoksugung wall.

Sejong Centre for the Performing Arts (Map 8)

Conveniently located in the downtown area, this centre *(☎ 399 1700; W www.sejongpac.or.kr)* is a lively arts complex that puts on numerous drama, music and art shows, including an annual drum festival. It has a grand hall, a small theatre and three art galleries.

Hoam Art Hall (Map 9)

Hoam Art Hall *(☎ 751 9614)* is a performing arts centre with a seating capacity of 1000 and puts on a varied programme of events.

Theatre Restaurants

The **Sheraton Walker Hill Hotel** *(Map 2; ☎ 455 5000; W www.walkerhill.co.kr)* puts on a 1½-hour show twice nightly that includes traditional Korean music and dance and a Western-style glitzy cabaret revue. The two shows and dinner costs W69,000.

Korea House *(Map 9; ☎ 2266 9101; W www.koreahouse.or.kr; open noon-2pm, 5.30pm-7pm & 7.30pm-8.50pm daily)* offers a sumptuous buffet of traditional Korean food and drink for W30,000 (lunch) or W33,000 (dinner) in a restored *yangban* house. Set menus of court food cost W50,000 to W80,000. Every evening top performers put on a one-hour folk music and dance show, which costs W29,000. The shows start at 7pm and 8.50pm every day, except Sunday when only one show is performed at 8pm.

CASINOS

The only casino *(Map 2; ☎ 456 2121)* in Seoul is at the Sheraton Walker Hill Hotel. Open 24 hours a day, it offers the usual ways of losing money – machines, roulette, poker, black jack, baccarat, big wheel and *tai-sa*. Snacks – cornflakes, sandwiches and rice and noodle dishes – are free. Free drinks are also available at the gaming tables. Minimum bets start at W2500 or W5000. There is no dress code and Korean nationals are not allowed.

To get here, take subway Line 5 to Gwangnaru station and leave by Exit 2. Then take a taxi (W2000) as it's a 1km, 20-minute uphill walk.

SEOUL RACECOURSE (MAP 2)

Seoul Racecourse *(☎ 509 2337, fax 509 2309; admission W800; open 11am-5.30pm Sat & Sun, but closed 5 weekends of the year)* offers foreigners a special luxury suite in the impressive grandstand – take lift No 6 up to the 6th floor. You get a great view of the horse racing and the surrounding hillsides from the suite and the English-speaking staff will help you fill in the betting slips. A booklet in English gives the form of the horses and all sorts of other information.

Two giant outdoor screens on the course (as well as numerous small screens in the suite) show close-ups of the racing action. Short races over 1km or 2km take place every half-hour between 11am and 5.30pm at the weekend.

The only other horse-racing track is far away on Jejudo and options for gamblers in Seoul are limited, so race days are crowded with some 30,000 mainly male punters, but everything is organised and convenient – the only problem is picking the winners.

To get here, take subway Line 4 to Seoul Racecourse station, leave by Exit 2 and go along the covered walkway to the entrance.

ROCK CONCERTS

Concerts featuring top local bands and famous groups from Western countries usually take place in one of the stadiums in Olympic Park (Map 7) or Jamsil Sports Complex (Map 7). Ticket prices are W40,000 to W70,000. Check the newspapers, websites or **KNTO** *(Map 8; ☎ 757 0086; W www.knto.or.kr)* for details about any big musical events.

SPECTATOR SPORTS

Watching live sport is something all visitors can enjoy on a visit to Seoul. It is relatively inexpensive and there is no language barrier. Check with the **KNTO** *(Map 8; ☎ 757 0086; W www.knto.or.kr)* for dates, times and details of matches and tournaments.

Baseball

South Korea won a bronze medal for baseball at the Sydney Olympics in 2000 and has had a professional league since 1982, with teams sponsored by local *jaebol* corporations. General admission to matches is W5000, and the season runs from April to July and from August to October.

Matches are held at Jamsil Baseball Stadium (Map 7) and at a baseball stadium in Dongdaemun (Map 4) – you can get a free view from the food court of the nearby mall.

Soccer

Soccer has become much more popular due to the heroic efforts of the South Korean team in the 2002 FIFA World Cup finals, which were cohosted by South Korea and Japan. Although most of their players came from the semiprofessional home league, the South Korean team reached the semifinals and defeated multimillion dollar teams from Europe. See the boxed text 'Asia's Best Soccer Team' for more information. Soccer matches are played from April to October at Olympic Stadium (Map 7) and World Cup Stadium (Map 2).

Asia's Best Soccer Team

The FIFA World Cup finals of 2002 were cohosted by South Korea and Japan and the two countries (normally arch-rivals) cooperated to put on a very successful tournament. South Korea spent billions of won building 10 new soccer stadiums around the country, even though each one only hosted three matches.

Seoul became a sea of red on the days that the Korean team was playing, as soccer fans watched the matches on giant outdoor screens put up around the capital. Up to two million people packed the streets sporting 'Be The Reds' T-shirts and red headscarves and with the national flag painted on their faces. The cheering and chanting started hours before the matches began and continued late into the night whenever the team won, which was quite often. The celebrations were the wildest seen in Seoul in recent times. Any player who scored a goal became an instant national hero whose name was on everyone's lips.

The Korean team, inspired by the fervent public support and guided by their experienced Dutch coach, Guus Hiddink, were skillful, fast and hard-working. Incredibly, they defeated Poland, Portugal, Spain and then Italy before losing 1-0 to Germany, and became the first Asian team to reach the semifinals of the World Cup.

Keeping ahead of their main Asian neighbours and rivals, Japan and China, is South Korea's aim in the future – and not just on the soccer field.

Basketball

Ten teams play in the Korean basketball league and matches are played from November to April, usually at Jamsil Gymnasium (Map 7). Two foreign players (usually Americans) are allowed in each team.

Ssireum

Ssireum is Korean-style wrestling, which is more similar to Mongolian wrestling than Japanese sumo wrestling. Wrestlers start off kneeling, then grab their opponent's piece of cloth, called *satba,* which is tied around the waist and thighs, and try to throw each other to the ground. Tournament winners are given the title of *changsa,* 'the strongest man in the world' and they used to be given a live bull as a prize. National tournaments were first held in 1959.

You can watch *ssireum* at Jangchung Gymnasium (Map 9).

Taekwondo

The headquarters and main hall for taekwondo competitions is at the World Taekwondo Federation (Map 6), which has equipment shops and a small museum as part of the complex. See the Activities section of the Things to See & Do chapter for more details.

Shopping

Seoul is a shopper's paradise, with plenty of traditional markets, electronics bazaars, underground arcades, upmarket department stores and glitzy malls full of fashion boutiques and brand-name goods.

TAX REFUNDS

Global Refund *(☎ 776 2170, fax 776 2177; W www.globalrefund.com)* and **Korea Refund** *(☎ 537 1755)* are the two companies offering schemes that give you a partial refund on the VAT that is included in the prices of all the goods you buy in Korea. If you spend more than W30,000 or W50,000 in certain shops, you can claim a cash refund at Incheon International Airport before you fly out of the country.

Just shop at a department store, mall or souvenir shop that participates in one of the schemes. The retailer gives you a special receipt, which you must show, together with the goods you bought, to a customs officer at one of the customs declaration desks in Incheon airport. Go there before checking in your luggage, as the customs officer will want to see the items before stamping your receipt.

Go through immigration and show your stamped receipt at the relevant refund desk, which you will find next to the duty-free shops. They will give you your won refund in cash or by cheque. There is a bank nearby if you want to change your won into a foreign currency, or you can spend your refund in one of the many shops and restaurants.

But don't get too excited – the refunds range from 5% to 7%. Spend W100,000 and you will receive a W5000 refund, spend W500,000 and you will get W34,000 back.

WHAT TO BUY

Popular items for foreign tourists and merchants to buy in Seoul include clothes, shoes and bags, which are available from Namdaemun Market (Map 9) and Dongdaemun Market (Map 4). Large sizes in clothes and shoes can be difficult to find but should be obtainable in Itaewon (Map 11). Electronic goods are also popular – try Yongsan Electronics Market (Map 6) and Techno Mart (Map 7). For sports equipment try Dongdaemun Market (Map 4); spectacles are available at Namdaemun Market (Map 9) and National Souvenir Centre in Myeong-dong (Map 9). To purchase red ginseng look around Gyeongdong Market (Map 4) and Namdaemun Market (Map 9). Joseon-dynasty antiques and traditional handicrafts can be found at Insadong (Map 8) and Janghanpyeong Antiques Market (Map 2).

Make Your Own Korean Teas

The following ingredients can all be bought at Gyeongdong Market (Map 4).

Omijacha First buy some dried *omija* (it looks like peppercorns) – the cheaper quality is good enough. Put one heaped tablespoon of *omija* into a large cup, half fill the cup with water and leave it to soak overnight. Next morning, strain out the *omija*, fill the cup with water, add one heaped tablespoon of sugar or honey and heat it up in a microwave or saucepan. This delicious fruit tea is said to combine five different flavours. Most people prefer to drink it cold but you can also drink it hot.

Nokcha Put two heaped tablespoons of green tea leaves into a large cup. Pour in boiling water and stand for five minutes. Take out the green tea leaves and drink. Nokcha has a mild and delicate flavour.

Daechucha Buy some dried *daechu* (jujubes or dried Chinese red dates), cut up 15 of them and put them in a saucepan with three cups of water. Simmer for 30 minutes, then mash the dates, add two level tablespoons of sugar and simmer for another 10 minutes. Strain immediately and let it cool before putting it in the fridge – it should be enough to make one cup.

Prices for foreigners are dependent on the exchange rate but there are lots of good buys, although real bargains are harder to find.

Ginseng

Ginseng, the wonder root, is always a popular purchase, especially with Asian visitors, and it appears in all sorts of products. You can chew it, eat it, drink it, clean yourself with it or bath in it. Ginseng tea, ginseng wine, ginseng soup, ginseng chewing gum, ginseng chocolate, ginseng soap and ginseng bath salts are just some of the ways of benefiting from its well-known health-giving properties.

Teas

A wide range of unusual teas are available in department stores and supermarkets. Powdered instant teas are not as good as the authentic tea you can drink in a tea shop, but they are easy to carry home. Ginseng tea is expensive (red ginseng tea is likely to cost W9000 for 150g) but the others, such as ginger, lemon, pine needle and green tea, are reasonably priced. The **Tea Museum Café** *(Map 6; ☎ 515 2350, open 10.30am-9pm)* in Apgujeong sells teas from around the world.

Regional Liquors

An amazing range of alcoholic drinks are produced in the different regions of Korea, and they are sold in all kinds of glass and ceramic bottles.

Prize-winning rice wines include Baekseju, which is 13% alcohol and is made from rice, yeast, ginseng and 10 medicinal herbs. A 375ml bottle costs W3200 – less than a cup of tea in a teashop. Geumsan Insamju is similar but without the medicinal herbs and the recipe is 600 years old. Daechusul is flavoured with malt, pine needles and jujube.

Jirisan Bokbunja comes from Jeollabukdo and is made from wild berries, while Royal King is expensive and made from *naju* pears. Time of Kings is based on a royal-court recipe and is made from rice, chrysanthemum flowers, pine needles and ginseng.

Jeonju Leegangju is a 25% proof *soju* flavoured with pear, ginger, cinnamon and honey. Moonbaesool is another *soju*-like liquor based on a 1000-year-old recipe.

Ppeondaegi

This silkworm larvae snack is sure to delight your friends and can be bought in a tin at supermarkets and convenience stores and taken home as a souvenir.

Leather

Leather jackets, belts, wallets, purses, bags and shoes are a Seoul speciality. A huge range of locally produced and reasonably priced leather goods are available.

CDs

Expect to pay around W11,000 for a Korean CD and W14,000 for a foreign album. **Musicland** *(Map 8; ☎ 278 2422)* and **Kyobo Bookshop** *(Map 8; ☎ 3973 5100)* have large, well-organised selections of local and Western rock, jazz and classical music, as well as the latest releases. Small music stores in the Hongik University area (Map 3) often specialise in one particular type of music.

South of the river there are a couple of good CD stores near Gangnam subway station (Line 2): try **TPA** *(Map 6)* on one side of the road and **Tube** *(Map 6; ☎ 523 7742)* on the other. In the COEX Mall (Map 7), **Evan** *(☎ 602 1000)* has a café and a wide selection of music.

DVDs

DVD prices vary with the title but around W22,000 is usual. If you want to buy Korean feature films on DVD with English subtitles, **Seoul Selection Bookshop** *(Map 8; ☎ 734 9565)* has an interesting range to choose from.

Books

There are three large bookshops downtown: **Kyobo Bookshop** *(Map 8; ☎ 3973 5100)*, **Yeongpung Bookshop** *(Map 8; ☎ 399 5600)* and **Jongno Bookshop** *(Map 8; ☎ 732 2331)*, sell English-language books and magazines. However, **Bandi & Luni's** *(☎ 6002 6002; open 10.30am-9pm daily)* in the COEX Mall (Map 7) probably has the best selection and is worth a browse. **Seoul Selection Bookshop** *(Map 8; ☎ 734 9565)* has books about all aspects of Korean culture in English. **Shoestring Travel** *(Map 3; ☎ 333 4151)* near Hongik University

Hanbok

The striking traditional clothing worn by Koreans is known as *hanbok* and is as much part of the local culture as *hangeul* and *gimchi*. Traditionally the women wore a loose-fitting short blouse with long sleeves and a voluminous long skirt, while the men wore a jacket and baggy trousers. In winter, overcoats were worn over the top. The exact designs varied over the centuries but maintained their basic pattern of simple lines and were an elegant and stylish costume. Generally using plain colours, some parts could be embroidered and the very rich could afford silk *hanbok*.

Hanbok style followed Confucian principles of unadorned modesty. In those days you could tell a person's occupation and status from the *hanbok* they wore, as clothes were a symbol of status and were strictly regulated. For instance, only the *yangban* could wear the black horse-hair hats that were a badge of their rank. Scholars (invariably male in those days) wore plain white as did the peasant class. Yellow was reserved for royalty.

In today's markets and shops you can buy modern or traditional *hanbok*. The everyday kind of *hanbok* is reasonably priced but the formal styles, made of silk and intricately embroidered, cost an arm and a leg.

Nowadays *hanbok* is usually only worn at weddings and other special occasions. Men prefer Western suits or casual wear, and most women find *hanbok* uncomfortable and unflattering. It restricts their movements, has no pockets and is difficult to clean.

is the Lonely Planet agent and is the place to go for a particular Lonely Planet book.

Lacquerware

A Korean speciality is lacquerware, which is made using a black paint that comes from the sap of the lacquer tree; Wonju city is a famous production centre. In the past, taxes could be paid to the government in the form of lacquer. Lacquerware is often inlaid with mother-of-pearl or ox horn.

Souvenirs

Colourful macramé and embroidery, boxes made of handmade paper *(hanji)*, wooden masks, lacquerware boxes inlaid with mother-of-pearl, painted wooden wedding ducks and fans can be found in the souvenir shops. More expensive items include pale green celadon pottery, reproduction Joseon-dynasty furniture and *hanbok* dresses – the more embroidery on it, the more expensive it will be. Silk, fur or leather clothes are other options. Shirts or blouses made of lightweight *ramie* material are an unusual fashion item that you can buy.

If you fall in love with dried seaweed *gim* or pickled cabbage *gimchi*, you can buy them in sealed packages and take them home with you.

Good-quality handicraft souvenirs are available in Insadong (Map 8), in the **National Souvenir Centre** *(Map 9; ☎ 778 6529; W www.souvenir.or.kr; open 10.30am-9pm daily)* – see the Myeong-dong section later for details – and in the **Korea House Souvenir Shop** *(Map 9)* near Namsangol Traditional Village.

WHERE TO SHOP

Dongdaemun Market (Map 4)

This huge, sprawling wholesale and retail shopping area combines traditional markets and street stalls with modern high-rise shopping malls. The 30,000 stores and stalls are supplied by 50,000 local manufacturing companies. The area is buzzing with activity all day and all night and it never completely closes, as different parts of the market have different days off.

Basic clothing, leather jackets and goods, local fashion brands and shoes are reasonably priced, and many Russian merchants come here regularly and have offices near the market. You can even eat in **PYCCKUU**, a Russian restaurant (see the Places to Eat chapter for details). A complete new kit of trousers, a shirt, socks, underwear and backpacker sandals can cost less than W40,000 if you bargain.

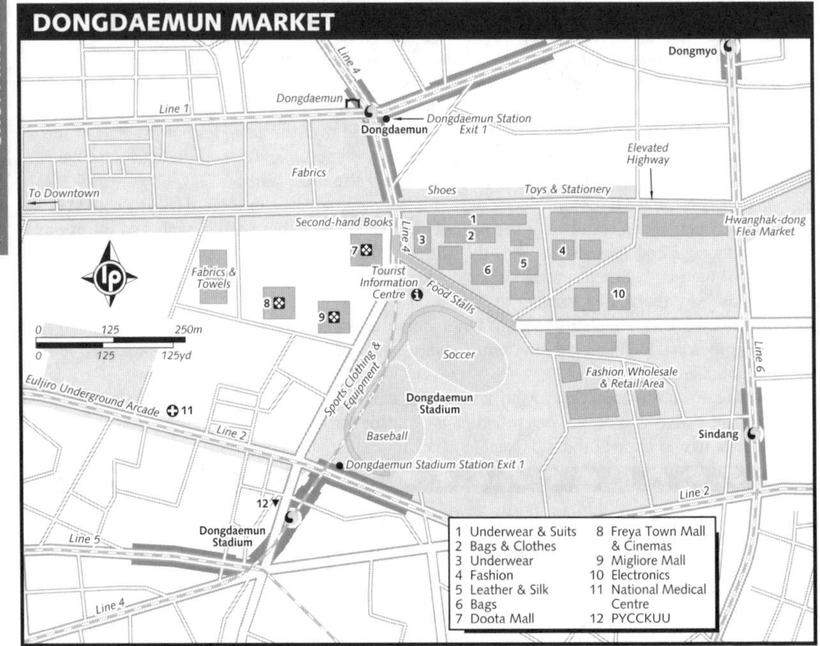

Doosan Tower (Doota), **Migliore** and **Freya Town** are three new high-rise shopping malls with food courts and entertainment areas. Each building is occupied by more than 2000 small retailers who sell mainly clothes, accessories, shoes, toys and imported goods. Freya Town has a whole floor of toys. All three malls are open from 10.30am to 5am every day except Monday, so insomniacs can shop all night. Freya Town's 10-screen **cinema multiplex** is also open all night and shows films 24 hours a day – night-owls are well catered for in Seoul. Concerts and talent shows sometimes take place in the evening on the open-air stages near the entrances to the malls.

The **Dongdaemun Market Information Centre** *(☎ 2254 3300, fax 2254 1676; W www.dongdaemun.com; open noon-10pm daily)* on the 2nd floor of the Tourist Information Centre in front of the baseball stadium provides translation and export advice services for big spenders.

To get to the market, take subway Line 1 or 4 to Dongdaemun station and leave by Exit 6 or 7. An alternative is to take subway Line 2, 4 or 5 to Dongdaemun Stadium station and leave by Exit 1.

Namdaemun Market (Map 9)

This is another traditional day-and-night retail and wholesale market, which is mixed in with new fashion malls (such as **Good & Good** and **Mesa**) and **Shinsegae**, an upmarket department store with a supermarket in the basement that opens from 10.30am to 7.30pm daily (closed the 1st and 3rd Monday of each month). Mesa sells mainly clothes and accessories, has restaurants on the 8th and 9th floors, and is open from 11am to 7am Monday to Saturday.

Smaller and more compact than Dongdaemun, Namdaemun offers a wider range of goods and services and never closes, as some parts are always open for business. Backpacking equipment, *hanbok,* children's clothes, ginseng, dried seaweed, fresh food and flowers, imported and household goods, spectacles, watches and handicrafts can all be found in the market area. Namdaemun underground arcade sells those food and drink items you might be missing from home, such as peanut butter, chocolate spread, tortilla chips and Scotch whiskey. The variety and cheap prices attract both tourists and locals.

Food stalls and restaurant alleys in the market offer cheap meals. The small restaurants have plastic models of the meals and clearly marked prices, which makes choosing what to eat easy.

The **Namdaemun Market Information Centre** *(☎ 2128 7800, fax 2128 7803; W www.namdaemunmarket.co.kr; open noon-10pm daily)*, on the 13th floor of Mesa Fashion Town, can help serious shoppers with translation, export procedures and so on.

To get here, take subway Line 4 to Hoehyeon station, leave by Exit 5 and you will be in the market near Gate 6 with the tourist information bureau on your right.

Gyeongdong Market (Map 4)

This market specialises in traditional Asian herbal medicines and dried food, but also has a good fruit and vegetable section, and general merchandise is sold on the fringes. Leaves, bark, herbs, seeds, roots, flowers, mushrooms, seaweed, fruit, prawns, fish and frogs are all dried and put on sale here.

Bark is sold to be made into medicinal soup, while *gine* is a long millipede that is boiled to make a soup or eaten dry. It is said to be good for backache and a handful costs W6000. Prickly pear fruit is sold as a remedy for coughs and colds, aloe leaves are said to be good for your skin and stomach, and the dried fungus is said to lower blood pressure.

Turn left at the Chohung bank for two arcades that specialise in ginseng, honey and dried mushrooms – one is underground and one is on the 2nd floor.

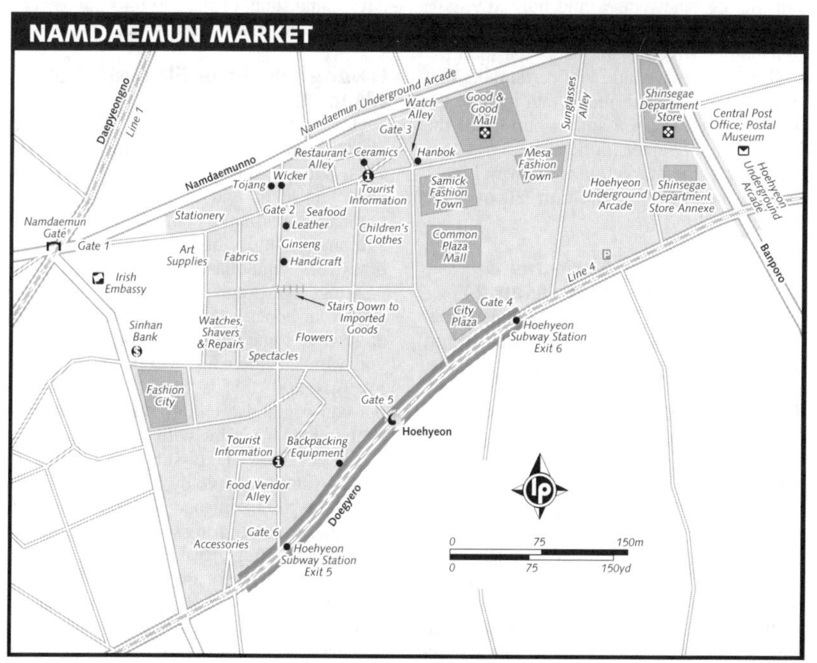

Most stalls in the fresh fruit and vegetable section have prices marked, which makes shopping here convenient. Unusual fruits like mulberries turn up when they are in season.

Gyeongdong market opens from 8am to 6.30pm but is partly closed on the first and third Sunday of each month.

To get here, take subway Line 1 to Jegi-dong station and leave by Exit 2.

Noryangjin Fish Market (Map 5)

This is the largest fish and seafood market in Seoul, and every kind of marine life imaginable is swimming around in tanks, buckets and bowls – it's a free aquarium show that is well worth a visit. The market is south of Yeouido and is open daily from 1am to 9pm.

Giant octopus, prawns, mussels and crabs are on view and on sale. Dried and pickled sea food is also available, but the fresh fish is the big attraction. A large plate of raw fish on salad costs W15,000, which is a good deal considering what you would normally have to pay. The strangest looking and tasting item is *meongge,* which is an orange sea squirt.

Upstairs are a handful of restaurants that specialise in raw fish meals that include the bones cooked up in a spicy soup – see the Places to Eat chapter for details.

To get to the market, take subway Line 1 to Noryangjin station and turn left over the railway tracks.

Janghanpyeong Antiques & Collectables Market (Map 2)

This market, open 10am to 7pm daily but closed on the first and third Sunday of the month, is made up of **Samhui Arcade**, **Woosung Arcade** and **Songwha Arcade**. They house numerous small antique shops that are crammed from floor to ceiling with all kinds of things that are either old or have been made to look old.

Wood carvings, paintings, embroidery, furniture, books, musical instruments, swords, celadon pottery and teapots are piled up in the dusty shops. Large stone statues are lined up outdoors and even the corridors are full of vintage items. Some shops specialise in old clocks, radios, telephones, cameras and other collectables. Prices aren't cheap – US$600 for a reproduction Joseon-dynasty chest and W800,000 for a *heungbae,* the embroidered status symbol worn by Joseon scholars, generals and government officials.

The atmosphere is quiet and uncrowded compared to the other markets, and coming here is like stepping into a time machine and going back into Seoul's past when tea-drinking Joseon-dynasty scholars debated Confucian principles and dabbled in calligraphy and art.

To get here, take subway Line 5 to Dapsimni station and leave by Exit 2. Over on the right is an orange-tiled building, which is Samhui Building No 6. Next door is Samhui No 5 and a few minutes further down the road is Samhui No 2. Walk back past the subway and continue walking for five minutes and you reach the Woosung and Songwha arcades. Outside Exit 3 of Dapsimni subway station is a cheap lunch counter called **Jenkseokjeomun** – W2000 for *gimbap* (sushi) and soup, or W2500 for *jajangmyeon* (noodles with black-bean sauce).

Hwanghak-dong Flea Market (Map 4)

Nicknamed Dokkaebi (Goblin Market), tens of thousands of second-hand LPs, cassettes, CDs, videos and DVDs are for sale on pavement stalls and in small shops at this market. Second-hand clothes, shoes, sporting equipment, tools, bric-a-brac, collectables, brasswork, Buddhas, musical instruments, paintings, books and pottery turn the area into a giant car-boot sale open from 8am to 6.30pm daily (but some stalls close on Sunday). If you want a video for W1000 or a bicycle for W10,000, this is the place to come – but you could also end up taking some very strange luggage home with you.

To get here, take subway Line 2 to Sindang station, leave by Exit 1 and then go left along the main road for 50m. Turn left into the covered **Jungang Market**, which sells food and general items. At the end of the market, carry on straight ahead and you will come to the flea market spread out in front of the elevated highway. It's a 15-minute walk from the subway station.

Yongsan Electronics Market (Map 6)

The Yongsan Electronics Market is probably the largest electronics market in Asia, with 5000 small shops spread around almost a dozen buildings. Everything from household appliances and lighting fixtures to the very latest mobile phones, digital cameras, video cameras, DVD players, music players, wide-screen TVs, computers and computer accessories are on sale. If you can plug it in, you can find it here. Prices are lower than elsewhere but are not generally marked on the products. The market is open from 9.30am to 7.30pm daily, although some sections close on the first and third Sunday of each month.

Surprisingly, there are few food options at present, but **Monghyeop Supermarket** has food on the 1st floor and gift items, such as ginseng, tea and souvenirs, on the top floor.

To get here, take subway Line 1 to Yongsan station and you will find yourself on the 3rd floor of the terminal complex. To leave the building via the covered walkway, go down to the 2nd floor. Four other covered walkways in other parts of the market help you get from building to building.

Techno Mart (Map 7)

Techno Mart is another electronics mall that fills up most of a high-rise building. It is less overwhelming than Yongsan Electronics Market and easier to find your way around. A fun feature is the food court on the B1 floor, which has 40 outlets that offer banquet-sized meals on large platters and giant ice-cream desserts at very reasonable prices. On the 10th floor is a **cinema multiplex**. Techno Mart is open from 10am to 8pm daily, but most shops close on the second and fourth Tuesday of every month.

To get here, take subway Line 2 to Gangbyeon station and leave by Exit 1.

Itaewon (Map 11)

This 1.5km shopping street has sprung up to cater to the American soldiers stationed at the nearby Yongsan military base. Most of the 2000 retailers speak some English, and tailor-made suits and shirts are a speciality. Custom-made shoes in leather, ostrich skin and eel skin are also available. Such diverse items as antique and modern furniture, hip-hop fashion clothes and purple amethyst jewellery are on sale along with piles of T-shirts and handicraft souvenirs. Opticians in this area speak some English if you want to buy a pair of glasses. Shops are generally open from 9am to 9pm and street stalls help to create a market atmosphere.

Insadong (Map 8)

This fascinating shopping street is traffic-free on Sunday, a scheme that is likely to extend to other days too, which will make shopping a more pleasant experience. Numerous small shops sell art and craft goods,such as pottery, antiques, calligraphy brushes and *hanji*. Works of art can be viewed and bought in more than 50 small art galleries and Korean traditional snacks can be bought from stalls that generally operate at the weekend.

A novelty shop to look out for is the **North Korea Souvenir Shop**. Not much is on display here, but you can buy North Korean cigarettes, ginseng and liquor, as well as oddities such as painted pebbles for W10,000 and Demilitarized Zone (DMZ) barbed wire for W22,000.

Buddhist items, such as cassettes of monks chanting, incense sticks, candles, and even monk's and nun's clothing, can be bought in shops that are grouped around nearby Jogyesa temple. The winding back alleys are full of traditional teashops and restaurants, including vegetarian ones.

Myeong-dong (Map 9)

The traffic-quiet narrow streets of Myeong-dong in the central downtown area make up one of the leading fashion centres of Seoul. Every evening crowds come here to shop for local and imported clothes, shoes, bags, accessories, cosmetics and CDs. Cafés, restaurants, department stores and new high-rise shopping malls with food courts and cinema multiplexes have made this area popular with young people. **Utoozone Mall** *(open 11.30am-9.30pm daily)* and **Migliore Mall** *(open 10.30am-3am Tues-Sun)* are two malls selling clothing and accessories.

The **National Souvenir Centre** *(☎ 778 6529; w www.souvenir.or.kr; open 10.30am-9pm daily)* has a wide range of handicrafts and other items for sale. You can buy a pair of glasses for around W50,000 (and get a 5% VAT refund at Incheon airport), which will be ready within 24 hours. Ginseng and other Korean food and drink is also on sale, and there's a teashop on the top floor. A smaller branch shop is in Insadong (Map 8).

Ahyeon-dong Wedding Street (Map 3)

Starting at Ewha Women's University subway station (Line 2), nearly 200 small wedding outfitters line both sides of the street that heads east. At the end of the wedding shops is a footbridge so you can cross over the road safely. In this street of romantic dreams you can see elaborate and expensive *hanbok* and Western-style wedding gowns and suits displayed in the shop windows – it's a free fashion show.

Ewha Women's University (Map 3)

Outside this famous Christian university a busy neighbourhood of shops and stalls has been established to provide clothes, bags, accessories and beauty treatments to the fashion conscious who study at the university. Cafés, fast-food outlets and ice-cream shops have set up here to catch the eye of the passers-by. New trends begin here and the alleys are free of traffic.

Apgujeong (Map 6)

Don't expect to find any cheap bargains in Apgujeong, as it is a wealthy part of Seoul with luxury apartments nearby. Deluxe department stores, foreign boutiques and high-class hairdressers, beauty salons and cosmetic surgeons can be found here. Even dogs and other pets have their own beauty parlours, surgeons and cafés. People come here to see the latest styles on sale in the designer shops and to gaze at the fashions being worn by the people walking in the street. Most shops open from 10am to 10pm daily.

Yegi-dong Jewellery & Watch Alley (Map 8)

The area that stretches from Jongno 2-ga to Jongno 5-ga is filled with jewellery shops and stalls that offer a glittering array of locally produced and imported jewellery and watches. If you are looking for something made of gold, silver or precious stones, this is the place to visit.

Nakwon-dong Rice-Cake Shops (Map 8)

Around the Nakwon elevated arcade lots of small shops have been selling *tteok* (home-made rice cakes) since the 1920s. The shops were originally started by rice-cake makers who had worked in the nearby royal palaces, but were out of a job after Japan abolished the monarchy in 1910. Descendants of the royal *tteok* makers still run some of the shops.

Rice cakes cost W3000 a packet and are flavoured with nuts, red beans, sesame, honey and other ingredients. Other traditional snacks are also on sale.

Nakwon Arcade (Map 8)

On the 2nd floor of this elevated arcade are 200 small shops selling all kinds of musical instruments. Locally made guitars and flutes are a good buy. On the 3rd floor is the **Hollywood Cinema**.

Department Stores

Lotte *(Maps 5, 7 & 9)*, **Hyundai** *(Maps 3, 6 & 7)*, **Shinsegae** *(Maps 5, 6 & 9)*, **Galleria** *(Map 6)* and **Metro Midopa** *(Map 9)* are some of the well-known department stores. Since prices are fixed, so it can be a good idea to check out prices in department stores before venturing into the hurly-burly of the markets. Prices are higher than in the markets, but everything is under one roof and you can try on clothes or test cosmetics before you buy. Look out for sales when prices are heavily discounted.

Department stores offer good-quality **restaurants** usually on a high floor with good views. They also offer reasonably priced food courts in the basement. So if you have trouble finding somewhere to eat, just head for a department store.

MARTIN VINCENT ROBINSON

Fashion victim on Myeong-dong

PATRICK HORTON

Shoppers, Namdaemun market

MARTIN VINCENT ROBINSON

Teashops in Insadong exude the rustic charm of a bygone era

MARTIN MOOS

Take a hike in Bukhansan National Park

ERIC L WHEATER

Korean Folk Village temple wall

MARTIN MOOS

The ancient fortress wall at Suwon

BILL WASSMAN

The massive white granite peaks and verdant forests of Bukhansan National Park just north of Seoul

Department stores also have **supermarkets** in their basements and are useful because other supermarkets are rare in Seoul. Local liquors, rice cakes, souvenirs and special gift packs are on sale.

Yeongdeungpo (Map 5) and Myeong-dong (Map 9) are two areas where department stores are concentrated.

Opening hours for department stores are generally from 10am to 7.30pm daily, although some may close one day per week.

Underground Arcades

Sometimes it seems as if half of central Seoul is underground. Underpasses have been built to allow pedestrians to cross under busy roads, and these often link up with subway stations and the basements of high-rise buildings.

The longest underground arcade is **Euljiro** *(Map 9)*, which runs all the way from City Hall to Dongdaemun Stadium (almost 3km) following subway Line 2. Other underground shopping arcades include **Jongno** *(Map 8)* around Jonggak subway station (Line 1), **Lotte** *(Map 9)*, **Myeong-dong** and **Sogong** *(Map 9)*, which all connect up, and **Hoehyeon** *(Map 9)* southwest of Myeong-dong. Shops in the upmarket Sogong underground arcade sell ginseng, stationery, antiques, handicrafts, clothing and accessories. The biggest shopping warren of all is in the **Namdaemun Market Underground Arcade** *(Map 9)*, where huge quantities of goods are piled up and you can find mini restaurants huddled under stairways.

Exploring underground central Seoul is a particularly good idea if the weather above ground is too hot, too cold or too wet.

Above-Ground Arcades

Seoul has one above-ground arcade that runs for four blocks in a straight north-south line. The northern end of the arcade is across the street from Jongmyo Park (Map 8), just east of the Jongno 3-ga subway station (Line 1, 3 or 5). The southern end is close to Chungmuro subway station (Map 9; Line 3 or 4).

The arcade changes its name on each block. It's known as the **Seun Arcade** in the north and then becomes the **Taerim Arcade**, **Sampung Arcade** and **Shinseong Arcade**. The Seun Arcade is full of electronic equipment and home appliances, while the others sell tools, hardware and a wide range of household goods. Prices are cheaper than elsewhere.

Supermarkets

There are very few supermarkets in central Seoul except in department stores (see the Department Stores section earlier).

The **Goryeo Supermarket** (Map 8) is fairly small but is centrally located near the Sejong Centre for Performing Arts. Another supermarket is located in the Yongsan Electronics Market (Map 6) and has an entire floor devoted to gifts and souvenirs. Also try the supermarket in Itaewon, near King Club (Map 11).

Duty-Free Shops

Large duty-free shops can be found all over Seoul and stock the usual perfumes, cameras, watches, clothing and accessories, alcoholic drinks, cigarettes and souvenirs. You can pay in US dollars, Japanese yen or Korean won or by credit card. The shops are easy to find and have a wide variety of goods under one roof, but expect high prices. You have to pick up the goods at the airport when you leave, so you can't use them during your stay in Seoul. Hours vary but most shops are open from 10am to 8pm daily.

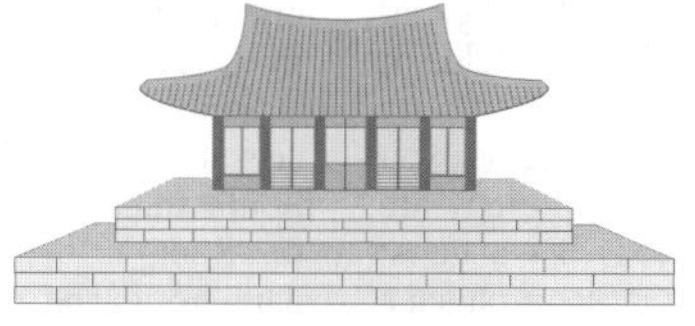

Excursions

PANMUNJEOM & THE DMZ TOUR

Situated 55km north of Seoul, the truce village of Panmunjeom is the only place in the Demilitarized Zone (DMZ) where visitors are permitted. This is the village established on the ceasefire line at the end of the Korean War in 1953. In the blue buildings in Panmunjeom the endless peace discussions continue.

There's nowhere else in South Korea where you can get so close to North Korea and North Korean soldiers without being arrested or shot, and the tension is palpable. Occasionally gun battles erupt in this frontier village – the last one was in 1984 when a Russian defector escaped from the North to the South.

Other chilling incidents have occurred here and are described by the US military personnel who conduct the tour within the DMZ, a strip of land 4km wide and 240km long, that divides the two Koreas and is one of the most heavily fortified borders in the world. High fences topped with barbed wire, watchtowers, antitank obstacles and minefields line both sides of the DMZ.

More than 5000 US and South Korean troops live in Camp Bonifas, which is 'In Front of Them All' and would face the brunt of any surprise attack from the North.

There are only two villages in the DMZ, and they're both near Panmunjeom – and within hailing distance of each other if you have a big enough loudspeaker. On the south side is Daesong, a subsidised village with high tax-free incomes. Each family there lives in a modern house and farms seven hectares. All 240 residents must be at home by the 11pm curfew, and soldiers stand guard while the villagers work in the rice fields or tend their ginseng plants.

The North Korean village, Gijong, is even more unusual because all the buildings are empty and always have been. It's a ghost town whose only function is to broadcast propaganda to anyone around for six to 12 hours a day, using ultra-powerful loudspeakers as big as a house that any rock band would love to own.

The village also has an Eiffel Tower–like structure, 160m high, flying a flag that weighs nearly 300kg. The North Korean flag is larger than the one on the South Korean side. Giant *hangeul* letters on the northern hillsides spell out slogans such as 'Follow the way of the Leader', while on the South Korean side the message 'Freedom, Abundance and Happiness' is lit up at night.

Panmunjeom is where important diplomatic talks are still held. On the South Korean side is a pagoda-style building, from where you can look down on the three blue UN buildings that straddle the border. On the North Korean side is a large concrete building, guarded by soldiers, and some watchtowers.

The tour includes a visit inside one of the UN buildings, which looks like a temporary classroom with simple tables and chairs. Both sides constantly monitor the rooms so everything you say can be overheard. On the ceasefire line soldiers from the North and South stand only centimetres apart. Despite the South's 'sunshine policy' this is still a dangerous and frightening front line and visiting it is a sobering experience.

DMZ National Park?

The Demilitarised Zone (DMZ) separates North and South Korea. It is 4km wide and 240km long, surrounded by tank traps, mines and electrical fences, and is virtually sealed off to all human beings. Ironically, this has made it something of an environmental paradise. No other place in the world with a temperate climate has been so well preserved. This has been a great boon to wildlife – for example, the DMZ is home to flocks of Manchurian cranes, whooper cranes and white herons, as well as rare plants. Environmentalists hope that the day the two Koreas cease hostilities, the DMZ will be kept as a nature reserve.

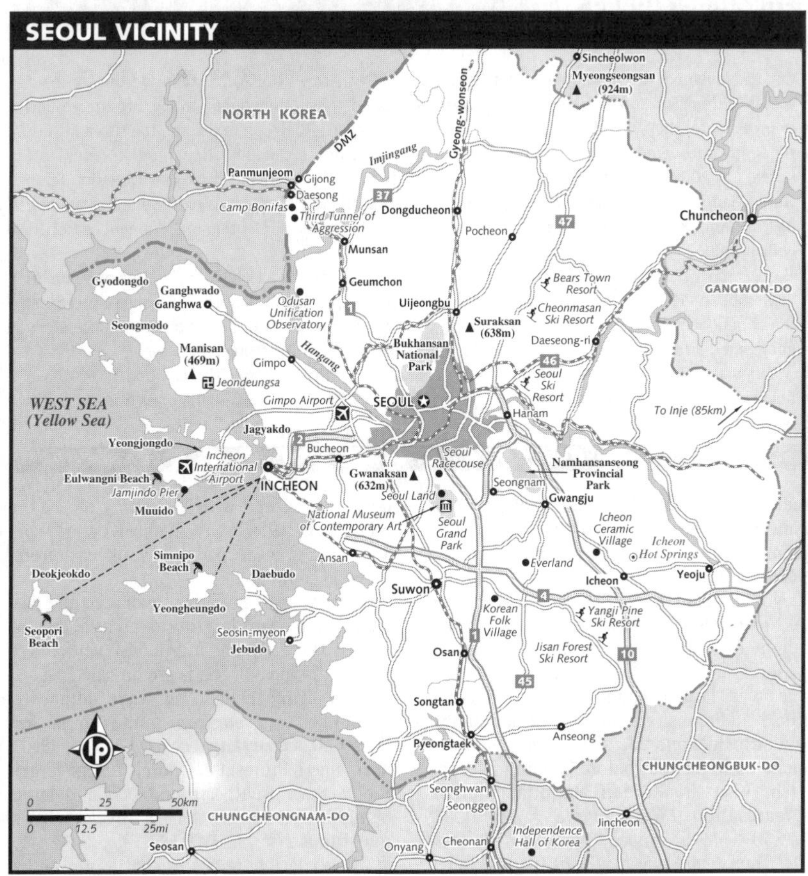

Getting There & Away

Access to Panmunjeom is permitted for tour groups only – this is not a do-it-yourself trip. You must have your passport or you won't be allowed to board the bus. There's also a dress and behaviour code, and before you enter the DMZ all visitors must sign a document absolving the UN and the South Korean government of responsibility in case of any injuries due to 'enemy action' while on the tour.

The **United Service Organizations** *(USO; ☎ 724 7003, fax 723 4106; W www.uso.org/korea)*, the US army's social and entertainment organisation at the Yongsan base, runs twice-weekly tours that cost US$40 and include the Third Tunnel, but not lunch. They start early at 7.30am and finish at 3pm. To reach USO take subway Line 1 to Namyeong station.

Half-day tours with Korean companies cost around W40,000 and full-day tours cost around W60,000. Make sure they include Panmunjeom. On these tours your Korean guide will accompany you to Camp Bonifas on the southern side of the DMZ, where your group will eat lunch. You are

The Underground War

A brass plaque in Panmunjeom gives this account of the North Koreans' tunnelling activities:

On 15 November 1974, members of a Republic of Korea Army (ROKA) patrol inside the southern sector of the DMZ spotted vapour rising from the ground. When they began to dig into the ground to investigate, they were fired upon by North Korean snipers. ROKA units secured the site and subsequently uncovered a tunnel dug by the North Koreans which extended 1.2km into the Republic of Korea. On 20 November, two members of the United Nations Command (UNC) investigation team were killed inside the tunnel when dynamite planted by the North Koreans exploded. The briefing hall at Camp Kitty Hawk is named after one of the officers killed, Lieutenant Commander Robert N Ballinger.

In March 1975, a second North Korean tunnel was discovered by a UNC tunnel detection team. In September of 1975, a North Korean engineer escaped and provided valuable intelligence concerning the communist tunnelling activities. Acting on the information, a tunnel-detection team successfully intercepted a third tunnel in October 1978, less than 2km from Panmunjeom.

Today the North Koreans continue to dig tunnels beneath the DMZ. The UN and ROKA have fielded tunnel-detection teams which drill around the clock in hope of intercepting these tunnels of aggression.

then given a slide show and briefing by an American soldier, who will then accompany your group on a military bus into the Joint Security Area of Panmunjeom.

Not all the tours are the same. Some tours take in a visit to the Third Tunnel, which was dug by the North Koreans. The discovery of a fourth tunnel was announced in 1990 – this one was large enough to accommodate trucks and tanks. Visiting one of the tunnels is worthwhile and you should make sure it's included in the tour before handing over the cash. Visit the **Korean National Tourism Organisation** *(KNTO; Map 8; ☎ 757 0086; W www.knto.or.kr; open 9am-6pm daily Mar-Oct, 9am-5pm daily Nov-Feb)* for brochures and details on the various tour options.

INCHEON

☎ 032 • pop 2.5 million

Thirty-six kilometres southeast of Seoul, Incheon is Seoul's seaport and airport.

The **City Bus Tour** runs hourly between 10am and 6pm, and costs only W1000 for an exhaustive four-hour, 80km ride around Incheon city, but the tour is conducted in Korean. Another option is to pay W2500 and hop on and off all day.

Jayu Park has good views and a statue of General MacArthur who changed the destiny of Korea with his daring attack on Incheon in 1950 early in the Korean War. The park is a steep uphill walk east from Incheon station.

Sinpodong is the downtown area and has an enormous **underground arcade** that is almost 1km long and a ground-level market where all kinds of goods are on sale.

Near Dong-Incheon subway station are a number of *yeogwan* with rooms for W25,000. **Daeyang** *(☎ 032-772 4892)* near Naeri Protestant Church offers larger rooms than usual, a round bed and large bath. Incheon also has a **backpacker's guesthouse** *(☎ 032-747 1872, fax 746 2513; W www.guesthouseinkorea.com; dorm beds/singles/doubles & twins W15,000/25,000/35,000)*, where breakfast, tea and coffee, Internet access, use of the washing machine, bicycle and fishing gear hire, and pick-ups are all free.

An interesting budget restaurant is **Inhasamchijip**, which is full of men, noise and cigarette smoke. A kettle of *makgeolli* costs W3000 and the excellent barbecued fish, *sanchi,* is only W2000.

Chinatown is being brought back to life. Originally established in 1883, it is being renovated and some Chinese shops, bakeries and restaurants are open for business.

Yeonan Pier is the departure point for regular **international ferries** to a number of Chinese cities – see the Boat section of the Getting There & Away chapter. The pier also has a **domestic ferry terminal** where boats leave for 14 of the larger inhabited islands in the West Sea. The ferries cost from W5500 to W24,700 depending on the distance and the speed of the ferry. The ferries provide a more frequent service in summer when many holiday-makers head out to the beaches and seafood restaurants on these unspoilt and relaxing islands.

To get to Yeonan Pier, take bus No 12 or 24 from Incheon station or hail a taxi (around W4400).

Songdo Resort *(☎ 032-832 0011; admission W3000)* has a fairground with thrill rides, paddle boats, a water slide and swimming in a large saltwater lake that is popular in summer.

Also in Songdo is the **Incheon Landing Memorial Monument Hall** *(admission free; open 9am-5.30pm Tues-Sun Mar-Oct; 9am-4.30pm Tues-Sun Nov-Feb)*. Old newsreel films of the Korean War reveal the ugly reality of modern warfare. Sixteen countries sent troops or medical units to help South Korea, and 70,000 UN and South Korean troops took part in the surprise landing in Incheon in 1950, supported by 260 warships.

Next door is **Incheon Municipal Museum** *(admission W400; open 9am-5.30pm Mon-Sat Mar-Oct; 9am-4.30pm Mon-Sat Nov-Feb)*, which has an excellent collection of celadon pottery that spans 19 centuries.

To get to Songdo from Incheon station, hop on bus No 6 or 16, or take a taxi (W5000).

Wolmido is the most attractive place in Incheon and has sea breezes and a wide promenade along the sea front with views of boats and islands. Lined with seafood restaurants (raw-fish meals are W50,000), bars and smart cafés, the promenade has an outdoor concert area. In summer young people gather here in the evening to listen to music, drink alcohol and let off fireworks.

An amusement park has the usual rides for around W3000 each. Cruises on the *Harmony* and *Cosmos* pleasure boats are popular with middle-aged Koreans – a 1½-hour cruise with live music and dancing girls is W10,000.

To get to Wolmido, it's a 20-minute walk from Incheon station or a W1500 taxi ride.

Getting There & Away

Take subway Line 1 to Incheon station. It costs W1100 and takes 70 minutes from Seoul Station. Incheon has its own subway system but it doesn't cover the tourist areas.

ISLAND HOPPING IN THE WEST SEA

Sandy beaches, sea views, rural scenery, vineyards, fresh air and fresh seafood – the West Sea islands are a different world to Seoul. To go island hopping, take subway Line 1 to Incheon station and then a taxi (W1500) to Wolmido. On the promenade is the ticket office for the car ferry to Yeongjongdo. The adult fare is W1500 for the 20-minute trip and ferries run every half-hour from 7am to 9.30pm daily.

Yeongjongdo wharf has a market that sells fish, shellfish, crabs and other seafood, and nearby restaurants will cook and serve it for W5000. Behind the market, take the Jamjindo bus (or ask the driver of the bus to the western beaches to drop you near Jamjindo). The bus ride takes 15 minutes and costs W1200. In the latter case, walk over the causeway from Yeongjongdo to **Jamjindo**, while enjoying the sea and island views. A 15-minute walk brings you to the small ferry to Muuido, which costs W1000 and leaves at least every hour.

On **Muuido Wharf**, try a delicious fresh shellfish BBQ – a big bowl costs W25,000 and octopus *pajeon* is W4000. Then it's a 10-minute walk to a fishing village, where you can turn right and walk over the hill past cherry trees and grapevines for 15 minutes to **Keunmuri Resort** *(admission Sept-Jun W1000, July & Aug W2000; huts Sept-Jun W30,000, Jul & Aug W42,000)* where there are camp sites and huts. The resort is pleasant, with pine trees, a sandy beach and a swimming pool. At low tide you can walk across to the unspoilt, uninhabited **Silmido**.

ISLAND HOPPING IN THE WEST SEA

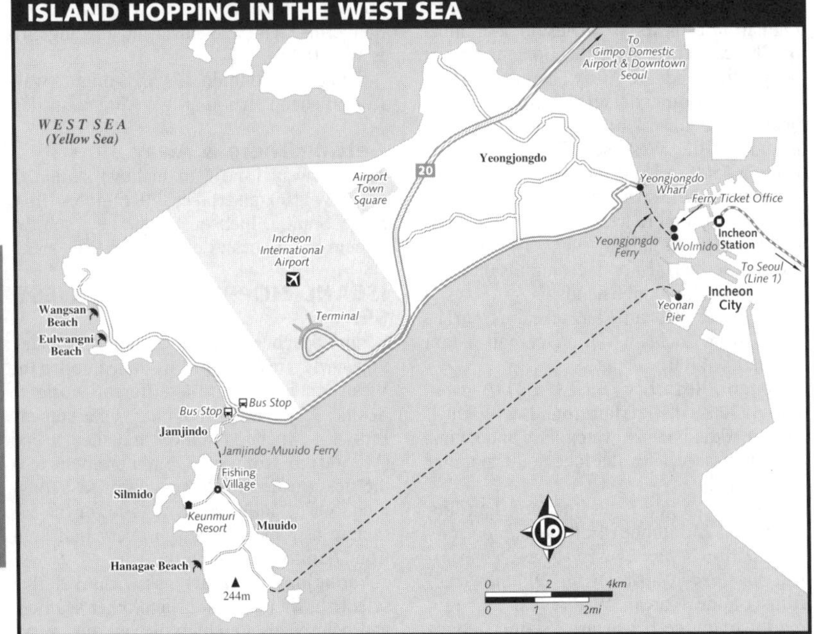

Return the same way you came and you can catch a bus on Yeongjongdo to the popular western beaches. **Eulwangni Beach** is 10 minutes from the Jamjindo drop-off point by bus, and has motels, minbak, *noraebang* and hundreds of restaurants. It's popular because the sea doesn't disappear at low tide leaving behind huge mud flats. For a quieter beach, walk north on to **Wangsan**.

The western beaches, set among rice fields and vineyards, are still attractive despite the nearby Incheon International Airport. Surprisingly you won't hear or see any aircraft from the beaches.

Other attractive, but more distant, islands that can be visited include **Deokjeokdo**, which is 70km from Incheon city. This 36-sq-km island has camping grounds, *yeogwan* and 40 *minbak* on the 2km-long Seopori Beach, which is a 20-minute bus ride from the wharf. The island is a popular destination for swimming, fishing off the rocky headlands, hiking up Bijosan (292m) or just lazing about on the sandy beach, which is fringed by pine trees. Ferries to the island leave at 9.30am and 4pm, but run more frequently on weekends, public holidays, and in July and August. In summer people crowd on to the island to escape from the high temperatures and humidity in Seoul. From the wharf, boats leave for other nearby islands and beaches. A return trip from Yeonan Pier to Deokjeokdo costs W33,000 on the fast ferry, which takes less than an hour, while the slower ferry takes two hours and costs W22,800.

Another option not so far away is **Yeongheungdo**, where Simnipo Beach in the northwest corner of the island is popular.

HIKING AROUND THE WALLS OF SUWON FORTRESS

The fortress wall in Suwon city stretches for 5.7km and was originally built between 1794 and 1796 during the reign of King Jeongjo. Restored in the 1970s, 95% of the wall is intact and it's a Unesco World Heritage site well worth a visit.

Start at Paldalmun, the southern entrance gate, and follow the brown sign to Sojangdae. From here you walk along the wall up to the top of **Paldasan** (143m), a good viewpoint, where you might hear or see cuckoos. The wall is made of earth and faced with large stone blocks, while other features are made of brick or wood. Along the wall are command posts, observation towers, entrance gates, secret gates and a five-beacon platform for sending messages.

Half-way round, take the steps down from the wall at Hwahongmun to the popular **Yeonpo Restaurant** *(☎ 255 1337)* to eat the famous Suwon version of *galbitang*. An unsophisticated W5000 meal, it consists of big beef ribs in a broth with spicy side dishes. A *galbi* barbecue meal is W20,000.

A leisurely walk around takes two hours and there's a large market at the end that is worth exploring.

Getting There & Away

Take subway Line 1, but make sure the train has 'Suwon' written on it. It takes an hour from downtown Seoul and costs W900. Then take bus No 13, 36 or 39 from the left side of the train station for the W600, 10-minute ride to Paldalmun, the South Gate. A taxi costs around W2500. Buses back to the station leave from the line of bus stops on the opposite side of the gate.

KOREAN FOLK VILLAGE

The Korean Folk Village *(Seoul Vicinity Map; adult/12-24 year olds/under 12 W9000/6000/5000; open 9am-6.30pm daily, 9am-5.30pm daily Oct-Mar)*, south of Seoul, is a very large collection of thatched and tiled traditional houses that takes all day to look around. You can see a temple, Confucian school and shrine, a market, magistrate's house with examples of punishments, storehouses, a bullock pulling a cart, and all sorts of household furnishings and tools. In this historical and rural village atmosphere, *hanbok*-clad artisans create pots, make paper and weave bamboo, while other workers tend vegetable plots and chickens.

Korean meals, snacks and handicraft souvenirs are on sale, and restaurants are clustered around the entrance and the market area. Be careful on the traditional see-saw game, where you stand on the see-saw and jump up and down – it's difficult to keep your balance. The swing is safer.

Traditional musicians, dancers, acrobats and tightrope walkers put on displays and you can even watch a wedding ceremony. These events happen twice daily and usually start around 11pm and 3pm.

Next door is an **amusement park** for children (W2500 a ride), an **art gallery** *(admission W3000)* and a **world folk museum** *(admission W2500)*.

Getting There & Away

Take subway Line 1 to Suwon station. It takes an hour from downtown Seoul and costs W900. Leave the station, turn right, walk 150m and then cross the main road on the pedestrian crossing. On the left is the ticket office and free shuttle bus, which takes 30 minutes and runs every hour. Unfortunately, the last free shuttle bus leaves the Folk Village at 4pm. After that time, walk to the far end of the car park and catch city bus No 37 back to Suwon.

EVERLAND

An excellent amusement park, Everland *(☎ 759 1408; W www.everland.com)* is an hour southeast of Seoul by bus, but worth a visit. It is divided into four separate parts.

Caribbean Bay *(adult/child June W30,000/20,000, July & Aug W45,000/30,000; open 9.30am-6pm daily, later hrs July & Aug;)* is a world-class water park. The outdoor section is open from 1 June to 15 September and has a wave pool, sandy beach, tube rides, body slides, spa pools, a surf pool, lazy pool, an adventure pool and a scuba diving pool.

The indoor section *(adult/child W15,000/10,000)* is all that is open from September to May. It is similar to the outdoor section but smaller in scale. The advantage is that it is cheaper.

Festival World *(adult/child W18,000/13,000, passport ticket W26,000/18,000;*

EXCURSIONS

open 9.30am-10pm daily Apr-Sept, 9.30am-7pm daily Oct-Mar) follows the Disneyland formula with fantasy buildings, thrill rides, impressive gardens, parades, live-music entertainment, and lots of restaurants and fast-food outlets. One novelty feature is the 'real' **African safari** where lions and tigers live together.

Speedway is a motor racing track that is close to the other two sections. You can watch races for free from the grass bank. On some days visitors can drive a racing car – the cost varies with the horsepower of the vehicle.

The **Hoam Art Museum** *(☎ 031-320 1801; 🅆 www.hoammuseum.org; adult/child W3000/2000; open 10am-6pm Tues-Sun)* is a major art collection that contains 91 Korean national treasures, foreign 20th-century art and a sculpture garden. A free shuttle bus runs on the hour from outside Festival World Entrance B, which is near the buses to Seoul.

Getting There & Away

To get to Everland, take a direct bus (No 5002) from Seoul, which takes about an hour and costs W4000. Take subway Line 2 to Gangnam station, leave by Exit 6 and walk to the bus stop that is outside Kookmin Bank (Map 6).

Other buses go to Everland from Suwon (bus No 6000 or No 66, one hour), Sinchon or from outside Dong-Seoul bus terminal. Check the excellent Everland website for up-to-date transport details.

INDEPENDENCE HALL OF KOREA

This museum *(☎ 041-560 0114; 🅆 www.independence.or.kr; adult/12-24 year olds/child W2000/1100/700; open 9.30am-6pm Tues-Sun Mar-Oct, 9.30am-5pm Tues-Sun Nov-Feb)* is a large and impressive complex 90km south of Seoul that focuses on the Korean struggle for independence against Japanese colonialism between 1910 and 1945. It presents a different story to that put forward in Japanese school history books. Built on a grand scale, it has seven exhibition halls and some English-language description of the exhibits.

The active collaboration with the Japanese colonialists at all levels of society from ordinary policemen to the *yangban* elite is not covered in the exhibition. One display states that 'the entire Korean population participated in the March 1st Movement'. This opposition movement was widespread, but not everyone took part.

The Circle Vision Theatre has nine film projectors and 24 loudspeakers, and presents films on Korea's scenic beauty, traditions, customs and economic development, using the latest audio-visual techniques.

A pleasant wooded area surrounds the museum so you can take a picnic. Otherwise, you can eat in the museum's large restaurant where meals cost up to W5000, or buy a snack from one of the food stalls.

Getting There & Away

The museum is in Chungcheongnam-do. Take subway Line 3 to Nambu Bus Terminal station and leave by Exit 5. Walk up the steps into the terminal and take a bus to Cheonan (W3800, one hour) – they leave every hour. In Cheonan you have to catch another bus to Independence Hall (W800, 20 minutes).

GANGHWADO

Northwest of Seoul, this large island is connected to the mainland by bridge so it is easy to visit. The island has played a significant role in Korean history. It is where the Goryeo court took refuge during the Mongol invasions of the 13th century, and where the Koreans resisted French and American troops in the late 19th century.

Being an island fortress, Ganghwado has its fair share of fortifications, palaces, royal tombs and temples. Many prehistoric dolmens (stone tombs) can also be seen on the island, and hiking is popular especially in the fall when the hillsides are a riot of colour. Unfortunately everything is rather spread out, so the ideal situation is to find a local willing to drive you around. An alternative is to take a USO tour.

The main town is Ganghwa, where three fortress gates can be seen and the old fortifications of Ganghwasanseong are being rebuilt. You can walk there from the bus terminal in

10 minutes. **Ganghwa History Hall** *(☎ 032-930 3525; admission W1200; open 9am-6pm daily)* is the place to find out about the history of the island, but it's located outside the town near the bridge to the island.

Many tourists take a 40-minute bus ride (W1100) to **Manisan** *(admission W1000)*, 14km southwest of Ganghwa. This 469m mountain is famous for the altar, Chamseong-dang, dedicated to Dangun, the legendary figure credited with being the first Korean and originator of the Korean people. A ceremony is held here every year on 3 October, which is National Foundation Day. It's a 3km hike from the bus stop in Hwado village to the summit along a well-trodden path. Allow two hours for the climb up and down.

Another place to visit is **Jeondeungsa**, a temple that dates back to the 4th century and has been reconstructed and renovated many times over the years. It is inside a fortress just outside Onsu village. Regular buses (W1500) go to Onsu from Ganghwa.

Before you leave, check out the souvenirs. The beautiful rush mats woven in flower patterns, called *hwamunseok*, are very expensive and large. The other famous Ganghwado product is ginseng, which is also expensive but more portable.

Getting There & Away

Take subway Line 2 to Sinchon station and walk to Sinchon bus terminal (Map 3). The walk is less than five minutes. Regular buses leave from there for Ganghwa and take an hour.

ICHEON CERAMICS VILLAGE

Forty kilometres southeast of Seoul and 3km north of the town of Icheon (not to be confused with the city of Incheon) is Icheon Ceramics Village. It has been a centre of the pottery industry since the Goryeo dynasty or even earlier, and many traditional wood-burning kilns are still in operation. Celadon and white porcelain are both produced here. You can see huge displays from expensive reproductions of Goryeo-dynasty celadon to cheap everyday household articles, such as plates, bowls, cups and chopstick rests. In small studios potters are at work, and you can buy their products, and even try shaping a pot yourself (for a fee).

Haegang Ceramics Museum *(☎ 031-632 7017; adult/child W2000/500; open 9.30am-5.30pm Tues-Sun)* has displays on the history of Korean pottery and the manufacturing process as well as thousands of pottery items.

Between Seoul and Icheon town is another village, **Gwangju** which has more kilns and another museum. Icheon town itself is well known for its therapeutic hot springs and you can take a relaxing bath in one of the resort hotels.

These tourist attractions are rather spread out and require some effort to reach by public transport, so taking a guided tour is a good idea. See also the Excursions chapter for further information.

Getting There & Away

Buses run from Seoul Express bus terminal (Map 6) and Dong-Seoul bus terminal (Map 7) to Icheon, take an hour and cost W3300 one way. Tell the driver you want to get off at Icheon Ceramics Village and not Icheon, which is a few kilometres further on. If you land up in Icheon you can take a local bus out to the ceramics village.

Language

Korean is a knotty problem for linguists. Various theories have been proposed to explain its origins, but the most widely accepted is that it is a member of the Ural-Altaic family of languages. Other members of the same linguistic branch are Turkish and Mongolian. In reality Korean grammar shares much more with Japanese than it does with either Turkish or Mongolian. Furthermore, the Koreans have borrowed nearly 70% of their vocabulary from neighbouring China, and now many English words have penetrated the Korean lexicon.

Chinese characters *(hanja)* are usually restricted to use in maps and occasionally in newspapers and written names. For the most part Korean is written in *hangeul,* the alphabet developed under King Sejong's reign in the 15th century. Many users of the Korean language argue that the Korean script is one of the most scientific and consistent alphabets used today.

Hangeul consists of only 24 characters and isn't that difficult to learn. However, the formation of words using *hangeul* is very different from the way that Western alphabets are used to form words. The emphasis is on the formation of a syllable so that it resembles a Chinese character. Thus the first syllable of the word 'hangeul' (한) is formed by an 'h' (ㅎ) in the top left corner, an 'a' (ㅏ) in the top right corner and an 'n' (ㄴ) at the bottom, the whole syllabic grouping forming a syllabic 'box'. These syllabic 'boxes' are strung together to form words.

Romanisation

In July 2000, the Korean government adopted a new method of Romanising the Korean language. Most of the old Romanisation system was retained, but a few changes were introduced to ensure a more consistent spelling throughout Korea and overseas. The main changes involved the removal of the apostrophe and diacritical breve marker and the substitution of a few consonants.

The new system has been energetically promoted throughout the government and tourist bureaus, but it will take a long time for everyone to fall into line. Local governments have until 2005 to change all the road signs around the country and the central government is also actively encouraging the adoption of the new system overseas.

Travellers have to be careful with Romanisation during the years of transition. Lonely Planet has adopted the new Romanisation style throughout this book, but you will come across many spelling variations. To avoid confusion it's always best to go back to the original Korean script. In fact, it's well worth the few hours required to learn the Korean alphabet. To help make travel easier, we have provided Korean script throughout this book for map references and points of interest.

After familiarising yourself with *hangeul,* the next step towards Korean competency is listening to the way Koreans pronounce place names and to try and repeat their pronunciations.

The main changes to the Romanisation system are:

- the diacritical breve (**ŏ** or **ŭ**) has been dropped and an 'e' placed in front of the 'o' or 'u'; eg, Inch'ŏn and Chŏngŭp become Incheon and Jeongeup.
- the consonants ㄱ/ㄷ/ㅂ/ㅈ in initial position will always be transliterated as **g**/**d**/**b**/**j**; eg, Pusan and Kwangju become Busan and Gwangju.
- the voiceless consonants ㅋ/ㅌ/ㅍ/ㅊ will retain the letters **k**/**t**/**p**/**ch** but will lose their apostrophe. Previously, voiceless or aspirated consonants (those accompanied by a puff of air) were indicated by an apostrophe, as in P'ohang or Ch'ungju. But under the new system they'll be written Pohang and Chungju respectively.
- the form 시 will no longer be 'shi', but simply 'si'; eg, Shinch'on becomes Sinchon.
- official names of persons and companies will remain unchanged, but for all new names the new Romanisation system will be used.
- hyphens are rarely used, except where confusion may arise between two syllables; eg,

Chungangno becomes Jung-angno. Hyphens have been retained for administrative units; eg, Gyeonggi-do, Suncheon-si and Myeong-dong.

Pronunciation

Vowels

ㅏ	**a**	as in 'are'
ㅑ	**ya**	as in 'yard'
ㅓ	**eo**	as in 'of'
ㅕ	**yeo**	as in 'young'
ㅗ	**o**	as in 'go'
ㅛ	**yo**	as in 'yoke'
ㅜ	**u**	as in 'flute'
ㅠ	**yu**	as the word 'you'
ㅡ	**eu**	as the 'oo' in 'look'
ㅣ	**i**	as the 'ee' in 'beet'

Vowel Combinations

ㅐ	**ae**	as the 'a' in 'hat'
ㅒ	**yae**	as the 'ya' in 'yam'
ㅔ	**e**	as in 'ten'
ㅖ	**ye**	as in 'yes'
ㅘ	**wa**	as in 'waffle'
ㅙ	**wae**	as the 'wa' in 'wax'
ㅚ	**oe**	as the 'wa' in 'way'
ㅝ	**wo**	as in 'won'
ㅞ	**we**	as in 'wet'
ㅟ	**wi**	as the word 'we'
ㅢ	**ui**	as 'u' plus 'i'

Consonants

In the old McCune-Reischauer Romanisation system apostrophes were used to indicate consonant sounds that are aspirated (ie, accompanied by a puff of air). Aspirated consonants include ㅋ/ㅌ/ㅍ/ㅊ. Under the new Romanisation system they will retain the letters **k**/**t**/**p**/**ch**, but lose their apostrophe. Unaspirated consonants are generally difficult for English speakers to render. Under the new Romanisation system, word initial ㄱ/ㄷ/ㅂ/ㅈ will be transliterated as **g**/**d**/**b**/**j**. To those unfamiliar with Korean, an unaspirated **k** will sound like 'g', an unaspirated **t** like 'd', and an unaspirated **p** like 'b'.

Whether consonants in Korean are voiced or unvoiced depends on where they fall within a word – at the beginning, in the middle or at the end. The rules governing this are too complex to cover here – the following tables show the various alternative pronunciations you may hear.

Single Consonants

ㅅ is pronounced 'sh' if followed by the vowel ㅣ. In the middle of a word, ㄹ is pronounced 'n' if it follows ㅁ (**m**) or ㅇ (**ng**), but when it follows ㄴ (**n**) it becomes a double 'l' sound (**ll**).

ㄱ	**g/k**
ㄴ	**n**
ㄷ	**d/t**
ㄹ	**r/l/n**
ㅁ	**m**
ㅂ	**b/p**
ㅅ	**s/t**
ㅇ	**–/ng**
ㅈ	**j**
ㅊ	**ch**
ㅋ	**k**
ㅌ	**t**
ㅍ	**p**
ㅎ	**h**

Double Consonants

Double consonants are pronounced with more stress than their single consonants counterparts.

ㄲ	**kk**
ㄸ	**tt**
ㅃ	**pp**
ㅆ	**ss**
ㅉ	**jj**

Complex Consonants

These occur only in the middle or at the end of a word.

ㄱ ㅅ	**-ksk**
ㄴ ㅈ	**–/nj/n**
ㄴ ㅎ	**–/nh/n**
ㄹ ㄱ	**–/lg/k**
ㄹ ㅁ	**–/lm/m**
ㄹ ㅂ	**–/lb/p**
ㄹ ㅅ	**–/ls/l**
ㄹ ㅌ	**–/lt/l**
ㄹ ㅍ	**–/lp/p**
ㄹ ㅎ	**–/lh/l**
ㅂ ㅅ	**–/ps/p**

Polite Korean

Korea's pervasive social hierarchy means that varying degrees of politeness are codified into the grammar. Young Koreans tend to use the very polite forms a lot less than the older generations, but it's always best to use the polite form if you're unsure. The sentences in this section employ polite forms.

Greetings & Civilities

Hello.
annyeong hasimnikka (polite) 안녕하십니까
annyeong haseyo (less formal) 안녕하세요

Goodbye. (to person leaving)
annyeonghi gaseyo 안녕히가세요

Goodbye. (to person staying)
annyeonghi gyeseyo 안녕히계세요

Please.
putak hamnida 부탁합니다

Thank you.
gamsa hamnida 감사합니다

You're welcome.
gwaenchanseumnida 괜찮습니다

Yes.
ye/ne 예/네

No.
aniyo 아니요

Excuse me.
sillye hamnida 실례합니다

I'm sorry.
mianhamnida 미안합니다

My name is ...
je ireumeun ... imnida 제이름은 ... 입니다

I come from ...
jeoneun ... eseo watseumnida 저는 ... 에서 왔습니다

Getting Around

I want to get off here.
yeogie naeryeo juseyo 여기에 내려 주세요

I want to go to ...
... e gago sipseumnida 에 가고싶습니다

Where can I catch the bus to ...?
... haeng beoseuneun eodi e seo tamnikka? ... 행 버스는 어디에서 탑니까?

airport
gonghang 공항

airport bus
gonghang beoseu 공항버스

bus
beoseu 버스

bus card
beoseu kadeu 버스카드

bus stop
beoseu jeongnyujang 버스정류장

express bus terminal
gosok beoseu teomineol 고속버스 터미널

ferry boat
yeogaekseon 여객선

ferry crossing
naru 나루

ferry pier
budu 부두

immigration office
chulipguk gwalliso 출입국관리소

intercity bus terminal
sioe beoseu teomineol 시외버스 터미널

lockers
lakka 락카

lost & found office
bunsilmul bogwansenta 분실물보관센타

multiple-use subway ticket
jeong-aek seungchagwon 정액승차권

national timetable
sigakpyo 시각표

one-way (ticket)
pyeondo 편도

passport
yeogwon 여권

refund ticket
hwanbul 환불

return (ticket)
wangbok 왕복

subway station
jihacheol yeok 지하철역

taxi
taeksi 택시

train
gicha 기차

train station
gicha yeok 기차역

Necessities

antidiarrhoeal
seolsa yak 설사약
condoms
kondom 콘돔
electric mosquito coil
jeonja mogihyang 전자모기향
laxative
byeonbi yak 변비약
pain killer
jintongje 진통제
pharmacy
yakguk 약국
sanitary pads
saengnidae 생리대
tampons
tempo 템포
toilet
hwajangsil 화장실
toilet paper
hwajangji 화장지

Communication

aerogramme
hanggong bonghamnyeopseo
항공봉함엽서
airmail letter
hanggong seogan 항공서간
International Express Mail
gukje teukgeup upyeon
국제특급우편
post office
ucheguk 우체국
stamp
upyo 우표
telephone card
jeonhwa kadeu
전화카드
telephone office
jeonhwa guk
전화국
I'd like to know the telephone number here.
yeogi jeonhwabeonho jom gareuchyeo juseyo
여기 전화번호 좀 가르쳐 주세요

Money

bank
eunhaeng
은행
May I have change please?
jandoneuro bakkwo juseyo?
잔돈으로 바꿔 주세요?
How much does it cost?
eolmayeyo?
얼마예요?
Too expensive.
neomu bissayo
너무 비싸요
Can I have a discount?
jom ssage hae juseyo?
좀 싸게 해 주세요?
May I use a credit card?
kadeureul sseulsu isseumnikka?
카드를 쓸 수 있습니까?

Accommodation

hotel
hotel 호텔
guesthouse
yeogwan 여관
cheapest guesthouse
yeoinsuk 여인숙
homestay
minbak 민박
single room
singgeul lum 싱글룸
double room
deobeul lum 더블룸
towel
sugeon 수건
bathhouse
mogyoktang 목욕탕
without bath
yoksil eomneun bang juseyo
욕실 없는 방 주세요
with private bath
yoksil inneun bang juseyo
욕실 있는 방 주세요

May I see the room?
bang-eul bolsu isseoyo?
방을 볼 수 있어요?
Do you have anything cheaper?
deo ssan geoseun eopseumnikka?
더 싼 것은 없습니까?
May I have a namecard?
myeongham jom eodeul su isseulkkayo?
명함 좀 얻을 수 있을까요?
I will pay you now.
jigeum jibulhago sipeundeyo
지금 지불하고 싶은 데요

Emergencies

Fire!
buriya! 불이야!
Help!
saram sallyeo! 사람살려!
hospital
byeongwon 병원
Thief!
dodugiya! 도둑이야!

Call a doctor!
uisareul buleo juseyo!
의사를 불러 주세요!
Call an ambulance!
gugeupcha jom bulleo juseyo!
구급차 좀 불러 주세요!
Call the police!
gyeongchaleul bulleo juseyo!
경찰을 불러주세요!
I'm allergic to penicillin.
penisillin allereugiga isseoyo
페니실린 알레르기가 있어요
I'm allergic to antibiotics.
hangsaengje allereugiga isseoyo
항생제 알레르기가 있어요
I'm diabetic.
dangnyobyeong-i isseoyo
당뇨병이 있어요

Please give me a receipt.
yeongsujeung jom gatda juseyo
영수증 좀 갖다 주세요
I want to stay one more night.
hangru deo mukgo sipseumnida
하루 더 묵고 싶습니다
Please give me my key.
yeolsoe jom juseyo
열쇠 좀 주세요
Could you clean my room please?
bangcheongso jom hae juseyo?
방청소 좀 해 주세요?
Can you have my clothes washed?
setak sseobiseu doemnikka?
세탁 써비스 됩니까?

Numbers

Korean has two counting systems. One is of Chinese origin and the other a native Korean system. Korean numbers only go up to 99. Either Chinese or Korean numbers can be used to count days. Chinese numbers are used for minutes and kilometres. Korean numbers are used for hours. The Chinese system is used to count money, not surprising since the smallest Korean banknote is W1000.

Number	Chinese		Korean	
0			*yeong/gong*	영/공
1	*il*	일	*hana*	하나
2	*I*	이	*dul*	둘
3	*sam*	삼	*set*	셋
4	*sa*	사	*net*	넷
5	*o*	오	*daseot*	다섯
6	*yuk*	육	*yeoseot*	여섯
7	*chil*	칠	*ilgop*	일곱
8	*pal*	팔	*yeodeol*	여덟
9	*gu*	구	*ahop*	아홉
10	*sip*	십	*yeol*	열

Number	Combination	
11	*sib-il*	십일
20	*isip*	이십
30	*samsip*	삼십
40	*sasip*	사십
48	*sasippal*	사십팔
50	*osip*	오십
100	*baek*	백
200	*ibaek*	이백
300	*sambaek*	삼백
846	*palbaek sasip-yuk*	팔백사십육
1000	*cheon*	천
2000	*icheon*	이천
5729	*ocheon chilbaek isipgu*	오천칠백이십구
10,000	*man*	만

FOOD

Basics

restaurant
sikdang
식당
I'm a vegetarian.
chaesik juui imnida
채식주의 입니다
I want to eat spicy food.
maepge hae juseyo
맵게 해 주세요
I can't eat spicy food.
maeun eumsigeun meokji mothamnida
매운 음식은 먹지 못합니다

The menu, please.
menyureul boyeo juseyo
메뉴를 보여 주세요
The bill/check, please.
gyesanseo juseyo
계산서 주세요

noodles	*myeon/guksu*	면/국수
rice	*bap*	밥
steamed rice	*gonggibap*	공기밥

Seafood 생선요리

clam	*daehap*	대합
crab	*ge*	게
cuttlefish	*ojing-eo*	오징어
eel	*baemjang-eo*	뱀장어
fish	*saengseon*	생선
oyster	*gul*	굴
shrimp	*saeu*	새우

Meat 육류

beef	*sogogi*	소고기
chicken	*dakgogi*	닭고기
mutton	*yanggogi*	양고기
pork	*dwaejigogi*	돼지고기

Vegetables 야채요리

beans	*kong*	콩
capsicum	*gochu*	고추
cucumber	*oi*	오이
dried seaweed	*gim*	김
garlic	*maneul*	마늘
lotus root	*yeongeun*	연근
mushroom	*beoseot*	버섯
onion	*yangpa*	양파
potato	*gamja*	감자
radishes	*muu*	무우
soya-bean sprouts	*kongnamul*	콩나물
spinach	*sigeumchi*	시금치

Condiments 양념

black pepper	*huchu*	후추
butter	*beoteo*	버터
hot chilli pepper	*gochu garu*	고추가루
hot sauce	*gochujang*	고추장
jam	*jaem*	잼
ketchup	*kechap*	케찹
mayonnaise	*mayonejeu*	마요네즈
mustard	*gyeoja*	겨자
salt	*sogeum*	소금
soy sauce	*ganjang*	간장
soya-bean paste	*doenjang*	된장
sugar	*seoltang*	설탕
vinegar	*sikcho*	식초

Korean Dishes 한국음식

agujjim 아구찜
steamed spicy angler fish
beoseotjeongol 버섯전골
mushroom hotpot
bibim naengmyeon 비빔 냉면
spicy cold noodles without soup
bibimbap 비빔밥
rice, egg, meat & vegetables in chilli-pepper sauce
bibimguksu 비빔국수
cold-noodle broth, vegetables & hot sauce
bindaetteok 빈대떡
mung-bean pancake
bosintang 보신탕
dog-meat soup
bossam 보쌈
steamed pork & cabbage
bugeoguk 북어국
pollack (seafood) soup
bulgalbi 불갈비
marinated beef/pork-ribs grill
bulgogi 불고기
barbecued beef & vegetables grill
chamchi gimbap 참치 김밥
tuna sushi
chijeu gimbap 치즈 김밥
cheese sushi
chueotang 추어탕
mudfish soup
dakbaeksuk 닭백숙
soft-boiled stuffed chicken
dakgalbi 닭갈비
diced grilled chicken
doenjang jjigae 된장찌개
soya-bean paste stew
doganitang 도가니탕
ox-leg soup
dolsotbibimbap 돌솥비빔밥
bibimbap in a stone pot
dongchimi 동치미
pickled daikon radish
dotorimuk 도토리묵
acorn jelly

dubu jjigae 두부 찌개
tofu stew
dwaejigalbi 돼지갈비
barbecued pork-ribs grill
galbigui 갈비구이
barbecued beef-ribs grill
galbijjim 갈비찜
barbecued beef-ribs stew
galbitang 갈비탕
beef-ribs soup
gimbap 김밥
laver-wrapped sushi
gimchi gimbap 김치 김밥
gimchi sushi
gimchi jjigae 김치찌개
gimchi stew
gimchi 김치
pickled vegetables, garlic & chilli
gimchibokkeumbap 김치볶음밥
fried gimchi rice
gomtang 곰탕
beef soup
gopchangjeongol 곱창전골
tripe hotpot
guk/tang 국/탕
soup
haemultang 해물탕
spicy seafood soup
hanjeongsik 한정식
banquet
jang-eogui 장이구이
grilled eel
jeonbokjuk 전복죽
abalone porridge
jjigae 찌개
stew
jjimdak 찜닭
simmered chicken, noodles & potatoes
jokbal 족발
steamed pork hocks
kalguksu 칼국수
thick handmade noodles
kkorigomtang 꼬리곰탕
ox-tail soup
kongguksu 콩국수
noodle dish & soy-milk broth
kongnamulgukbap 콩나물국밥
spicy rice bean-sprout porridge
maeunmatjeyukbokkeum samgakgimbap
매운맛제유볶음 삼각김밥
triangular sushi with spicy fried pork
maeuntang 매운탕
spicy fish soup
makguksu 막국수
vegetables, meat, noodles & chicken broth
mandu 만두
dumplings
manduguk 만두국
soup with meat-filled dumplings
miyeokguk 미역국
brown seaweed soup
modeum gimbap 모듬 김밥
assorted sushi
mul naengmyeon 물 냉면
cold noodle soup
nakjijeongol 낙지전골
octopus hotpot
oksusu 옥수수
corn on the cob
omuraiseu 오므라이스
omelette with rice
pajeon 파전
spring-onion pancake
ppeondaegi 뻔대기
boiled silkworm snack
ramyeon 라면
noodle soup
ramyeonbokki 라면볶이
fried ramen noodles
samgakgimbap 삼각심밥
triangular sushi snack
samgyeopsal 삼겹살
barbecued bacon-type pork
samgyetang 삼계탕
ginseng chicken soup
seolleongtang 설렁탕
beef & rice soup
sinseollo 신선로
meat, fish & vegetable broth cooked at table
sogeumgui 소금구이
salted beef ribs
sogogi gimbap 쇠고기 김밥
beef sushi
sundae 순대
tofu, vegetable & noodle sausage
sundubu jjigae 순두부 찌개
tofu & clam stew
sutbulgochujangchikin samgakgimbap
숫불고치킨 삼각김밥
triangular sushi with chicken & hot sauce
tongdakgui 통닭구이
roasted chicken

tteokbokki 떡볶이
spicy rice rolls
tteokmanduguk 떡만두국
soup with dumplings, seaweed & rice cakes
twigim 튀김
seafood & vegetables fried in batter
yeolmu naengmyeon 열무 냉면
cold-noodle gimchi soup
yukgaejang 육개장
spicy beef soup
yukhoe 육회
seasoned raw beef

Desserts 디저트

aiseukeurim 아이스크림
ice cream
daepaesaenggangyeot 대패생강엿
shaved toffee
delimanjoo 데리만주
custard-filled minicakes
gwaja 과자
pastry
hotteok 호떡
sweet pita-bread snack
keikeu 케이크
cake
kkultarae 꿀타래
honey & cornflour threads with nuts
pai 파이
pie
patbingsu 팥빙수
red-bean parfait
pulppang 풀빵
waffles
tteok 떡
rice cake
wapeul 와플
waffles

Chinese Food 중국음식

Chinese restaurant
junggukjip 중국집

bokkeumbap 볶음밥
fried rice
buchujapchae 부추잡채
pork & spring-onion rice
ganjjajangmyeon 간짜장면
vegetables with noodles & black-bean sauce
gochujapchae 고추잡채
pork & green capsicum rice
gonggalpang 공갈팡
crispy pita bread
gunmandu 군만두
fried dumplings
gyerantang 계란탕
egg soup
japchae 잡채
fried vermicelli, meat & vegetables
japchaebap 잡채밥
fried rice with noodles
japtang 잡탕
assorted soup
japtangbap 잡탕밥
seafood, meat, vegetables & rice
jjajangmyeon 짜장면
noodles with black-bean sauce
jjamppong 짬뽕
spicy seafood noodle soup
keunsaeutwigim 큰새우튀김
prawns
nanjawanseu 난자완스
minced pork or beef balls
ohyangjangyuk 오향장육
sliced meats
palbochae 팔보채
seafood & vegetables
rajogi 라조기
spicy chicken dish
rajoyuk 라조육
spicy pork & beef dish
saeubokkeumbap 새우볶음밥
shrimp fried rice
saeutwigim 새우튀김
shrimp dish
samseonganjjajang 삼선간짜장
noodles & flavoured sauces
samseonjjajang 삼선짜장
noodles & spicy sauce
samseonjjamppong 삼선짬뽕
spicy noodles with vegetables
samseonudong 삼선우동
seafood noodles
samseonulmyeon 삼선울면
seafood soupy noodles
song-ideopbap 송이덮밥
rice with mushroom sauce
tangsuyuk 탕수육
sweet & sour pork
udong 우동
thick noodles with sauce
ulmyeon 울면
soupy noodles

Japanese Food 일식

Japanese restaurant
ilsikjib 일식집

chikinkkaseu 치킨까스
chicken cutlet
chobap 초밥
sushi
dakkoyakki 다꼬야끼
octopus balls
donkkaseu 돈까스
pork cutlet
saengseonhoe 생선회
sashimi (raw fish)
saengseonkkaseu 생선까스
fish cutlet
saengseontwigim 생선튀김
fish tempura
saeutwigim 새우튀김
shrimp tempura with vegetables
udon 우돈
noodles
yachaetwigim 야채튀김
vegetable tempura
yubuchobap 유부초밥
tofu-wrapped sushi

DRINKS

Baekseju 백세주
rice wine with ginseng
baemsul 뱀술
snake wine
boricha 보리차
barley tea
cha 차
tea
chanmul 찬물
cold water
chikcha 칡차
arrowroot tea
daechucha 대추차
jujube tea
deounmul 더운물
hot water
dongdongju 동동주
fermented rice wine
gugijacha 구기자차
Chinese matrimony vine tea
gwangcheonsu 광천수
mineral water
hongcha 홍차
black tea
Igangju 이강주
spicy rice wine
insamcha 인삼차
ginseng tea
insamju 인삼주
ginseng wine
jyuseu 쥬스
juice
keopi 커피
coffee
kkulcha 꿀차
honey tea
kkulsamcha 꿀삼차
honey-ginseng tea
kokoa 코코아
hot cocoa
maekju 맥주
beer
makgeolli 막걸리
milky-white rice brew
nokcha 녹차
green tea
omijacha 오미자차
five-flavours tea
orenjijyuseu 오렌지쥬스
orange juice
podoju 포도주
wine
remoncha 레몬차
lemon tea
saenggangcha 생강차
ginger tea
saengsu 생수
mineral water
Sansachun 산사춘
plain rice wine
sikhye 식혜
rice punch
soju 소주
yam or tapioca 'vodka'
ssanghwacha 쌍화차
herb tonic tea
ssukcha 쑥차
mugwort tea
sungnyungcha 륭차
burnt-rice tea
uyu 우유
milk
yujacha 유자차
citron tea
yulmu cha 율무차
pine nuts, walnuts & adlay tea

Glossary

ajumma – a married or older woman; a term of respect for a woman who runs a hotel, restaurant or other business
-am – hermitage
anju – snacks eaten when drinking alcohol

baduk – a Korean version of an old Chinese game of strategy; also known as *go*
bang – room; a PC *bang* is an Internet room and a DVD *bang* is a room where you can watch DVDs
bong – peak
buk – north
bukbu – northern area
buncheong – pottery decorated with simple folk designs

cha – tea
changgeuk – traditional Korean opera
changgi – Korean version of Chinese chess

dabang – tearoom
DMZ – the Demilitarized Zone that runs along the 38th parallel of the Korean peninsula, separating North and South
-do – province
do – island
-dong – ward
dong – east
dongbu – eastern area

-eup – town

-ga – section of a long street
gang – river
geobukseon – 'turtle ships'; iron-clad warships
gibun – harmonious feelings; face
gil – small street
go-stop – a popular card game
-gu – urban district
-gun – county
gung – palace
gugak – traditional Korean music
gut – shamanist ceremony
gyotongkadeu – subway and bus travel card

hae – sea
haesuyokjang – beach
hagwon – private schools where students study after school or work; foreigners are often employed here to teach English conversation
hanbok – traditional Korean clothing
hangeul – Korean phonetic alphabet
hanja – Chinese-style writing system
hanji – traditional Korean hand-made paper
hanok – traditional Korean one-storey wooden house with a tiled roof
ho – lake
hof – bar or pub

insam – ginseng

jaebeol – huge family-run corporate conglomerate
jeon – hall of a temple
jeong – pavilion

KNTO – Korean National Tourism Organisation

minbak – a private home with rooms for rent
mobeom – deluxe taxi
mudang – shaman, usually female
mugunghwa – limited express train
mun – gate
-myeon – township

nam – south
nambu – southern area
neung – tomb
no – large street, boulevard
noraebang – karaoke, a room for singing songs

oncheon – hot-spring bath
ondol – underfloor heating

pansori – traditional Korean opera
pungsu – Korean geomancy
pyeong – a unit of measurement equal to 3.3 sq m

-ri – village
reung – tomb
ro – large street, boulevard
ROK – Republic of Korea (South Korea)
ru – pavilion

sa – temple
saemaeul – luxury express train
samulnori – traditional farmer's dance
san – mountain
sandaenori – a type of mask dance
sanjang – mountain hut
sanseong – mountain fortress
seo – west
seobu – western area
Seon – a version of Zen Buddhism native to Korea
seowon – Confucian academies
si – city
sicheong – city hall
sinae – local, as in local bus terminal
ssireum – Korean-style wrestling
sunim – monk

taegyeon – the original form of taekwondo
taekwondo – Korean martial arts
tang – a bathhouse that usually includes a sauna
tap – pagoda
tojang – personal seal with your name carved on it
tongil – slow local train

USO – United Service Organizations, which provides leisure services for US troops and civilians

yak – medicine
yangban – aristocrat
yeogwan – small family-run hotel, usually with a private bathroom
yeoinsuk – small family-run budget hotel with shared toilets and bathrooms
yo – padded quilt which serves as a futon or mattress for sleeping on the floor
yut – a game played with sticks that is similar to ludo

LONELY PLANET

You already know that Lonely Planet produces more than this one guidebook, but you might not be aware of the other products we have on this region. Here is a selection of titles that you may want to check out as well:

Beijing Condensed
ISBN 1 74059 386 3
US$12.99 • UK£6.99

Tokyo Condensed
ISBN 1 74059 069 4
US$11.99 • UK£5.99

Korean Phrasebook
ISBN 1 74059 166 6
US$7.99 • UK£4.50

Korea
ISBN 0 86442 697 6
US$19.99 • UK£12.99

Japan
ISBN 0 86442 693 3
US$25.99 • UK£15.99

Tokyo
ISBN 1 74059 059 7
US$15.99 • UK£9.99

Mongolia
ISBN 1 86450 064 6
US$17.99 • UK£11.99

Taiwan
ISBN 1 86450 211 8
US$19.99 • UK£12.99

Shanghai
ISBN 0 86442 507 4
US$15.99 • UK£9.99

China
ISBN 1 74059 117 8
US$29.99 • UK£17.99

Beijing
ISBN 1 74059 281 6
US$15.99 • UK£9.99

Hong Kong & Macau
ISBN 1 86450 230 4

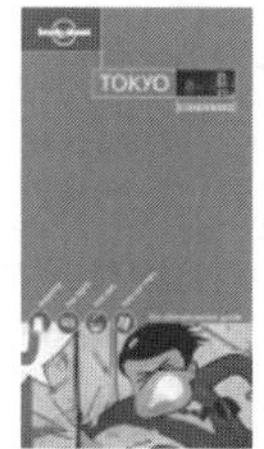

Lonely Planet Guides by Region

Lonely Planet is known worldwide for publishing practical, reliable and no-nonsense travel information in our guides and on our Web site. The Lonely Planet list covers just about every accessible part of the world. Currently there are 16 series: Travel guides, Shoestring guides, Condensed guides, Phrasebooks, Read This First, Healthy Travel, Walking guides, Cycling guides, Watching Wildlife guides, Pisces Diving & Snorkeling guides, City Maps, Road Atlases, Out to Eat, World Food, Journeys travel literature and Pictorials.

AFRICA Africa on a shoestring • Botswana • Cairo • Cairo City Map • Cape Town • Cape Town City Map • East Africa • Egypt • Egyptian Arabic phrasebook • Ethiopia, Eritrea & Djibouti • Ethiopian Amharic phrasebook • The Gambia & Senegal • Healthy Travel Africa • Kenya • Malawi • Morocco • Moroccan Arabic phrasebook • Mozambique • Namibia • Read This First: Africa • South Africa, Lesotho & Swaziland • Southern Africa • Southern Africa Road Atlas • Swahili phrasebook • Tanzania, Zanzibar & Pemba • Trekking in East Africa • Tunisia • Watching Wildlife East Africa • Watching Wildlife Southern Africa • West Africa • World Food Morocco • Zambia • Zimbabwe, Botswana & Namibia
Travel Literature: Mali Blues: Traveling to an African Beat • The Rainbird: A Central African Journey • Songs to an African Sunset: A Zimbabwean Story

AUSTRALIA & THE PACIFIC Aboriginal Australia & the Torres Strait Islands •Auckland • Australia • Australian phrasebook • Australia Road Atlas • Cycling Australia • Cycling New Zealand • Fiji • Fijian phrasebook • Healthy Travel Australia, NZ & the Pacific • Islands of Australia's Great Barrier Reef • Melbourne • Melbourne City Map • Micronesia • New Caledonia • New South Wales • New Zealand • Northern Territory • Outback Australia • Out to Eat – Melbourne • Out to Eat – Sydney • Papua New Guinea • Pidgin phrasebook • Queensland • Rarotonga & the Cook Islands • Samoa • Solomon Islands • South Australia • South Pacific • South Pacific phrasebook • Sydney • Sydney City Map • Sydney Condensed • Tahiti & French Polynesia • Tasmania • Tonga • Tramping in New Zealand • Vanuatu • Victoria • Walking in Australia • Watching Wildlife Australia • Western Australia
Travel Literature: Islands in the Clouds: Travels in the Highlands of New Guinea • Kiwi Tracks: A New Zealand Journey • Sean & David's Long Drive

CENTRAL AMERICA & THE CARIBBEAN Bahamas, Turks & Caicos • Baja California • Belize, Guatemala & Yucatán • Bermuda • Central America on a shoestring • Costa Rica • Costa Rica Spanish phrasebook • Cuba • Cycling Cuba • Dominican Republic & Haiti • Eastern Caribbean • Guatemala • Havana • Healthy Travel Central & South America • Jamaica • Mexico • Mexico City • Panama • Puerto Rico • Read This First: Central & South America • Virgin Islands • World Food Caribbean • World Food Mexico • Yucatán
Travel Literature: Green Dreams: Travels in Central America

EUROPE Amsterdam • Amsterdam City Map • Amsterdam Condensed • Andalucía • Athens • Austria • Baltic States phrasebook • Barcelona • Barcelona City Map • Belgium & Luxembourg • Berlin • Berlin City Map • Britain • British phrasebook • Brussels, Bruges & Antwerp • Brussels City Map • Budapest • Budapest City Map • Canary Islands • Catalunya & the Costa Brava • Central Europe • Central Europe phrasebook • Copenhagen • Corfu & the Ionians • Corsica • Crete • Crete Condensed • Croatia • Cycling Britain • Cycling France • Cyprus • Czech & Slovak Republics • Czech phrasebook • Denmark • Dublin • Dublin City Map • Dublin Condensed • Eastern Europe • Eastern Europe phrasebook • Edinburgh • Edinburgh City Map • England • Estonia, Latvia & Lithuania • Europe on a shoestring • Europe phrasebook • Finland • Florence • Florence City Map • France • Frankfurt City Map • Frankfurt Condensed • French phrasebook • Georgia, Armenia & Azerbaijan • Germany • German phrasebook • Greece • Greek Islands • Greek phrasebook • Hungary • Iceland, Greenland & the Faroe Islands • Ireland • Italian phrasebook • Italy • Kraków • Lisbon • The Loire • London • London City Map • London Condensed • Madrid • Madrid City Map • Malta • Mediterranean Europe • Milan, Turin & Genoa • Moscow • Munich • Netherlands • Normandy • Norway • Out to Eat – London • Out to Eat – Paris • Paris • Paris City Map • Paris Condensed • Poland • Polish phrasebook • Portugal • Portuguese phrasebook • Prague • Prague City Map • Provence & the Côte d'Azur • Read This First: Europe • Rhodes & the Dodecanese • Romania & Moldova • Rome • Rome City Map • Rome Condensed • Russia, Ukraine & Belarus • Russian phrasebook • Scandinavian & Baltic Europe • Scandinavian phrasebook • Scotland • Sicily • Slovenia • South-West France • Spain • Spanish phrasebook • Stockholm • St Petersburg • St Petersburg City Map • Sweden • Switzerland • Tuscany • Ukrainian phrasebook • Venice • Vienna • Wales • Walking in Britain • Walking in France • Walking in Ireland • Walking in Italy • Walking in Scotland • Walking in Spain • Walking in Switzerland • Western Europe • World Food France • World Food Greece • World Food Ireland • World Food Italy • World Food Spain
Travel Literature: After Yugoslavia • Love and War in the Apennines • The Olive Grove: Travels in Greece • On the Shores of the Mediterranean • Round Ireland in Low Gear • A Small Place in Italy

Lonely Planet Mail Order

Lonely Planet products are distributed worldwide. They are also available by mail order from Lonely Planet, so if you have difficulty finding a title please write to us. North and South American residents should write to 150 Linden St, Oakland, CA 94607, USA; European and African residents should write to 72-82 Rosebery Ave, London, EC1R 4RW, UK; and residents of other countries to Locked Bag 1, Footscray, Victoria 3011, Australia.

INDIAN SUBCONTINENT & THE INDIAN OCEAN Bangladesh • Bengali phrasebook • Bhutan • Delhi • Goa • Healthy Travel Asia & India • Hindi & Urdu phrasebook • India • India & Bangladesh City Map • Indian Himalaya • Karakoram Highway • Kathmandu City Map • Kerala • Madagascar • Maldives • Mauritius, Réunion & Seychelles • Mumbai (Bombay) • Nepal • Nepali phrasebook • North India • Pakistan • Rajasthan • Read This First: Asia & India • South India • Sri Lanka • Sri Lanka phrasebook • Tibet • Tibetan phrasebook • Trekking in the Indian Himalaya • Trekking in the Karakoram & Hindukush • Trekking in the Nepal Himalaya • World Food India **Travel Literature**: The Age of Kali: Indian Travels and Encounters • Hello Goodnight: A Life of Goa • In Rajasthan • Maverick in Madagascar • A Season in Heaven: True Tales from the Road to Kathmandu • Shopping for Buddhas • A Short Walk in the Hindu Kush • Slowly Down the Ganges

MIDDLE EAST & CENTRAL ASIA Bahrain, Kuwait & Qatar • Central Asia • Central Asia phrasebook • Dubai • Farsi (Persian) phrasebook • Hebrew phrasebook • Iran • Israel & the Palestinian Territories • Istanbul • Istanbul City Map • Istanbul to Cairo • Istanbul to Kathmandu • Jerusalem • Jerusalem City Map • Jordan • Lebanon • Middle East • Oman & the United Arab Emirates • Syria • Turkey • Turkish phrasebook • World Food Turkey • Yemen **Travel Literature**: Black on Black: Iran Revisited • Breaking Ranks: Turbulent Travels in the Promised Land • The Gates of Damascus • Kingdom of the Film Stars: Journey into Jordan

NORTH AMERICA Alaska • Boston • Boston City Map • Boston Condensed • British Columbia • California & Nevada • California Condensed • Canada • Chicago • Chicago City Map • Chicago Condensed • Florida • Georgia & the Carolinas • Great Lakes • Hawaii • Hiking in Alaska • Hiking in the USA • Honolulu & Oahu City Map • Las Vegas • Los Angeles • Los Angeles City Map • Louisiana & the Deep South • Miami • Miami City Map • Montreal • New England • New Orleans • New Orleans City Map • New York City • New York City City Map • New York City Condensed • New York, New Jersey & Pennsylvania • Oahu • Out to Eat – San Francisco • Pacific Northwest • Rocky Mountains • San Diego & Tijuana • San Francisco • San Francisco City Map • Seattle • Seattle City Map • Southwest • Texas • Toronto • USA • USA phrasebook • Vancouver • Vancouver City Map • Virginia & the Capital Region • Washington, DC • Washington, DC City Map • World Food New Orleans **Travel Literature**: Caught Inside: A Surfer's Year on the California Coast • Drive Thru America

NORTH-EAST ASIA Beijing • Beijing City Map • Cantonese phrasebook • China • Hiking in Japan • Hong Kong & Macau • Hong Kong City Map • Hong Kong Condensed • Japan • Japanese phrasebook • Korea • Korean phrasebook • Kyoto • Mandarin phrasebook • Mongolia • Mongolian phrasebook • Seoul • Shanghai • South-West China • Taiwan • Tokyo • Tokyo Condensed • World Food Hong Kong • World Food Japan
Travel Literature: In Xanadu: A Quest • Lost Japan

SOUTH AMERICA Argentina, Uruguay & Paraguay • Bolivia • Brazil • Brazilian phrasebook • Buenos Aires • Buenos Aires City Map • Chile & Easter Island • Colombia • Ecuador & the Galapagos Islands • Healthy Travel Central & South America • Latin American Spanish phrasebook • Peru • Quechua phrasebook • Read This First: Central & South America • Rio de Janeiro • Rio de Janeiro City Map • Santiago de Chile • South America on a shoestring • Trekking in the Patagonian Andes • Venezuela **Travel Literature**: Full Circle: A South American Journey

SOUTH-EAST ASIA Bali & Lombok • Bangkok • Bangkok City Map • Burmese phrasebook • Cambodia • Cycling Vietnam, Laos & Cambodia • East Timor phrasebook • Hanoi • Healthy Travel Asia & India • Hill Tribes phrasebook • Ho Chi Minh City (Saigon) • Indonesia • Indonesian phrasebook • Indonesia's Eastern Islands • Java • Lao phrasebook • Laos • Malay phrasebook • Malaysia, Singapore & Brunei • Myanmar (Burma) • Philippines • Pilipino (Tagalog) phrasebook • Read This First: Asia & India • Singapore • Singapore City Map • South-East Asia on a shoestring • South-East Asia phrasebook • Thailand • Thailand's Islands & Beaches • Thailand, Vietnam, Laos & Cambodia Road Atlas • Thai phrasebook • Vietnam • Vietnamese phrasebook • World Food Indonesia • World Food Thailand • World Food Vietnam

ALSO AVAILABLE: Antarctica • The Arctic • The Blue Man: Tales of Travel, Love and Coffee • Brief Encounters: Stories of Love, Sex & Travel • Buddhist Stupas in Asia: The Shape of Perfection • Chasing Rickshaws • The Last Grain Race • Lonely Planet ... On the Edge: Adventurous Escapades from Around the World • Lonely Planet Unpacked • Lonely Planet Unpacked Again • Not the Only Planet: Science Fiction Travel Stories • Ports of Call: A Journey by Sea • Sacred India • Travel Photography: A Guide to Taking Better Pictures • Travel with Children • Tuvalu: Portrait of an Island Nation

Index

Text

Bold indicates maps.

Places to Stay

Places to Eat

Boxed Text

Entertainment

Locality Guide

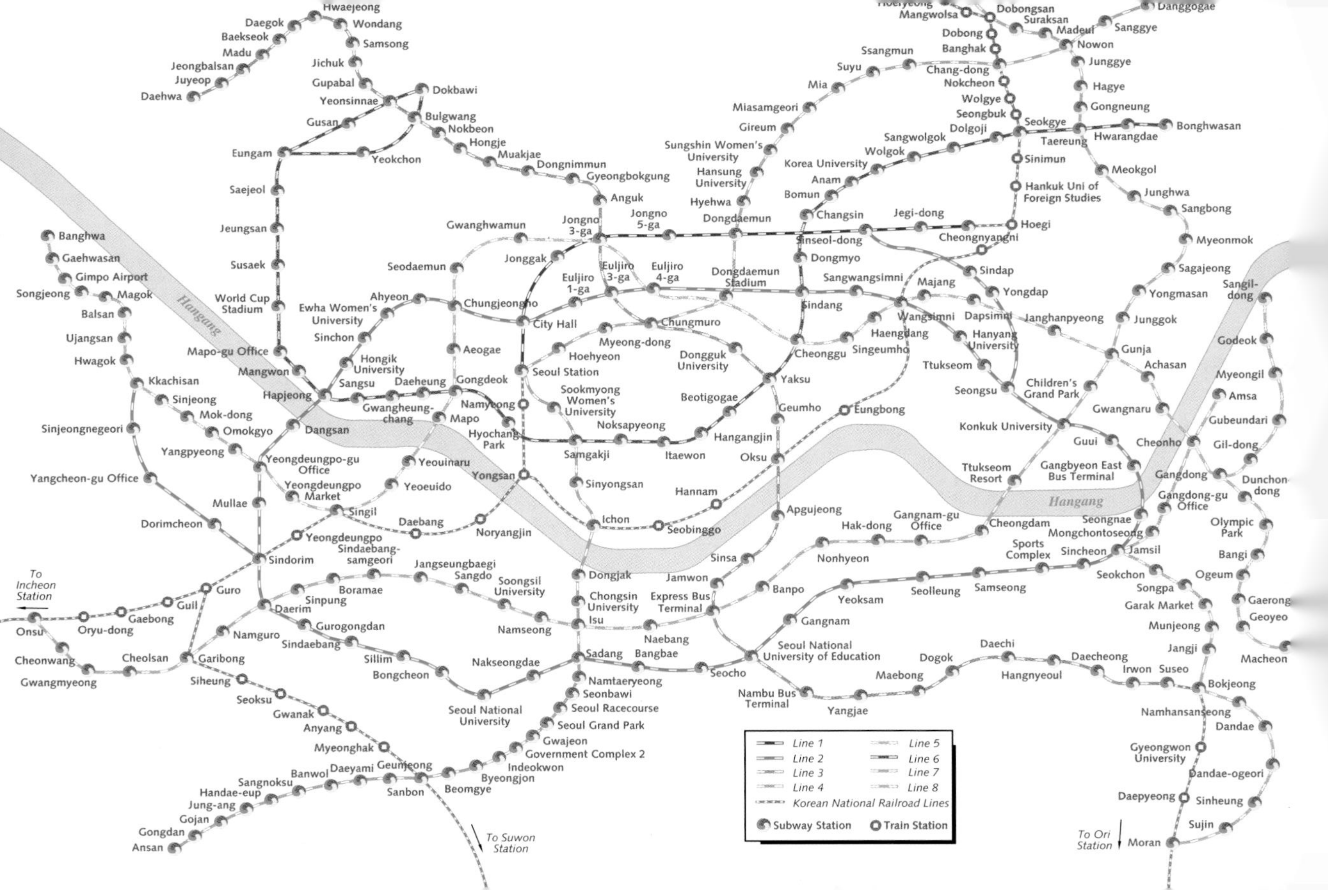

Line 1
Line 2
Line 3
Line 4
Line 5
Line 6
Line 7
Line 8
Korean National Railroad Lines
Subway Station
Train Station
Hangang
Hangang
To Incheon Station
To Suwon Station
To Ori Station
Hwaejeong
Wondang
Samsong
Daegok
Baekseok
Madu
Jeongbalsan
Juyeop
Daehwa
Jichuk
Gupabal
Yeonsinnae
Dokbawi
Bulgwang
Nokbeon
Hongje
Muakjae
Dongnimmun
Gyeongbokgung
Anguk
Gusan
Yeokchon
Eungam
Saejeol
Jeungsan
Susaek
World Cup Stadium
Mapo-gu Office
Mangwon
Hapjeong
Banghwa
Gaehwasan
Gimpo Airport
Songjeong
Magok
Balsan
Ujangsan
Hwagok
Kkachisan
Sinjeong
Mok-dong
Omokgyo
Sinjeongnegeori
Yangpyeong
Yangcheon-gu Office
Dorimcheon
Mullae
Yeongdeungpo-gu Office
Yeongdeungpo Market
Dangsan
Sindorim
Guro
Guil
Gaebong
Oryu-dong
Onsu
Cheonwang
Gwangmyeong
Cheolsan
Garibong
Siheung
Seoksu
Gwanak
Anyang
Myeonghak
Geumjeong
Sanbon
Beomgye
Daeyami
Banwol
Sangnoksu
Handae-eup
Jung-ang
Gojan
Gongdan
Ansan
Namguro
Daerim
Sindaebang
Gurogongdan
Sillim
Bongcheon
Seoul National University
Nakseongdae
Sinpung
Boramae
Sindaebang-samgeori
Yeongdeungpo
Jangseungbaegi
Sangdo
Soongsil University
Namseong
Singil
Daebang
Noryangjin
Yeouinaru
Yeoeuido
Yongsan
Sinchon
Ewha Women's University
Ahyeon
Sangsu
Hongik University
Daeheung
Gwangheung-chang
Gongdeok
Mapo
Aeogae
Seodaemun
Chungjeongno
Gwanghwamun
Jonggak
Jongno 3-ga
Jongno 5-ga
Dongdaemun
City Hall
Euljiro 1-ga
Euljiro 3-ga
Euljiro 4-ga
Dongdaemun Stadium
Seoul Station
Namyeong
Hyochang Park
Sookmyong Women's University
Samgakji
Sinyongsan
Ichon
Seobinggo
Hannam
Hoehyeon
Myeong-dong
Chungmuro
Dongguk University
Yaksu
Beotigogae
Noksapyeong
Itaewon
Hangangjin
Geumho
Oksu
Apgujeong
Sinsa
Jamwon
Express Bus Terminal
Dongjak
Chongsin University
Isu
Sadang
Naebang
Bangbae
Seocho
Namtaeryeong
Seonbawi
Seoul Racecourse
Seoul Grand Park
Gwajeon
Government Complex 2
Indeokwon
Byeongjeon
Banpo
Nonhyeon
Hak-dong
Gangnam-gu Office
Cheongdam
Gangnam
Yeoksam
Seolleung
Samseong
Sports Complex
Sincheon
Seoul National University of Education
Nambu Bus Terminal
Yangjae
Maebong
Dogok
Daechi
Hangnyeoul
Daecheong
Irwon
Suseo
Bokjeong
Namhansanseong
Dandae
Gyeongwon University
Dandae-ogeori
Daepyeong
Sinheung
Sujin
Moran
Jamsil
Seokchon
Songpa
Garak Market
Munjeong
Jangji
Seongnae
Mongchontoseong
Gangdong-gu Office
Olympic Park
Bangi
Ogeum
Gaerong
Geoyeo
Macheon
Gangdong
Dunchon-dong
Gil-dong
Gubeundari
Amsa
Myeongil
Godeok
Sangil-dong
Cheonho
Gwangnaru
Achasan
Gunja
Junggok
Yongmasan
Sagajeong
Myeonmok
Sangbong
Junghwa
Meokgol
Guui
Gangbyeon East Bus Terminal
Ttukseom Resort
Konkuk University
Children's Grand Park
Seongsu
Ttukseom
Hanyang University
Wangsimni
Haengdang
Singeumho
Cheonggu
Sindang
Sangwangsimni
Majang
Dapsimni
Janghanpyeong
Yongdap
Sindap
Eungbong
Cheongnyangni
Hoegi
Jegi-dong
Changsin
Sinseol-dong
Dongmyo
Hyehwa
Hansung University
Sungshin Women's University
Gireum
Miasamgeori
Mia
Suyu
Ssangmun
Bomun
Anam
Korea University
Wolgok
Sangwolgok
Dolgoji
Seokgye
Sinimun
Hankuk Uni of Foreign Studies
Taereung
Hwarangdae
Bonghwasan
Gongneung
Hagye
Junggye
Nowon
Madeul
Suraksan
Dobongsan
Mangwolsa
Dobong
Banghak
Chang-dong
Nokcheon
Wolgye
Seongbuk
Sanggye
Danggogae

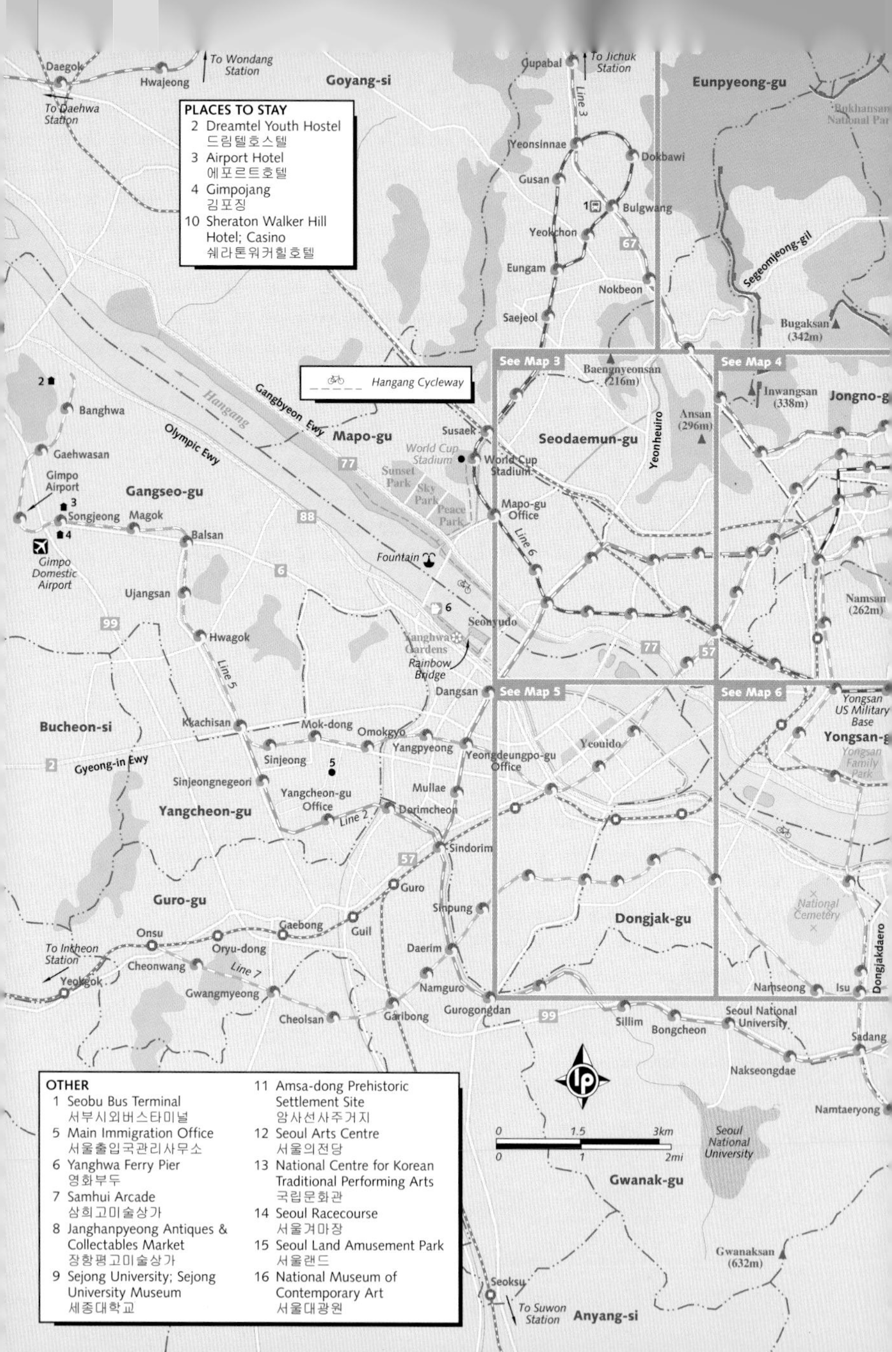

PLACES TO STAY
2 Dreamtel Youth Hostel
드림텔호스텔
3 Airport Hotel
에포르트호텔
4 Gimpojang
김포장
10 Sheraton Walker Hill Hotel; Casino
쉐라톤워커힐호텔
Hangang Cycleway
OTHER
1 Seobu Bus Terminal
서부시외버스터미널
5 Main Immigration Office
서울출입국관리사무소
6 Yanghwa Ferry Pier
영화부두
7 Samhui Arcade
삼희고미술상가
8 Janghanpyeong Antiques & Collectables Market
장항평고미술상가
9 Sejong University; Sejong University Museum
세종대학교
11 Amsa-dong Prehistoric Settlement Site
암사선사주거지
12 Seoul Arts Centre
서울의전당
13 National Centre for Korean Traditional Performing Arts
국립문화관
14 Seoul Racecourse
서울겨마장
15 Seoul Land Amusement Park
서울랜드
16 National Museum of Contemporary Art
서울대광원
See Map 3
See Map 4
See Map 5
See Map 6
Daegok
Hwajeong
To Wondang Station
To Daehwa Station
Goyang-si
Gupabal
To Jichuk Station
Line 3
Eunpyeong-gu
Bukhansan National Park
Yeonsinnae
Dokbawi
Gusan
Bulgwang
Yeokchon
Eungam
Nokbeon
Saejeol
Segeomjeong-gil
Bugaksan (342m)
Baengnyeonsan (216m)
Inwangsan (338m)
Jongno-gu
Ansan (296m)
Yeonheuiro
Seodaemun-gu
Banghwa
Gaehwasan
Gimpo Airport
Songjeong
Magok
Gangseo-gu
Balsan
Gimpo Domestic Airport
Hangang
Gangbyeon Ewy
Olympic Ewy
Mapo-gu
Susaek
World Cup Stadium
Sunset Park
Sky Park
Peace Park
Mapo-gu Office
Line 6
Fountain
Ujangsan
Hwagok
Line 5
Seonyudo
Yanghwa Gardens
Rainbow Bridge
Dangsan
Namsan (262m)
Yongsan US Military Base
Yongsan-gu
Yongsan Family Park
Bucheon-si
Kkachisan
Mok-dong
Omokgyo
Yangpyeong
Yeongdeungpo-gu Office
Yeouido
Gyeong-in Ewy
Sinjeong
Sinjeongnegeori
Yangcheon-gu Office
Mullae
Yangcheon-gu
Line 2
Dorimcheon
Sindorim
Guro
Guro-gu
Sinpung
Dongjak-gu
National Cemetery
Gaebong
Guil
Onsu
Oryu-dong
To Incheon Station
Daerim
Cheonwang
Line 7
Yeokgok
Namguro
Gwangmyeong
Cheolsan
Garibong
Gurogongdan
Namseong
Isu
Dongjakdaero
Sillim
Bongcheon
Seoul National University
Sadang
Nakseongdae
Namtaeryong
Gwanak-gu
Gwanaksan (632m)
Seoksu
To Suwon Station
Anyang-si
0 1.5 3km
0 1 2mi

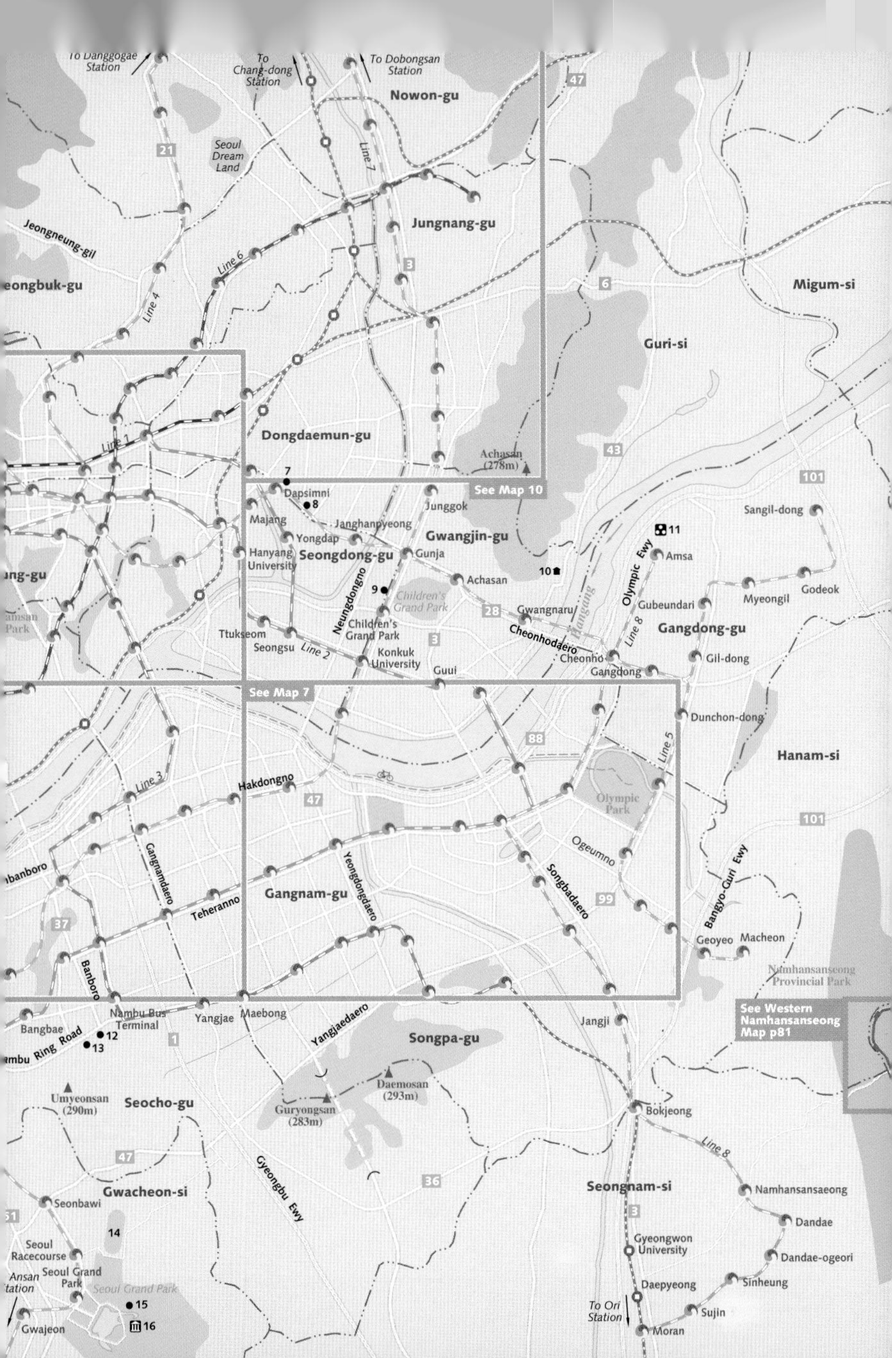

To Danggogae Station
To Chang-dong Station
To Dobongsan Station
Nowon-gu
Seoul Dream Land
Line 7
Jungnang-gu
Jeongneung-gil
Line 6
Line 4
eongbuk-gu
Migum-si
Guri-si
Dongdaemun-gu
Line 1
Achasan (278m)
See Map 10
7
Dapsimni
8
Majang
Janghanpyeong
Junggok
Gwangjin-gu
Yongdap
Hanyang University
Seongdong-gu
Gunja
Achasan
10
11
Amsa
Olympic Ewy
Sangil-dong
ung-gu
9
Children's Grand Park
Neungdongno
Gwangnaru
Hangang
Gubeundari
Myeongil
Godeok
Ttukseom
Seongsu
Line 2
Children's Grand Park
Konkuk University
Cheonhodaero
Cheonho
Gangdong
Line 8
Gangdong-gu
Gil-dong
Guui
See Map 7
Dunchon-dong
Line 5
Hanam-si
Line 3
Hakdongno
Olympic Park
Ogeumno
Gangnamdaero
Yeongdongdaero
Songbadaero
Bangyo-Guri Ewy
nbanboro
Gangnam-gu
Teheranno
Geoyeo
Macheon
Namhansanseong Provincial Park
Banboro
Nambu Bus Terminal
Yangjae
Maebong
Yangjaedaero
Jangji
See Western Namhansanseong Map p81
Bangbae
12
13
mbu Ring Road
Songpa-gu
Daemosan (293m)
Umyeonsan (290m)
Seocho-gu
Guryongsan (283m)
Bokjeong
Line 8
Gyeongbu Ewy
Gwacheon-si
Seongnam-si
Seonbawi
Namhansansaeong
Dandae
14
Seoul Racecourse
Gyeongwon University
Dandae-ogeori
Ansan Station
Seoul Grand Park
Seoul Grand Park
Daepyeong
Sinheung
15
16
To Ori Station
Sujin
Gwajeon
Moran
21
47
3
6
43
101
28
88
37
99
1
36

Baengnyeonsan (216m)
Euijuro
Line 3
Jeungsan
Line 6
Seodaemun-gu
Ansan (296m)
Susaegno
Yeonheuiro
To Downtown
Yonsei University
Seongsanno
Ewha Women's University
To World Cup Stadium
Mangwondonggil
Seogyoro
Hapjeongno
To Central Seoul
Hongik University
Donggyoro
Line 2
Sinchon
Mangwon
Sogang University
Wausan-gil
Hongik University
Picasso St
Hapjeong
Sangsu
Daeheungno
Gwangheungchang
Daeheung
Seogangno
Taeheungno
Hangang Cycleway
Tochonggil
Gangbyeon Ewy
Yanghwa Bridge
Seogang Bridge
Hangang
To Yeouido
Bamseom Island Bird Sanctuary
Mapo
Line 5
0 400 800m
0 400 800yd

MAP 3 – HONGIK, SINCHON & EWHA

PLACES TO STAY

6 Guesthouse Korea
게스트하우스코리아
19 Yeongbinjang
영빈장
20 Mirabeau Hotel
미라보호텔
21 Prince Hotel
프린스호텔
22 Geurin Motel
그린모텔
23 Onyangjang
온영장
41 Dongbojang; Geumsil Motel; Cheongsujang; Gallery Hotel
도보장
51 Seogyo Hotel
서교호텔
66 Kims' Guesthouse
킴스게스트하우스

PLACES TO EAT

3 Sandong Shui Jao Daewang
산동싀자오대왕
4 Jen Beijing
젠베이징
7 Mei Hwa
메이화
8 Hongbok
홍복
9 Hsiang Yuan
호시앙유안
15 Andrew's
앤드루스
16 idame
이댐
24 Chicken Rice
칙큰라이스
25 Naniwa (Sinchon)
나니와
30 Zen Zen
젠젠
37 Huedeura Ramyeon
후에드라라면
44 Coco's
코코스
47 Naniwa (Hongik)
나니와
48 Dangang Andong Jjimdak
단강안동찜닭
49 Pizza Hut
피자헛
50 Nolboo
놀부
53 Haejeodon
해저돈
59 Gio
기오

OTHER

1 Bongwonsa
봉원사
2 Seoul Foreign School
서울외국인학교
5 Sareoga Shopping Centre
사러가쇼핑센타
10 Birdland
버드랜드
11 Severance Hospital
세브란스병원
12 Yonsei Taekwondo Centre
연세태권도협회
13 Ewha Women's University Museum & Gallery
이화여자대학교박물관
14 Bubble Tea Shop
법블칫집
17 Ahyeon-dong Wedding Street
아현동웨딩거리
18 Post Office
우체국
26 Blue Monkeys
블루만키스
27 Wallflowers
월플러워스
28 Free Crocodiles
아어를풀어놔봐
29 Beatles
비틀즈
31 Voodoo
부두바
32 Woodstock
우드스탁
33 Doors
도어스바
34 Rolling Stones
롤링스톤스
35 Haeyuljae
해율재
36 Indoor Market
실내시장
38 Hyundai Department Store
현대백화점
39 Grand Mart & Cinema
크랜드백화점
40 Bagdad Magic Cafe
백대드매직까페
42 Sinchon Bus Terminal
신촌사외버스터미널
43 Macondo
마콘도
45 Bahia
바히아
46 Be Bop Jazz Club
비밥
52 Shoestring Travel
신발끈여행사거점
54 Y'sorno Cafe
이쏘르노
55 Hot House Live Jazz
훗하우스
56 Cinecastle
신니카실디비디방
57 Free Bird
프리버드
58 SLUG.er Disco
슬러거
60 Labris
라브리스
61 Gold
골드바
62 Sk@
스카
63 Drug
드럭
64 Hodge Podge
호지포지
65 Queen's Head
쿠에인스헤드
67 Seoul Foreigner's Cemetery
서울외인묘지
68 Jeoldusan Martyrs' Shrine & Museum
절두산수교성지

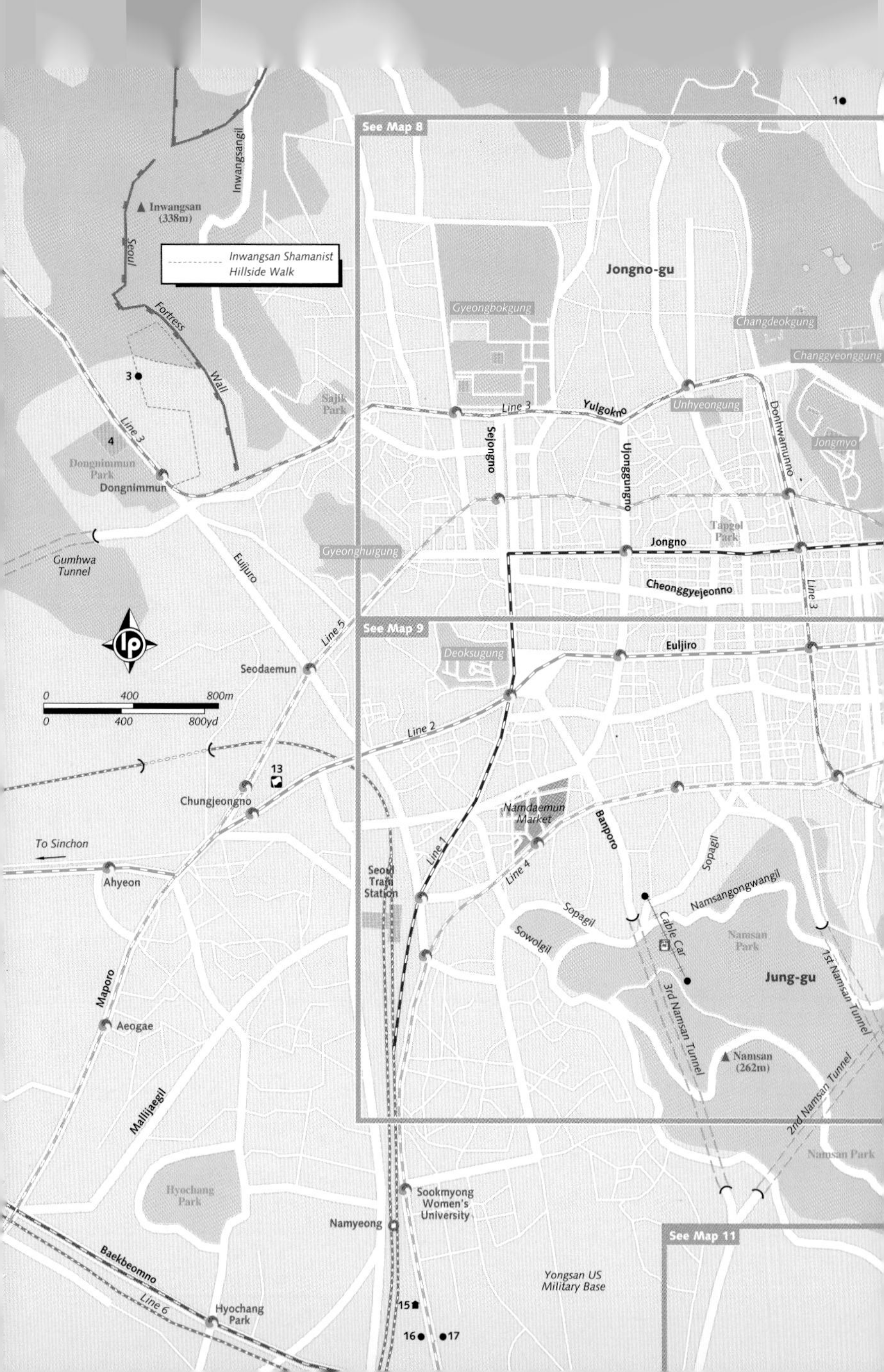

See Map 8
See Map 9
See Map 11
Inwangsan Shamanist
Hillside Walk
Inwangsan
(338m)
Inwangsangil
Seoul
Fortress
Wall
Sajik Park
Dongnimmun Park
Dongnimmun
Line 3
Gumhwa Tunnel
Euljiro
Gyeonghuigung
Gyeongbokgung
Jongno-gu
Changdeokgung
Changgyeongdung
Unhyeongung
Yulgokno
Sejongno
Ujongguno
Donhwamunno
Jongmyo
Tapgol Park
Jongno
Cheonggyejeonno
Deoksugung
Line 5
Seodaemun
Line 2
Line 1
Line 4
Chungjeongno
To Sinchon
Ahyeon
Namdaemun Market
Banporo
Sopagil
Namsangongwangil
Cable Car
Sowolgil
Seoul Train Station
Namsan Park
Jung-gu
3rd Namsan Tunnel
1st Namsan Tunnel
2nd Namsan Tunnel
Namsan
(262m)
Maporo
Aeogae
Mallijaegil
Hyochang Park
Sookmyong Women's University
Namyeong
Yongsan US Military Base
Baekbeomno
Line 6
0
400
800m
800yd
1
3
4
13
15
16
17

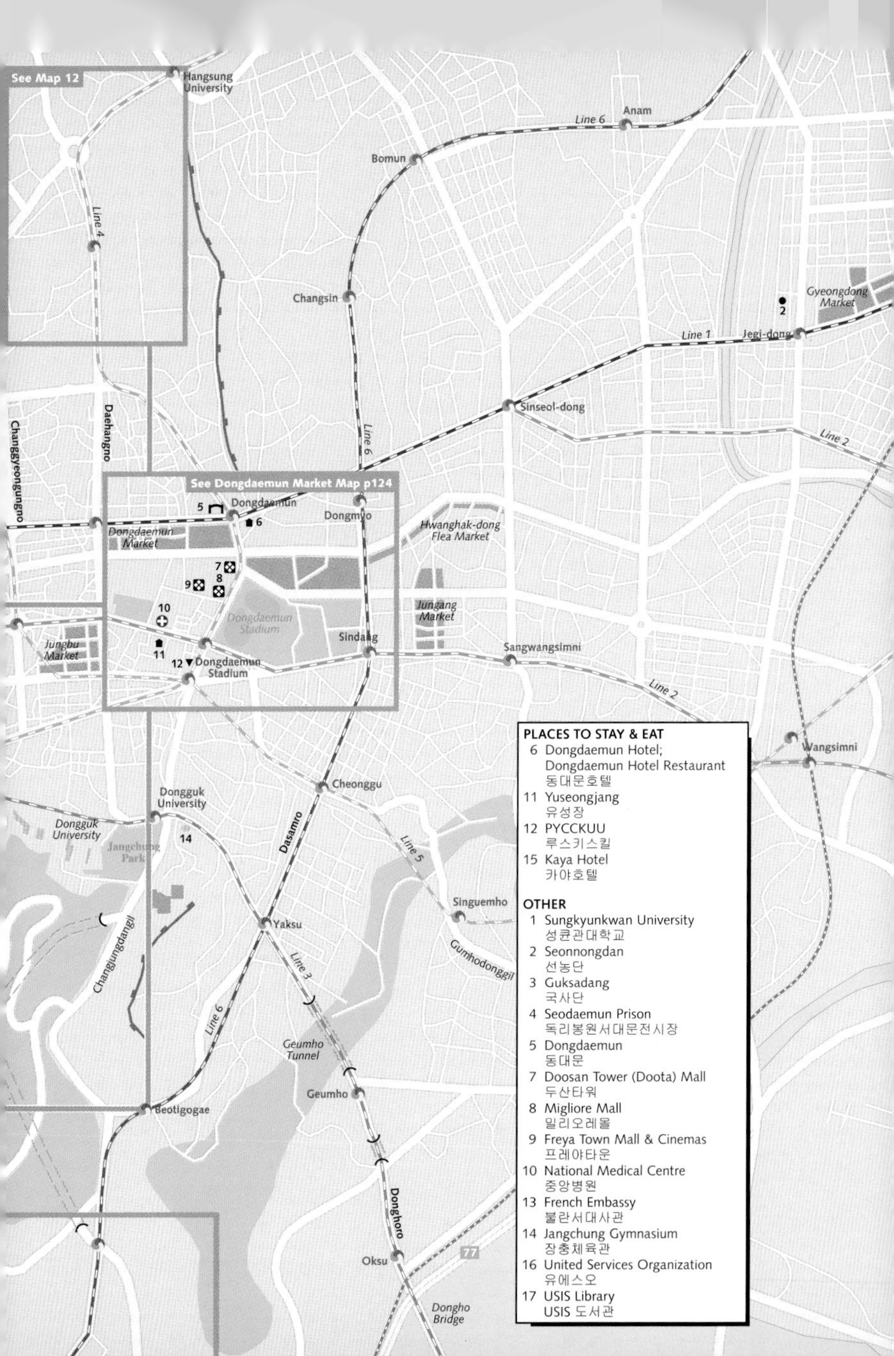
See Map 12
Hangsung University
Line 4
Line 6
Anam
Bomun
Changsin
Gyeongdong Market
2
Line 1
Jegi-dong
Sinseol-dong
Line 2
Daehangno
Changgyeongungno
See Dongdaemun Market Map p124
5
Dongdaemun
6
Dongmyo
Dongdaemun Market
Hwanghak-dong Flea Market
7
8
9
10
Dongdaemun Stadium
Jungang Market
Jungbu Market
11
12
Dongdaemun Stadium
Sindang
Sangwangsimni
Cheonggu
Wangsimni
Dongguk University
Dongguk University
14
Jangchung Park
Dasamro
Line 5
Singuemho
Yaksu
Gumhodonggil
Line 3
Changjungdangil
Geumho Tunnel
Geumho
Beotigogae
Donghoro
Oksu
77
Dongho Bridge
PLACES TO STAY & EAT
6 Dongdaemun Hotel; Dongdaemun Hotel Restaurant
동대문호텔
11 Yuseongjang
유성장
12 PYCCKUU
루스키스킬
15 Kaya Hotel
카야호텔
OTHER
1 Sungkyunkwan University
성균관대학교
2 Seonnongdan
선농단
3 Guksadang
국사단
4 Seodaemun Prison
독리봉원서대문전시장
5 Dongdaemun
동대문
7 Doosan Tower (Doota) Mall
두산타워
8 Migliore Mall
밀리오레몰
9 Freya Town Mall & Cinemas
프레야타운
10 National Medical Centre
중앙병원
13 French Embassy
불란서대사관
14 Jangchung Gymnasium
장충체육관
16 United Services Organization
유에스오
17 USIS Library
USIS 도서관

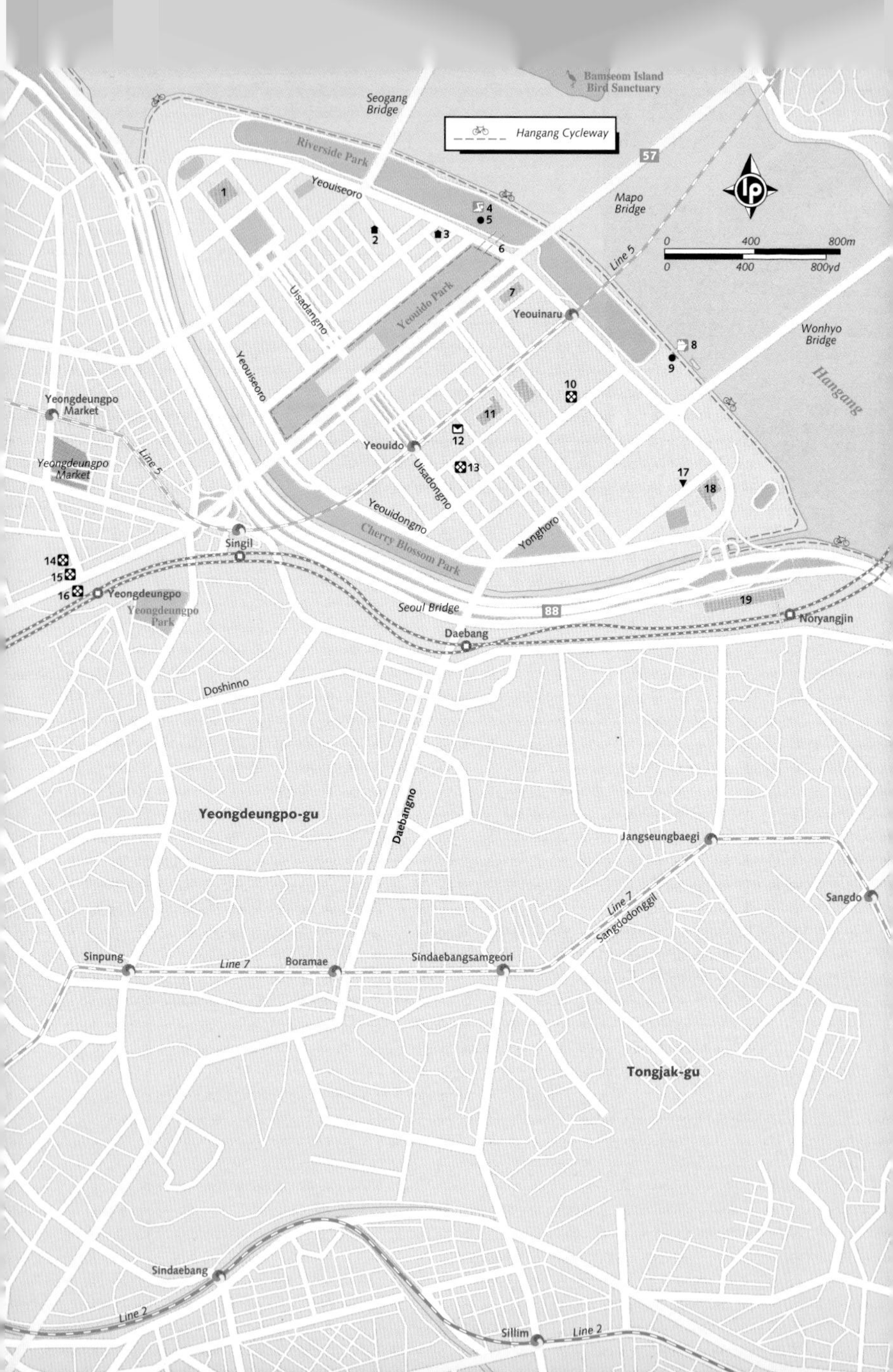

Bamseom Island Bird Sanctuary
Seogang Bridge
Hangang Cycleway
Riverside Park
57
Mapo Bridge
0
400
800m
0
400
800yd
Yeouiseoro
1
2
3
4
5
6
7
Line 5
Yeouido Park
Uisadangno
Yeouinaru
8
9
Wonhyo Bridge
Hangang
Yeouiseoro
10
11
12
Yeongdeungpo Market
Yeongdeungpo Market
Line 5
Yeouido
Uisadongno
13
17
18
Yeouidongno
Cherry Blossom Park
Yonghoro
Singil
14
15
16
Yeongdeungpo
Yeongdeungpo Park
Seoul Bridge
88
19
Noryangjin
Daebang
Doshinno
Yeongdeungpo-gu
Daebangno
Jangseungbaegi
Sangdo
Line 7
Sangdodonggil
Sinpung
Line 7
Boramae
Sindaebangsamgeori
Tongjak-gu
Sindaebang
Line 2
Sillim
Line 2

MAP 5 – YEOUIDO

PLACES TO STAY & EAT

2 New Manhattan Hotel
뉴맨해튼호텔

3 Yeouido Hotel
여의도호텔

17 Myeongdong Restaurant
명동식당

19 Noryangjin Fish Market Restaurants
노량진합어시장

OTHER

1 National Assembly
국회의사당

4 Swimming Pool
수영장

5 Bicycle Hire
자전거렌터

6 Cycleway Tunnel
터널

7 LG Twin Towers
엘지트윈타워즈

8 Yeouido Ferry Pier
여의도선착장

9 Bicycle Hire
자전거렌터

10 Yeouido Shopping Centre
여의도쇼핑센타

11 Korea Stock Exchange
증ㄱ권거래소

12 Yeouido Post Office
여의도우체국

13 Shopping Mall
쇼핑몰

14 Kyeongbang Phill Department Store
경방필백화점

15 Shinsegae Department Store
신세개백화점

16 Lotte Department Store
롯테백화점

18 63 Building
63빌딩

DENNIS JOHNSON

Detail of Changgyeonggung

BILL WASSMAN

Changgyeonggung – Palace of Flourishing Gladness

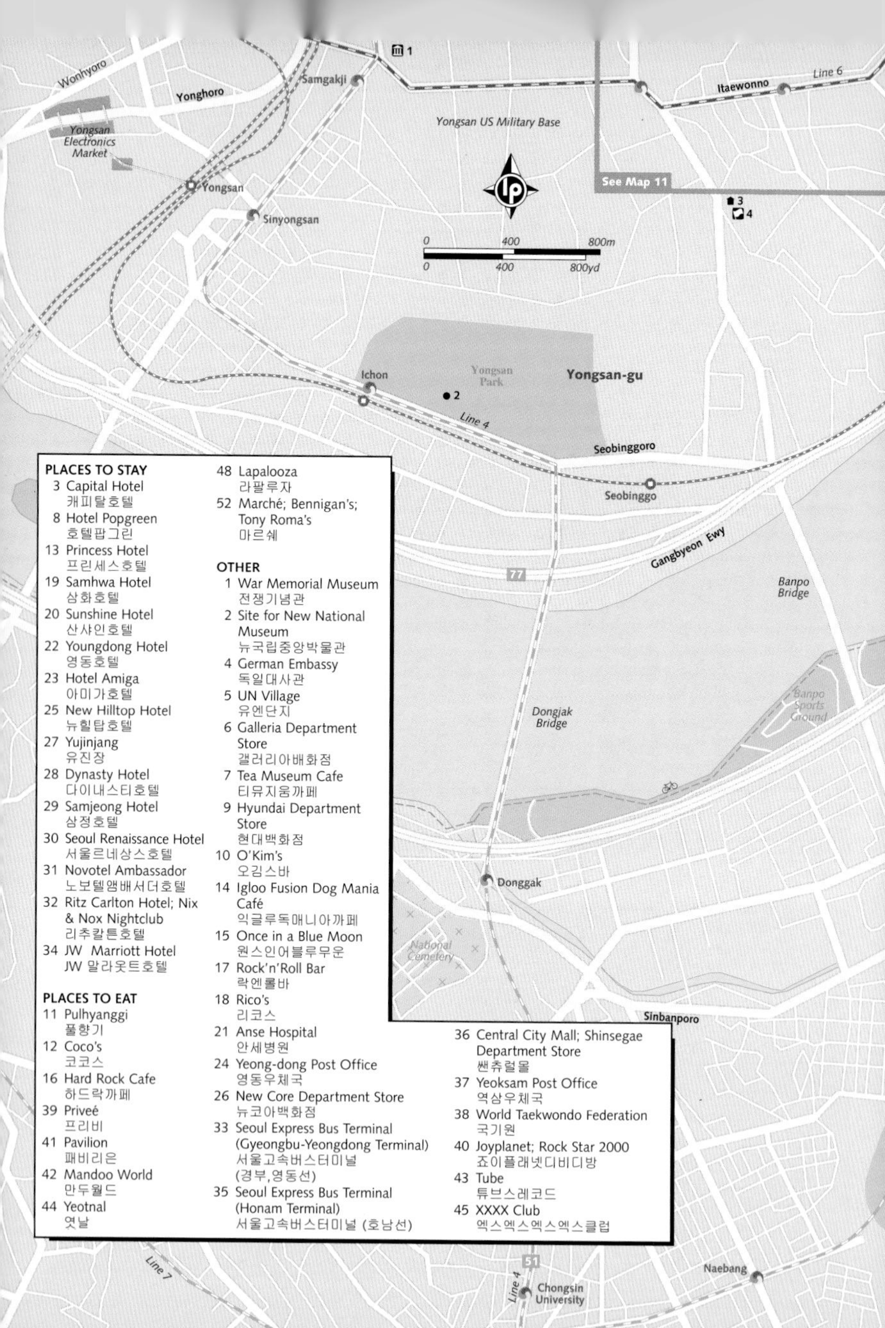

Wonhyoro
Yonghoro
Samgakji
1
Yongsan Electronics Market
Yongsan
Sinyongsan
Yongsan US Military Base
Itaewonno
Line 6
See Map 11
3
4
0 400 800m
0 400 800yd
Ichon
Yongsan Park
Yongsan-gu
2
Line 4
Seobinggoro
Seobinggo
Gangbyeon Ewy
77
Banpo Bridge
Banpo Sports Ground
Dongjak Bridge
Donggak
National Cemetery
Sinbanporo
Line 7
51
Line 4
Chongsin University
Naebang
PLACES TO STAY
3 Capital Hotel
캐피탈호텔
8 Hotel Popgreen
호텔팝그린
13 Princess Hotel
프린세스호텔
19 Samhwa Hotel
삼화호텔
20 Sunshine Hotel
산샤인호텔
22 Youngdong Hotel
영동호텔
23 Hotel Amiga
아미가호텔
25 New Hilltop Hotel
뉴힐탑호텔
27 Yujinjang
유진장
28 Dynasty Hotel
다이내스티호텔
29 Samjeong Hotel
삼정호텔
30 Seoul Renaissance Hotel
서울르네상스호텔
31 Novotel Ambassador
노보텔앰배서더호텔
32 Ritz Carlton Hotel; Nix & Nox Nightclub
리츠칼튼호텔
34 JW Marriott Hotel
JW 말라옷트호텔
PLACES TO EAT
11 Pulhyanggi
풀향기
12 Coco's
코코스
16 Hard Rock Cafe
하드락까페
39 Priveé
프리비
41 Pavilion
패비리은
42 Mandoo World
만두월드
44 Yeotnal
옛날
48 Lapalooza
라팔루자
52 Marché; Bennigan's; Tony Roma's
마르쉐
OTHER
1 War Memorial Museum
전쟁기념관
2 Site for New National Museum
뉴국립중앙박물관
4 German Embassy
독일대사관
5 UN Village
유엔단지
6 Galleria Department Store
갤러리아배화점
7 Tea Museum Cafe
티유지움까페
9 Hyundai Department Store
현대백화점
10 O'Kim's
오김스바
14 Igloo Fusion Dog Mania Café
익글루독매니아까페
15 Once in a Blue Moon
원스인어블루무운
17 Rock'n'Roll Bar
락엔롤바
18 Rico's
리코스
21 Anse Hospital
안세병원
24 Yeong-dong Post Office
영동우체국
26 New Core Department Store
뉴코아백화점
33 Seoul Express Bus Terminal (Gyeongbu-Yeongdong Terminal)
서울고속버스터미널 (경부,영동선)
35 Seoul Express Bus Terminal (Honam Terminal)
서울고속버스터미널 (호남선)
36 Central City Mall; Shinsegae Department Store
쎈츄럴몰
37 Yeoksam Post Office
역삼우체국
38 World Taekwondo Federation
국기원
40 Joyplanet; Rock Star 2000
죠이플래넷디비디방
43 Tube
튜브스레코드
45 XXXX Club
엑스엑스엑스엑스클럽

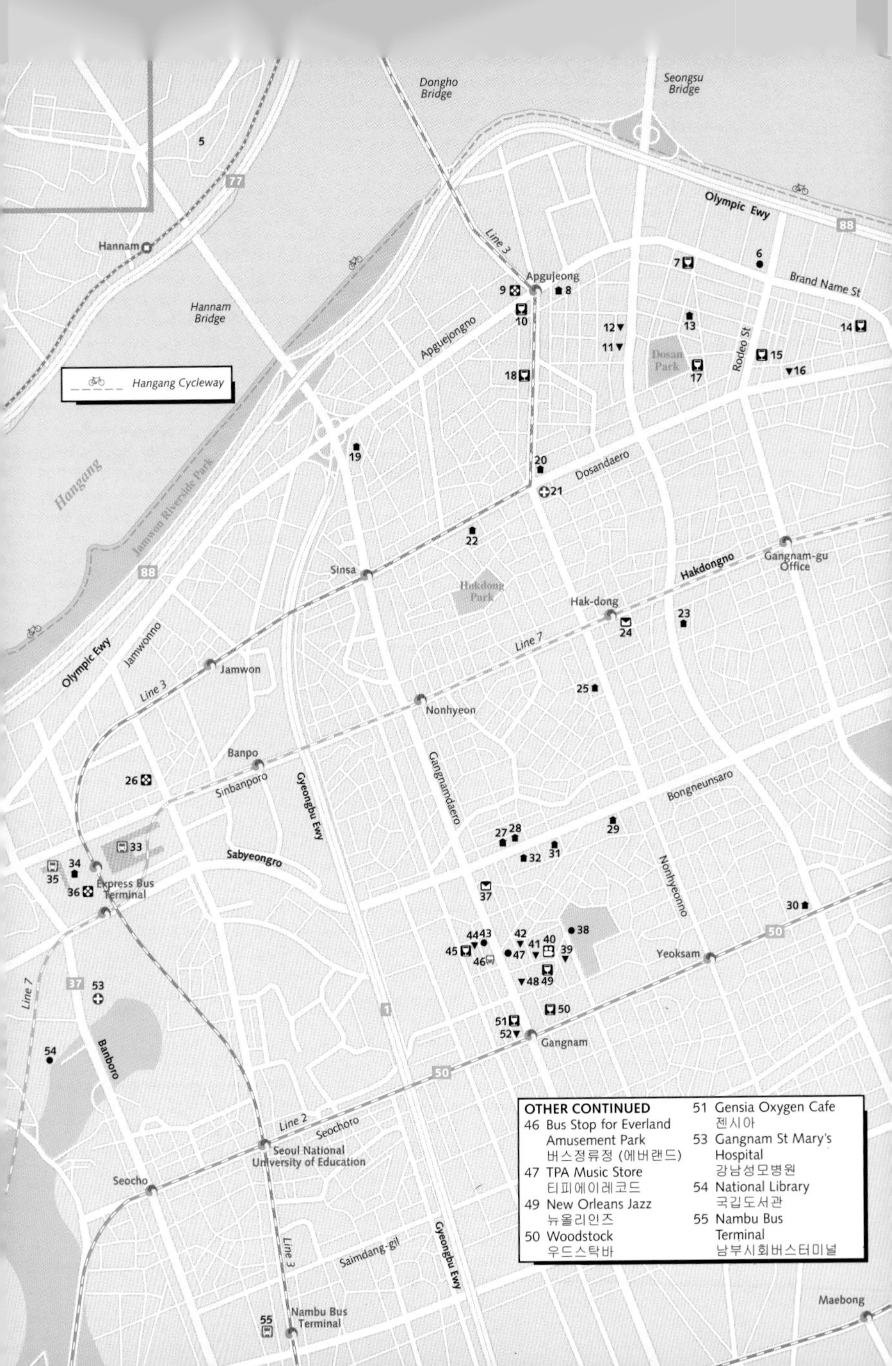

Dongho Bridge
Seongsu Bridge
Olympic Ewy
Brand Name St
Line 3
Apgujeong
Hannam
Hannam Bridge
Apguejongno
Rodeo St
Dosan Park
Hangang Cycleway
Hangang
Jamwon Riverside Park
Dosandaero
Sinsa
Hakdongno
Gangnam-gu Office
Hokdong Park
Hak-dong
Line 7
Olympic Ewy
Jamwonno
Jamwon
Line 3
Nonhyeon
Banpo
Sinbanporo
Gyeongbu Ewy
Gangnamdaero
Bongneunsaro
Sabyeongro
Express Bus Terminal
Nonhyeonno
Yeoksam
Line 7
Banboro
Gangnam
Line 2
Seochoro
Seoul National University of Education
Seocho
Line 3
Saimdang-gil
Gyeongbu Ewy
Nambu Bus Terminal
Maebong
OTHER CONTINUED
46 Bus Stop for Everland Amusement Park
버스정류정 (에버랜드)
47 TPA Music Store
티피에이레코드
49 New Orleans Jazz
뉴올리인즈
50 Woodstock
우드스탁바
51 Gensia Oxygen Cafe
젠시아
53 Gangnam St Mary's Hospital
강남성모병원
54 National Library
국립도서관
55 Nambu Bus Terminal
남부시회버스터미널

MAP 7 – JAMSIL & OLYMPIC PARK

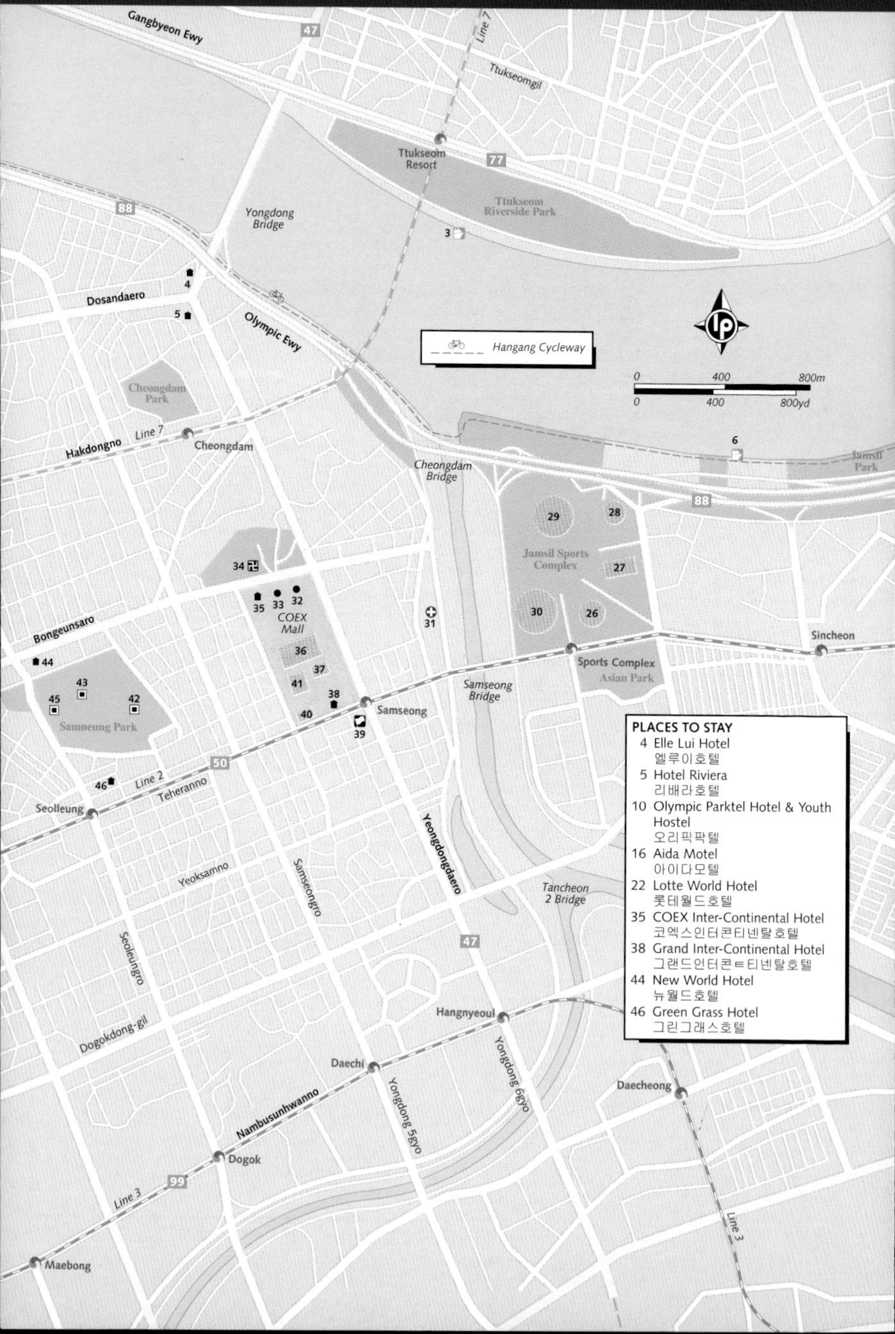
Gangbyeon Ewy
47
Line 7
Ttukseomgil
Ttukseom Resort
77
Ttukseom Riverside Park
88
Yongdong Bridge
3
4
Dosandaero
5
Olympic Ewy
Hangang Cycleway
0
400
800m
0
400
800yd
Cheongdam Park
Hakdongno
Line 7
Cheongdam
Cheongdam Bridge
6
Jamsil Park
88
29
28
Jamsil Sports Complex
27
34
35
33
32
COEX Mall
31
30
26
Bongeunsaro
Sincheon
Sports Complex
Asian Park
44
36
37
43
41
45
42
38
Samseong
Samseong Bridge
40
Samneung Park
39
50
46
Line 2
Teheranno
Seolleung
Yeongdongdaero
Yeoksamno
Samseongro
Tancheon 2 Bridge
Seoleungro
47
Dogokdong-gil
Hangnyeoul
Daechi
Yongdong 6gyo
Yongdong 5gyo
Daecheong
Nambusunhwanno
Dogok
99
Line 3
Maebong
Line 3

PLACES TO STAY

4 Elle Lui Hotel
엘루이호텔

5 Hotel Riviera
리베라호텔

10 Olympic Parktel Hotel & Youth Hostel
오리픽팍텔

16 Aida Motel
아이다모텔

22 Lotte World Hotel
롯테월드호텔

35 COEX Inter-Continental Hotel
코엑스인터콘티넨탈호텔

38 Grand Inter-Continental Hotel
그랜드언터콘ㅌ티넨탈호텔

44 New World Hotel
뉴월드호텔

46 Green Grass Hotel
그린그래스호텔

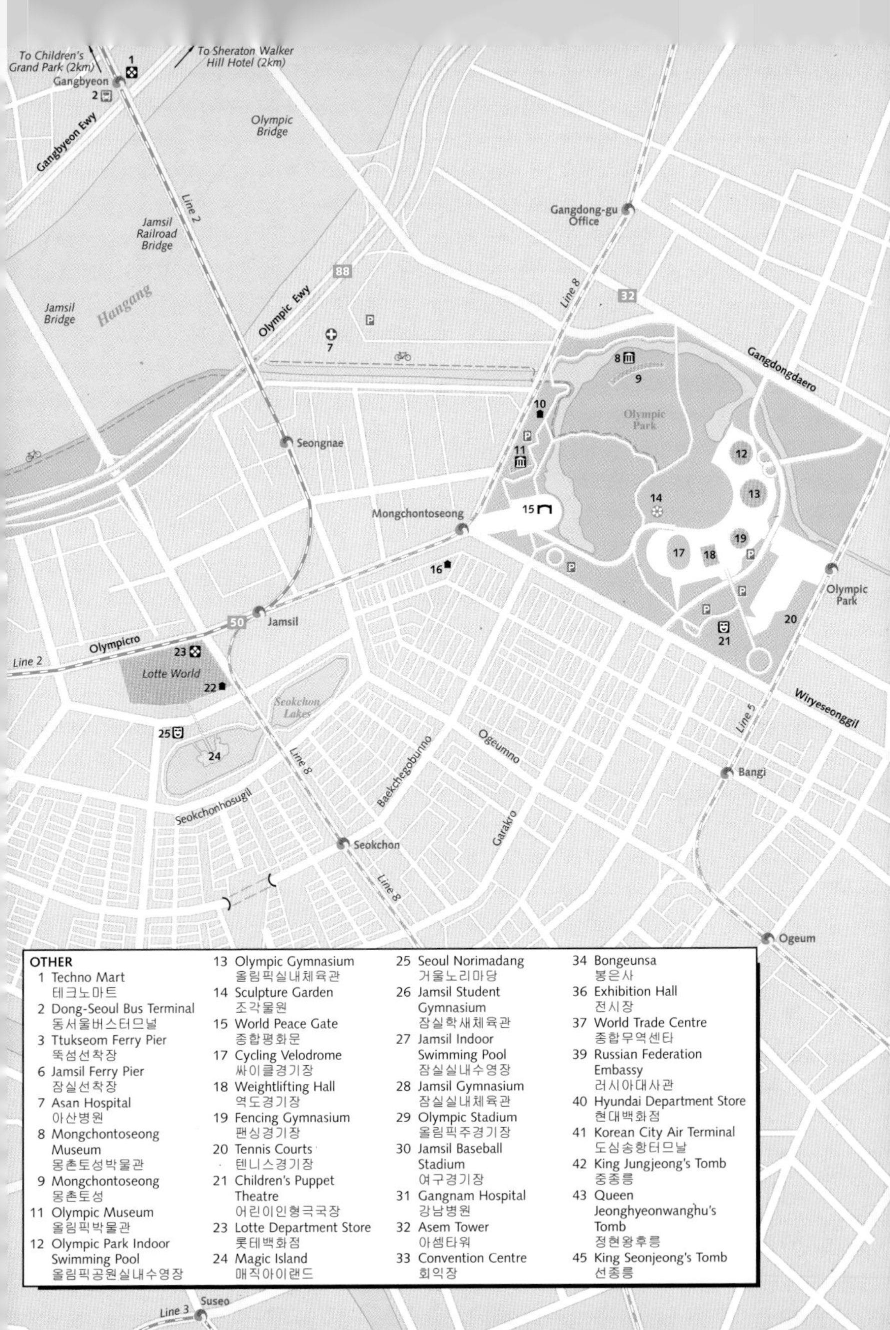

To Children's Grand Park (2km)
To Sheraton Walker Hill Hotel (2km)
Gangbyeon
Gangbyeon Ewy
Olympic Bridge
Line 2
Jamsil Railroad Bridge
Jamsil Bridge
Hangang
Olympic Ewy
88
Gangdong-gu Office
Line 8
32
Gangdongdaero
Olympic Park
Seongnae
Mongchontoseong
Jamsil
50
Olympicro
Line 2
Lotte World
Seokchon Lakes
Line 8
Baekchegobunno
Ogeumno
Garakro
Wiryeseonggil
Line 5
Bangi
Olympic Park
Seokchonhosugil
Seokchon
Line 8
Ogeum
Line 3
Suseo
OTHER
1 Techno Mart 테크노마트
2 Dong-Seoul Bus Terminal 동서울버스터미널
3 Ttukseom Ferry Pier 뚝섬선착장
6 Jamsil Ferry Pier 잠실선착장
7 Asan Hospital 아산병원
8 Mongchontoseong Museum 몽촌토성박물관
9 Mongchontoseong 몽촌토성
11 Olympic Museum 올림픽박물관
12 Olympic Park Indoor Swimming Pool 올림픽공원실내수영장
13 Olympic Gymnasium 올림픽실내체육관
14 Sculpture Garden 조각물원
15 World Peace Gate 종합평화문
17 Cycling Velodrome 싸이클경기장
18 Weightlifting Hall 역도경기장
19 Fencing Gymnasium 팬싱경기장
20 Tennis Courts 텐니스경기장
21 Children's Puppet Theatre 어린이인형극국장
23 Lotte Department Store 롯테백화점
24 Magic Island 매직아이랜드
25 Seoul Norimadang 거울노리마당
26 Jamsil Student Gymnasium 잠실학새체육관
27 Jamsil Indoor Swimming Pool 잠실실내수영장
28 Jamsil Gymnasium 잠실실내체육관
29 Olympic Stadium 올림픽주경기장
30 Jamsil Baseball Stadium 여구경기장
31 Gangnam Hospital 강남병원
32 Asem Tower 아셈타워
33 Convention Centre 회익장
34 Bongeunsa 봉은사
36 Exhibition Hall 전시장
37 World Trade Centre 종합무역센타
39 Russian Federation Embassy 러시아대사관
40 Hyundai Department Store 현대백화점
41 Korean City Air Terminal 도심송항터므날
42 King Jungjeong's Tomb 중종릉
43 Queen Jeonghyeonwanghu's Tomb 정현왕후릉
45 King Seonjeong's Tomb 선종릉

MAP 8 – GWANGHWAMUN, TAPGOL PARK & INSADONG

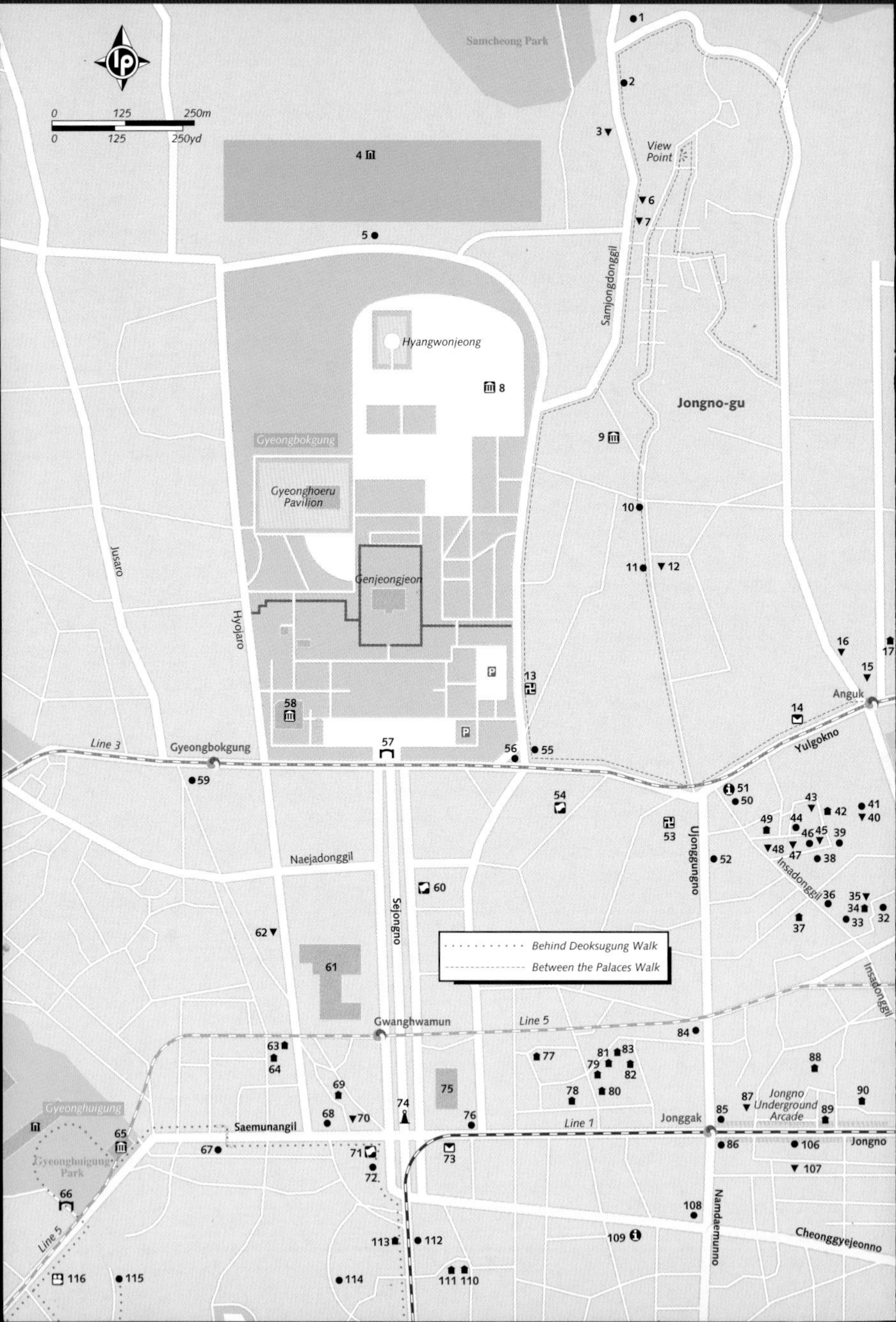

Samcheong Park
Samjongdonggil
View Point
Hyangwonjeong
Jongno-gu
Gyeongbokgung
Gyeonghoeru Pavilion
Genjeongjeon
Jusaro
Hyojaro
Line 3
Gyeongbokgung
Anguk
Yulgokno
Naejadonggil
Sejongno
Ujongungno
Insadonggil
Gwanghwamun
Line 5
Gyeonghuigung
Gyeonghuigung Park
Saemunangil
Line 1
Jonggak
Jongno Underground Arcade
Jongno
Namdaemunno
Cheonggyejeonno

Behind Deoksugung Walk
Between the Palaces Walk

0 125 250m
0 125 250yd

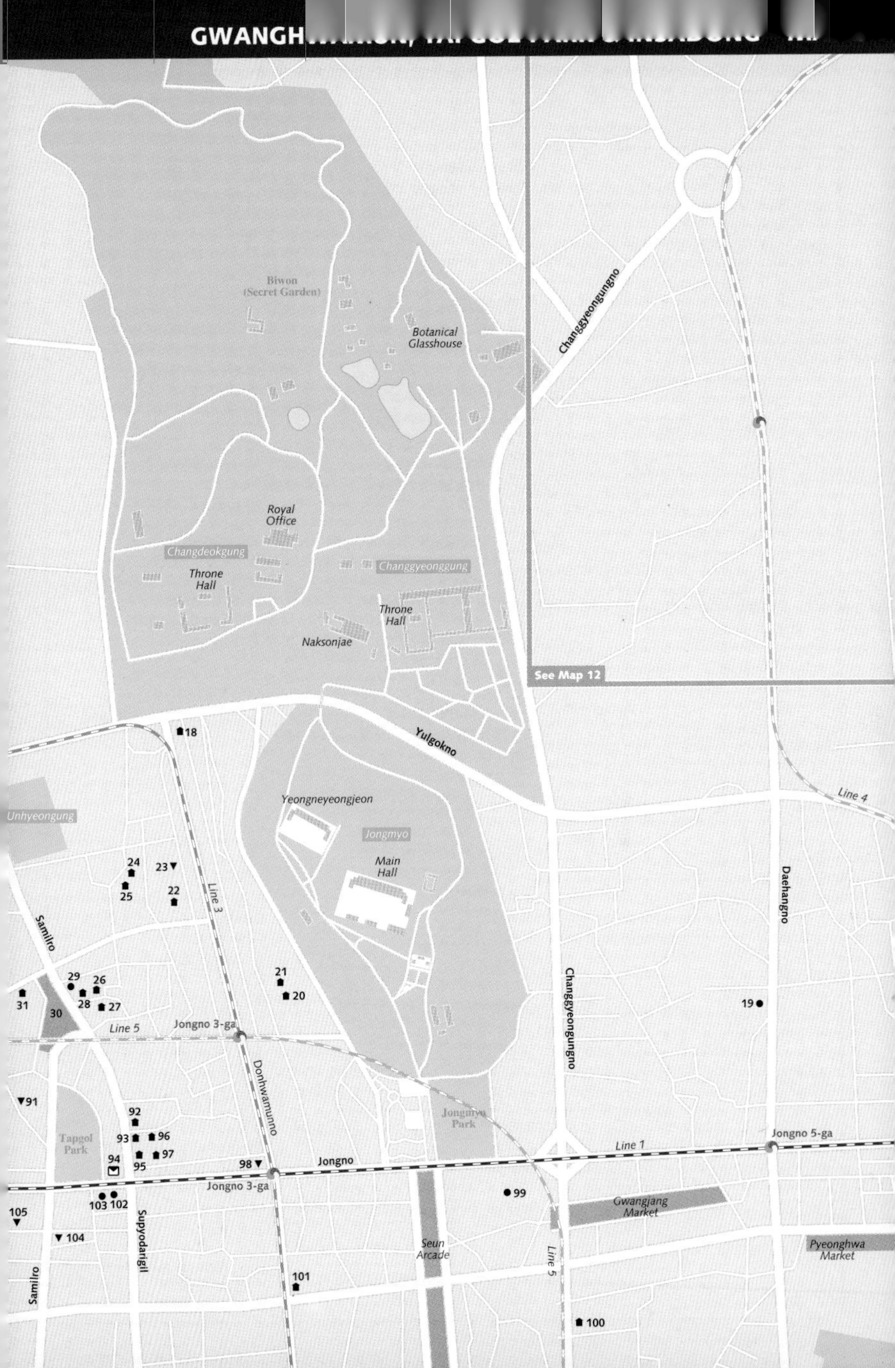
Biwon (Secret Garden)
Botanical Glasshouse
Changgyeongungno
Royal Office
Changdeokgung
Throne Hall
Changgyeonggung
Throne Hall
Naksonjae
See Map 12
18
Yulgokno
Line 4
Yeongneyeongjeon
Unhyeongung
Jongmyo
Main Hall
24
23
25
22
Line 3
Daehangno
Samilro
29
26
21
31
28
27
20
30
Changgyeongungno
19
Line 5
Jongno 3-ga
Donhwamunno
91
Jongmyo Park
92
Tapgol Park
93
96
Jongno 5-ga
Line 1
94
95
97
98
Jongno
Jongno 3-ga
103
102
99
Gwangjang Market
105
104
Supyodarigil
Seun Arcade
Line 5
Pyeonghwa Market
Samilro
101
100

MAP 8 – GWANGHWAMUN, TAPGOL PARK & INSADONG

PLACES TO STAY

17 Seoul Guesthouse
서울게스트하우스
18 Guesthouse Korea
게스트하우스코리아
20 New World Hotel
뉴월드모텔
21 Daerimjang
대림장
22 Seahwajang
세화장
24 Seoul Backpackers
서울백크팩크스
25 Motel Jongnowon
종로원모텔
26 Yongjin Yeogwan
융진여관
27 Hwaseong Yeogwan
화성여관
28 Emerald Hotel
애머릴드호텔
31 Fraser Apartments
트래이져
34 Yeongbinjang
영빈장
37 Saerim Hotel
세림호텔
42 Singungjang
신궁장
49 Gwanhunjang
관훈장
63 Deoksu Motel
덕수모텔
64 Gwanghwajang
광화장
69 Inn Daewon
대원여관
77 Gukjejang
국제장
78 Cheongjin Motel
청진모텔
79 Sinjinjang
신진장
80 Seoul Hotel
서울호텔
81 Dongwonjang
동원장
82 Useong Motel
우성장
83 Sejongjang
세종장
88 Paradise Motel (Jongno)
파라다이스모텔
89 YMCA; Top Travel; KISES Travel Agent
외엠씨에아
90 Wongap Inn
원갑여관
92 Ritz Hotel
리츠호텔
93 Paradise Motel (Tapgol Park)
파라다이스모텔
95 Gyeongbukjang
경북장
96 Yuhwajang
유화장
97 Cala Motel
카라모텔
100 Travelers A Motel
츄래빌러스에아모텔
101 Central Hotel
쌘츄럴호텔
110 New Kukje Hotel
뉴국제호텔
111 New Seoul Hotel
뉴서울호텔
113 Koreana Hotel
코리아나호텔

PLACES TO EAT

3 Yongsusan
용수산
6 Seoul Moemaeul
서울뫼마을
7 Hyangnamsegeuru
향남세그루
12 Kuay Yin Lo
쿠에이인로
15 Anjip
안집
16 Hanmoechon
한뫼촌
23 Jilsiru Tteok Café
질시루
35 Sanchon
산촌
40 Min's Club
민스클럽
43 Dimibang
디미방
44 Dagyeong
다경
45 Hayangim Pureunnae
하영김푸른내
47 Father's Restaurant & Teashop
아빠어려을적기
48 Yeongbin Garden
영빈가든
62 Hwanggeumjeong
황금정
70 Witch's Table
윗츠스테이블
87 Gamjatangjip
감자탕집
91 Shinpouri Mandu
신포우리
98 Midarae
미다래
104 Outback Steakhouse
아웃백스테이크하우스
105 Nutrition Centre
영양센타
107 Tomoko
토모코

OTHER

1 Antique Shop
이화당속품전몬
2 Seomulseoduljae Teashop
서물서둘재찻집
4 Cheongwadae
청와대
5 Main Entrance to Cheongwadae
8 National Folk Museum
국립민속박물관
9 Tibet Museum
티벳박물관
10 Art Sonje; Dal Restaurant
아트손제갤러리
11 Lotus Lantern International Buddhist Centre
연등회관
13 Beomyeonsa
범련사
14 Anguk Post Office
안국우체국
19 Royal Asiatic Society Korea Branch
로얄아시아협회
30 Nakwon Arcade; Hollywood Cinema; Nakwon-dong Rice-Cake Shops
낙원상가
32 Yetchatjip Teashop
옛잣집
33 Insa Art Plaza
인사아트갤러리

GWANGHWAMUN, TAPGOL PARK & INSADONG – MAP 8

36 North Korea Souvenir Shop
평양총유통

38 Hakgyo Jongi Ttaeng Ttaeng Ttaeng Teashop
학교종이땡땡땡

39 Dawon Teashop
다완

41 Suun Hall
구운괸

44 Dalsaeneun Dalman Saeng Gakhanda Teashop
달새는달만생각한다

50 To Art Gallery & Cafe
토아트갤러리

51 Tourist Information Bureau
괸굉인내소

52 Sinyetchatjip Teashop
신옛잣집

53 Jogyesa
조계사

54 Japanese Embassy
일본대사괸

55 Seoul Selection Bookshop
서울세렉슈은문고

56 Dongsipjagak
동십자각

57 Gwanghwamun
과ㅇ화문

58 National Museum
국립박물관

59 Immigration Office
적선현대빌딩

60 US Embassy
미국대사관

61 Sejong Centre for the Performing Arts
세종문화회관

65 Seoul Museum of History
서울역사박물관

66 Heunghwamun
흥화문

67 Statue of Hammering Man
망치쟁이동상

68 Goryeo Supermarket
고려슈핑푸드코트

71 Taiwan Mission
타이완영사관

72 Donghwa Duty-Free Shop
동화면세백화점

73 Gwanghwamun Post Office
광화문우체국

74 Admiral Yi Sun-shin's Statue
이순신장군동상

75 Kyobo Building; Australian Embassy; Dutch Embassy; New Zealand Embassy
교보빌딩

76 Kyobo Bookshop
교보문고

84 Jungang Map Shop
중앙지도

85 Jongno Tower; Top Cloud Restaurant; Top Cloud Cafe
종로타워

86 Bosingak
보싱각

94 Tapgol Post Office
탑골우체국

99 Yegi-dong Jewellery & Watch Alley
에지동금기겨도매상가

102 Musicland
뮤직랜드

103 Sisa Institute
시사학원

106 Jongno Bookshop
종로서점

108 Yeongpung Bookshop
영풍서점

109 KNTO Tourist Information Centre
힌국관광공사

112 Seoul Finance Centre; Buck Mulligan's Bar; Yongsusan Restaurant
서울재정센타

114 British Council
양국문화원

115 Russian Legation Tower
러씨은레개슈은타워

116 Star Six Cinema & Theatre
스타싯스국장

MARTIN MOOS

Downtown Seoul at dusk, seen from Namsan Park

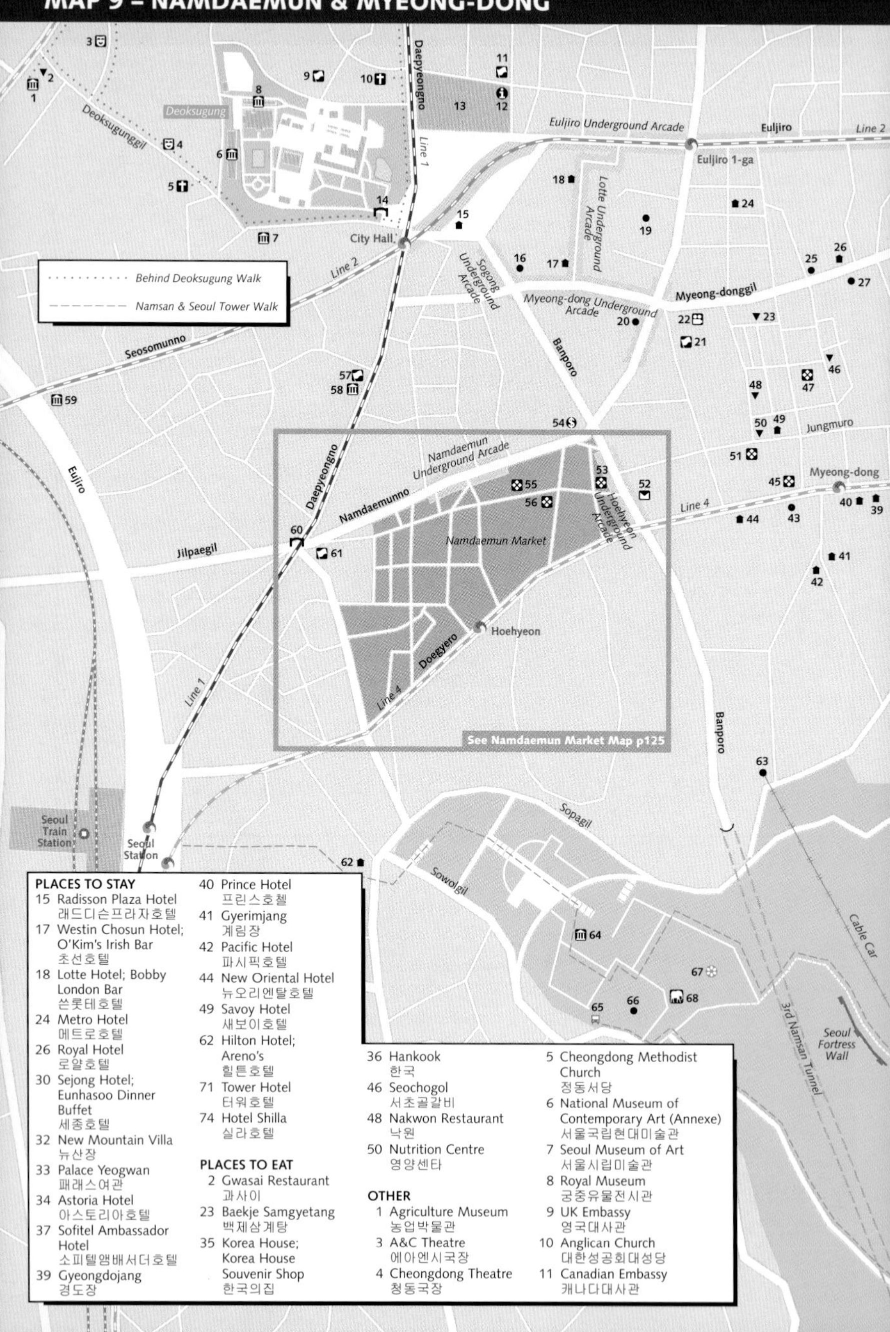
MAP 9 – NAMDAEMUN & MYEONG-DONG
Deoksugung
Deoksugunggil
Daepyeongno
Line 1
Euljiro Underground Arcade
Euljiro
Line 2
Euljiro 1-ga
Lotte Underground Arcade
City Hall
Sogong Underground Arcade
Myeong-dong Underground Arcade
Myeong-donggil
Banporo
Seosomunno
Behind Deoksugung Walk
Namsan & Seoul Tower Walk
Namdaemun Underground Arcade
Namdaemunno
Jilpaegil
Eujiro
Hoehyeon Underground Arcade
Namdaemun Market
Jungmuro
Myeong-dong
Line 4
Hoehyeon
Doegyero
See Namdaemun Market Map p125
Seoul Train Station
Seoul Station
Sopagil
Sowolgil
Cable Car
3rd Namsan Tunnel
Seoul Fortress Wall
PLACES TO STAY
15 Radisson Plaza Hotel
래드디슨프라자호텔
17 Westin Chosun Hotel; O'Kim's Irish Bar
조선호텔
18 Lotte Hotel; Bobby London Bar
쓴롯테호텔
24 Metro Hotel
메트로호텔
26 Royal Hotel
로얄호텔
30 Sejong Hotel; Eunhasoo Dinner Buffet
세종호텔
32 New Mountain Villa
뉴산장
33 Palace Yeogwan
패래스여관
34 Astoria Hotel
아스토리아호텔
37 Sofitel Ambassador Hotel
소피텔앰배서더호텔
39 Gyeongdojang
경도장
40 Prince Hotel
프린스호첼
41 Gyerimjang
계림장
42 Pacific Hotel
파시픽호텔
44 New Oriental Hotel
뉴오리엔탈호텔
49 Savoy Hotel
새보이호텔
62 Hilton Hotel; Areno's
힐튼호텔
71 Tower Hotel
터워호텔
74 Hotel Shilla
실라호텔
PLACES TO EAT
2 Gwasai Restaurant
과사이
23 Baekje Samgyetang
백제삼계탕
35 Korea House; Korea House Souvenir Shop
한국의집
36 Hankook
한국
46 Seochogol
서초골갈비
48 Nakwon Restaurant
낙원
50 Nutrition Centre
영양센타
OTHER
1 Agriculture Museum
농업박물관
3 A&C Theatre
에아엔시국장
4 Cheongdong Theatre
청동국장
5 Cheongdong Methodist Church
정동서당
6 National Museum of Contemporary Art (Annexe)
서울국립현대미술관
7 Seoul Museum of Art
서울시립미술관
8 Royal Museum
궁중유물전시관
9 UK Embassy
영국대사관
10 Anglican Church
대한성공회대성당
11 Canadian Embassy
캐나다대사관

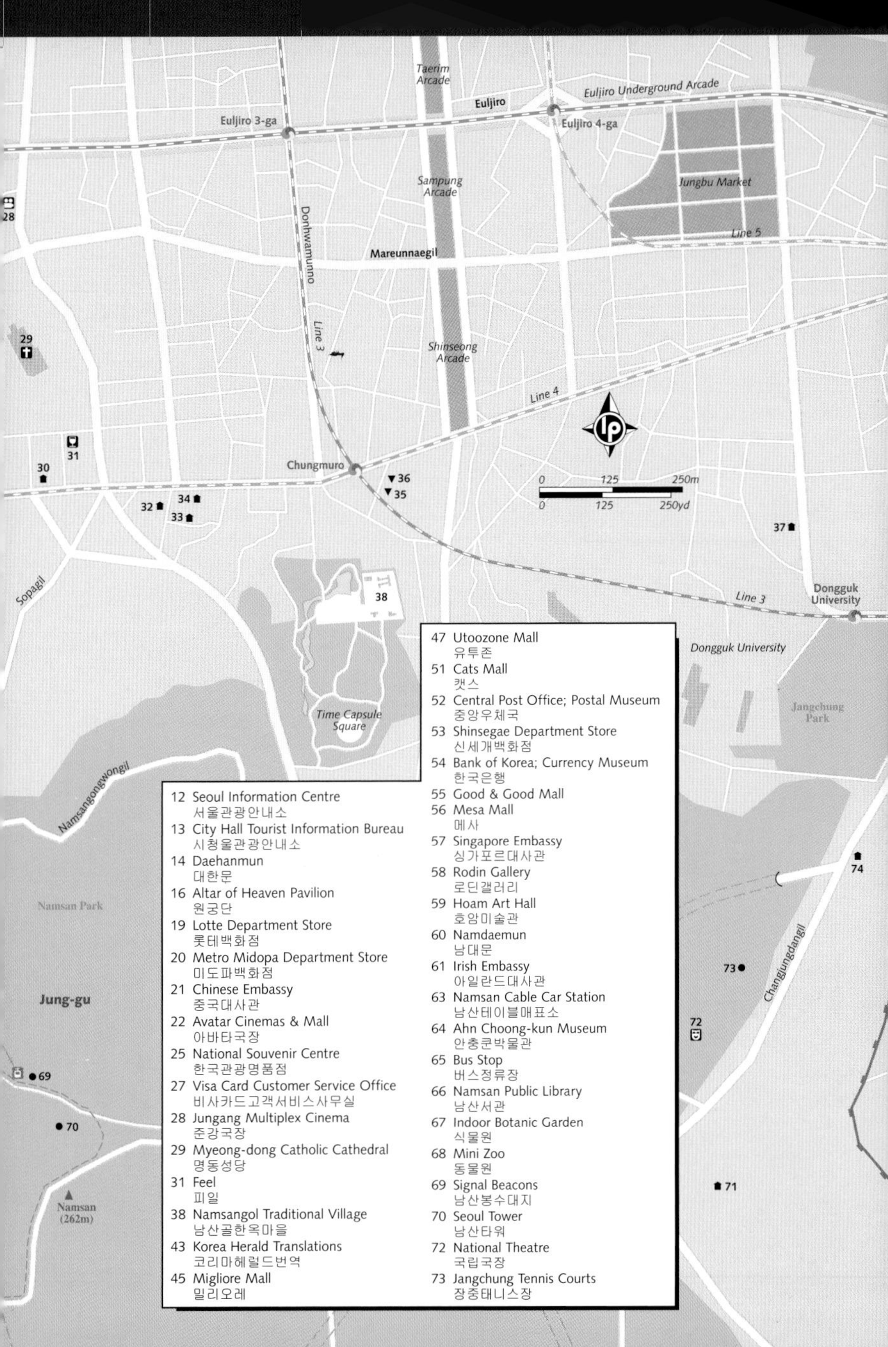
Taerim Arcade
Euljiro
Euljiro Underground Arcade
Euljiro 3-ga
Euljiro 4-ga
Sampung Arcade
Jungbu Market
Line 5
Dorhwamunno
Mareunnaegil
Line 3
Shinseong Arcade
Line 4
Chungmuro
0 125 250m
0 125 250yd
Sopagil
Line 3
Dongguk University
Dongguk University
Jangchung Park
Time Capsule Square
Namsangongwongil
Namsan Park
Jung-gu
Changjungdangil
Namsan (262m)
12 Seoul Information Centre
서울관광안내소
13 City Hall Tourist Information Bureau
시청울관광안내소
14 Daehanmun
대한문
16 Altar of Heaven Pavilion
원궁단
19 Lotte Department Store
롯데백화점
20 Metro Midopa Department Store
미도파백화점
21 Chinese Embassy
중국대사관
22 Avatar Cinemas & Mall
아바타극장
25 National Souvenir Centre
한국관광명품점
27 Visa Card Customer Service Office
비사카드고객서비스사무실
28 Jungang Multiplex Cinema
준강극장
29 Myeong-dong Catholic Cathedral
명동성당
31 Feel
피일
38 Namsangol Traditional Village
남산골한옥마을
43 Korea Herald Translations
코리마헤럴드번역
45 Migliore Mall
밀리오레
47 Utoozone Mall
유투존
51 Cats Mall
캣스
52 Central Post Office; Postal Museum
중앙우체국
53 Shinsegae Department Store
신세개백화점
54 Bank of Korea; Currency Museum
한국은행
55 Good & Good Mall
56 Mesa Mall
메사
57 Singapore Embassy
싱가포르대사관
58 Rodin Gallery
로딘갤러리
59 Hoam Art Hall
호암미술관
60 Namdaemun
남대문
61 Irish Embassy
아일란드대사관
63 Namsan Cable Car Station
남산테이블매표소
64 Ahn Choong-kun Museum
안충쿤박물관
65 Bus Stop
버스정류장
66 Namsan Public Library
남산서관
67 Indoor Botanic Garden
식물원
68 Mini Zoo
동물원
69 Signal Beacons
남산봉수대지
70 Seoul Tower
남산타워
72 National Theatre
국립국장
73 Jangchung Tennis Courts
장중태니스장

MAP 10 – BUKHANSAN NATIONAL PARK

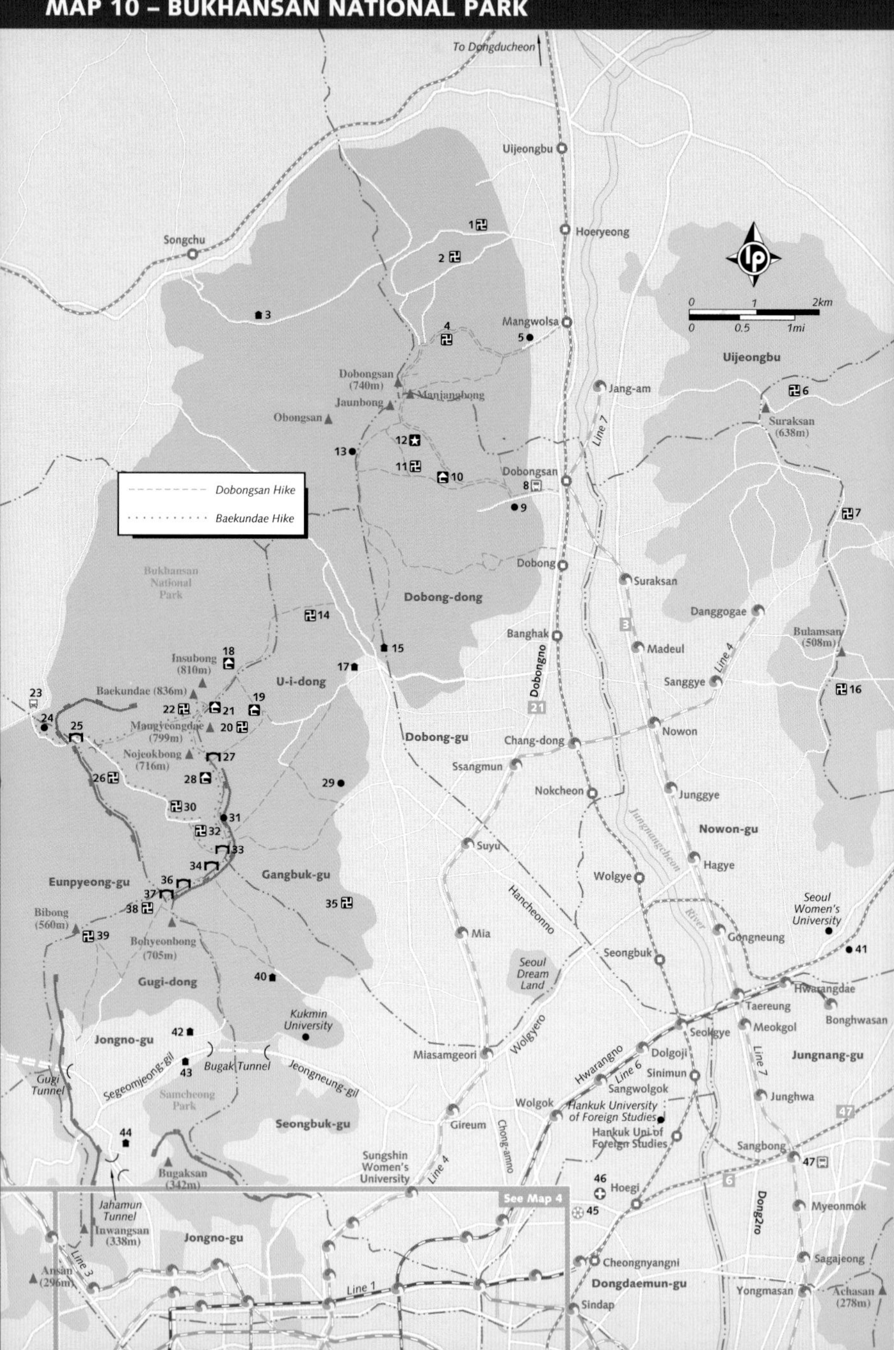

MAP 10 – BUKHANSAN NATIONAL PARK

PLACES TO STAY

3 Songchu Resort 송추유원지
10 Dobong Hut 도봉산장
15 U-I-dong Resort 우이동유원지
17 Green Park Hotel 그린파크호텔
18 Insu Hut 인수산장
19 U-i-Hut 우이산장
21 Baekundae Hut 백운대산장
28 Bukhansan Hut 북한산산장
40 Jeongneung Resort 정릉유원지
42 Bugak Park Hotel 부각파크호텔
43 Olympia Hotel 올림피아호텔
44 Exciting Korea Guesthouse 엑사이팅코리아 게스트하우스

OTHER

1 Seokcheonsa 석천사
2 Horyongsa 호룡사
4 Mangwolsa 망월사
5 Jangsuwon 장수원
6 Naewon-am 내원암
7 Heungguksa 흥국사
8 Bus Depot 버스정류장
9 Ticket Booth 도봉매표소
11 Cheonchuksa 천축사
12 Police Rescue Post 산악구조대
13 Gwaneumam 관음사
14 Yongdeoksa 용덕사
16 Bulamsa 불암사
20 Doseonsa 도선사
22 Yaksu-am 약수암
23 No 156 Bus Stop 버스정류장
24 Ticket Booth 잔정매표소
25 Daeseomun 대서문
26 Beopyongsa 법용사
27 Yongammun 용암문
29 4.19 Memorial Tower & Cemetery 4.19국립묘지
30 Yonghaksa 용학사
31 Dongjangdae 동장대
32 Taegosa 태고사
33 Daedongmun 대동문
34 Bogukmun 보국문
35 Hwagyesa 화계사
36 Daeseongmun 대성문
37 Daenammun 대남문
38 Munsusa 문수사
39 Seunggasa 승가사
41 Military Academy & Army Museums 륙군사관학교
45 Hongneung Arboretum 홍릉수목원
46 Kyunghee Oriental Hospital 경희대의대부속병원
47 Sangbong Bus Terminal 상봉시외버스터미널

JOHN ELK III

Calligraphy brushes in an art-supply shop

MAP 11 – ITAEWON

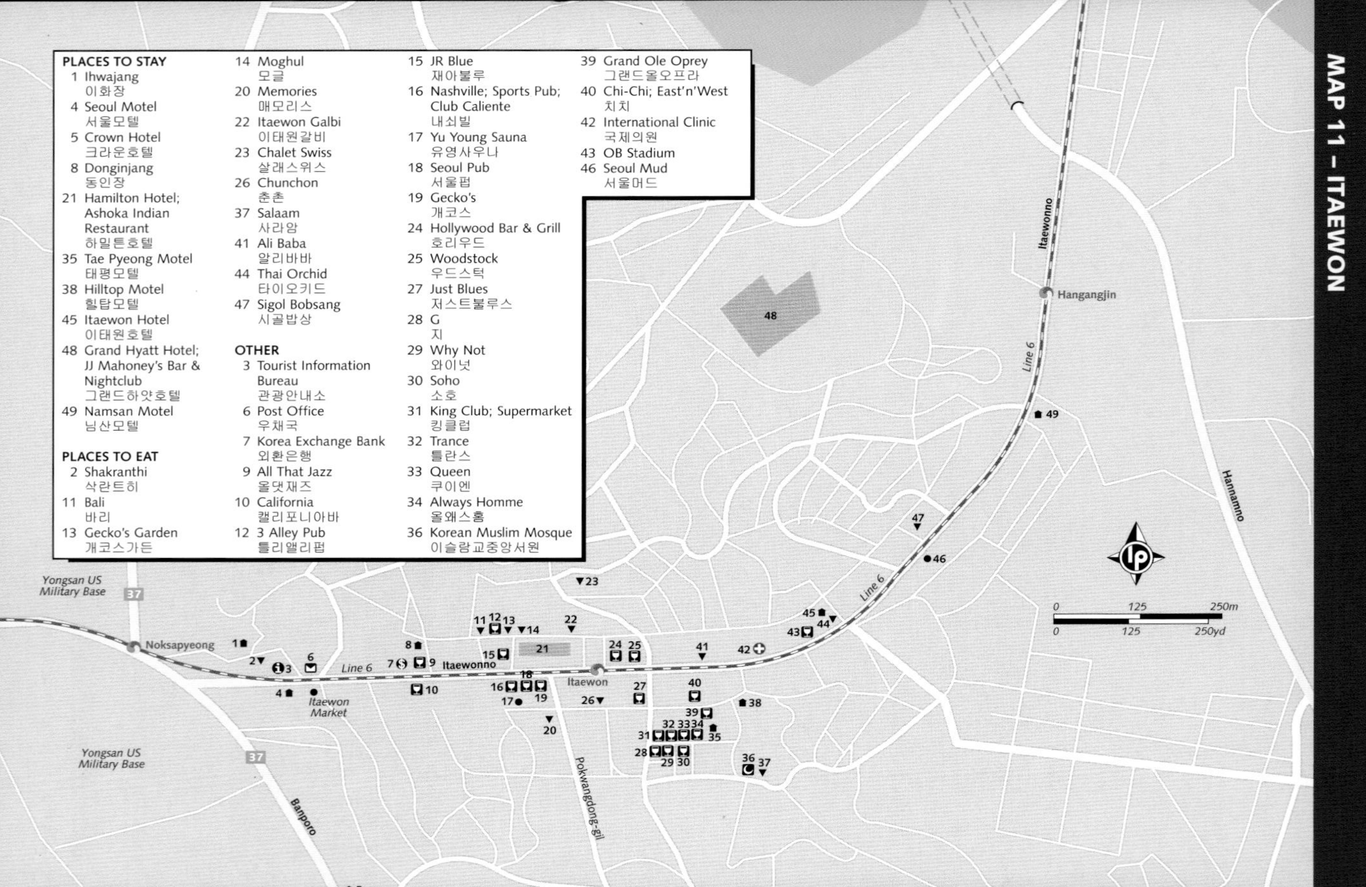

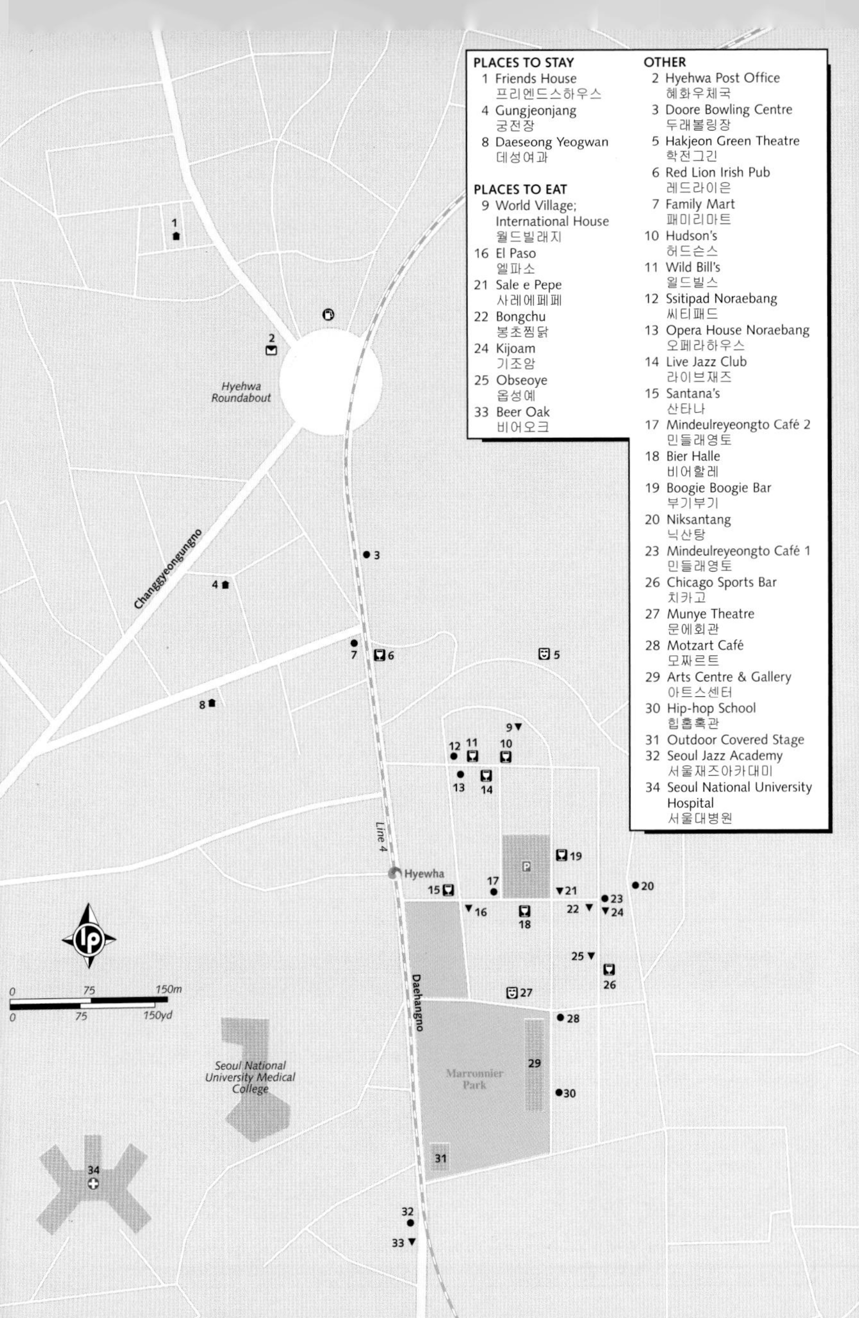

PLACES TO STAY
1 Friends House
프리엔드스하우스
4 Gungjeonjang
궁전장
8 Daeseong Yeogwan
데성여과
PLACES TO EAT
9 World Village; International House
월드빌래지
16 El Paso
엘파소
21 Sale e Pepe
사레에페페
22 Bongchu
봉초찜닭
24 Kijoam
기조암
25 Obseoye
옵성예
33 Beer Oak
비어오크
OTHER
2 Hyehwa Post Office
혜화우체국
3 Doore Bowling Centre
두래볼링장
5 Hakjeon Green Theatre
학전그긴
6 Red Lion Irish Pub
레드라이은
7 Family Mart
패미리마트
10 Hudson's
허드슨스
11 Wild Bill's
윌드빌스
12 Ssitipad Noraebang
씨티패드
13 Opera House Noraebang
오페라하우스
14 Live Jazz Club
라이브재즈
15 Santana's
산타나
17 Mindeulreyeongto Café 2
민들래영토
18 Bier Halle
비어할레
19 Boogie Boogie Bar
부기부기
20 Niksantang
닉산탕
23 Mindeulreyeongto Café 1
민들래영토
26 Chicago Sports Bar
치카고
27 Munye Theatre
문예회관
28 Motzart Café
모짜르트
29 Arts Centre & Gallery
아트스센터
30 Hip-hop School
힙홉혹관
31 Outdoor Covered Stage
32 Seoul Jazz Academy
서울재즈아카대미
34 Seoul National University Hospital
서울대병원
Hyehwa Roundabout
Changgyeongungno
Line 4
Hyehwa
Daehangno
Marronnier Park
Seoul National University Medical College
0 75 150m
0 75 150yd

MAP LEGEND

CITY ROUTES

Freeway .... Freeway
Highway .... Primary Road
Road .... Secondary Road
Street .... Street
Lane .... Lane
.... On/Off Ramp
.... Unsealed Road
.... One-Way Street
.... Pedestrian Street
.... Stepped Street
.... Tunnel
.... Footbridge

HYDROGRAPHY

.... River; Creek
.... Lake
.... Spring; Rapids
.... Waterfalls

REGIONAL ROUTES

.... Tollway; Freeway
.... Primary Road
.... Secondary Road
.... Minor Road

BOUNDARIES

.... International
.... State
.... Disputed
.... Fortified Wall

TRANSPORT ROUTES & STATIONS

.... Train
.... Underground Train
.... Metro
.... Cable Car; Chairlift
.... Ferry
.... Walking Trail
.... Path
.... Pier or Jetty

AREA FEATURES

.... Building
.... Park; Gardens
.... Market
.... Sports Ground
.... Beach
.... Cemetery
.... Campus
.... Plaza

POPULATION SYMBOLS

CAPITAL .... National Capital
CAPITAL .... State Capital
CITY .... City
Town .... Town
Village .... Village
.... Urban Area

MAP SYMBOLS

.... Place to Stay
.... Place to Eat
.... Point of Interest

.... Airport
.... Archaelogical Site
.... Bank
.... Bus Stop; Terminal
.... Bird Sanctuary
.... Buddhist Temple
.... Cable Car
.... Cave
.... Church
.... Cinema
.... Cycling
.... Golf Course
.... Hospital
.... Hut
.... Internet Cafe
.... Lookout
.... Monument
.... Mosque
.... Museum
.... National Park
.... Parking
.... Police Station
.... Post Office
.... Pub or Bar
.... Shopping Centre
.... Stately Home
.... Swimming Pool
.... Theatre
.... Tomb
.... Tourist Information
.... Winery
.... Zoo

Note: not all symbols displayed above appear in this book

LONELY PLANET OFFICES

Australia
Locked Bag 1, Footscray, Victoria 3011
☎ 03 8379 8000 fax 03 8379 8111
email: talk2us@lonelyplanet.com.au

USA
150 Linden St, Oakland, CA 94607
☎ 510 893 8555 TOLL FREE: 800 275 8555
fax 510 893 8572
email: info@lonelyplanet.com

UK
72-82 Rosebery Ave, London, EC1R 4RW
☎ 020 7841 9000 fax 020 7841 9001
email: go@lonelyplanet.co.uk

France
1 rue du Dahomey, 75011 Paris
☎ 01 55 25 33 00 fax 01 55 25 33 01
email: bip@lonelyplanet.fr
www.lonelyplanet.fr

World Wide Web: www.lonelyplanet.com or AOL keyword: lp
Lonely Planet Images: www.lonelyplanetimages.com